Do Small Groups Work?

SCM RESEARCH

Do Small Groups Work?

*A Study of Biblical Engagement
and Transformation*

Anna Clare Creedon

scm press

© Anna Clare Creedon 2021

Published in 2021 by SCM Press
Editorial office
3rd Floor, Invicta House,
108–114 Golden Lane,
London EC1Y 0TG, UK

www.scmpress.co.uk

SCM Press is an imprint of Hymns Ancient and Modern Ltd
(a registered charity)

Hymns Ancient & Modern

Hymns Ancient and Modern® is a registered trademark of
Hymns Ancient and Modern Ltd
13A Hellesdon Park Road, Norwich,
Norfolk NR6 5DR, UK

All rights reserved. No part of this publication may be reproduced,
stored in a retrieval system, or transmitted,
in any form or by any means, electronic, mechanical,
photocopying or otherwise, without the prior permission of
the publisher, SCM Press.

Anna Clare Creedon has asserted her right under the Copyright, Designs and
Patents Act 1988 to be identified as the Author of this Work

Scripture quotations are from New Revised Standard Version Bible: Anglicized
Edition, copyright © 1989, 1995 National Council of the Churches of Christ in
the United States of America. Used by permission. All rights reserved worldwide.

British Library Cataloguing in Publication data

A catalogue record for this book is available
from the British Library

978-0-334-06054-3

Typeset by Regent Typesetting
Printed and bound by
4edge Limited, UK

Contents

Acknowledgements   vii

1 Introduction   1
2 Transformation   12
3 Small Groups   35
4 Methodology and Methods   49
5 An 'Ordinary' Understanding of Transformation   72
6 Theme 1 – Expert   95
7 Theme 2 – Challenge   116
8 Theme 3 – Use of Materials   137
9 Transformation, Biblical Engagement and Small Groups: Some Practical and Theological Implications   159
10 Conclusion   167

Appendix A   172
Appendix B   174
Appendix C   177
Bibliography   178
Index of Names and Subjects   189

Acknowledgements

This book would not have been possible without a number of people.

First and foremost, I wish to thank the small group members who participated in this research. I am immensely grateful for your willingness to participate in this research and for the warm welcome I received: this research really wouldn't have been possible without you!

Immense thanks go to my two supervisors: Revd Dr Howard Worsley and Dr Andrew Rogers. Thank you both for your support, encouragement and guidance throughout the research process, and for many interesting conversations.

To all the students and staff at Trinity College, Bristol: it was wonderful to be part of such an amazing community, and thank you to all who supported and encouraged me, and shared your small group experiences. Special thanks to Dr Justin Stratis – my tutor and Director of Postgraduate Research – for developing and leading such a great research community.

Thank you to the Church of England for funding the majority of my tuition fees and also to St Luke's College Foundation for the grant towards both tuition fees and books.

Thank you to David Shervington and everyone else at SCM Press for supporting the publication of this book and guiding me through the process.

I have been supported by wonderful family and friends throughout this process. Special thanks go to my mother, Sally, proof-reader extraordinaire, not only for spotting the typos but also for asking various challenging questions. Thank you also to my father, Tim, for the loan of many books and for a number of very valuable discussions. Finally, thank you to my husband, Tim, who has been there through the inevitable highs and lows of the research and writing process, and has encouraged me to keep going!

This book would not have been possible without you all: thank you.

1

Introduction

'A lot has been written about transforming reading but very little about the conditions that reading (the Bible) must meet if change is intended.' (Hans de Wit, 2004a, p. 30)[1]

These words summarize well the focus of this book. My intention is to explore whether the context of a small group provides the necessary conditions for transformative biblical engagement to take place.

My initial interest in this area grew out of a long-running fascination with how peoples' behaviours are shaped by their beliefs. My preliminary thinking focused on the idea of biblical literacy and how someone's level of biblical knowledge and understanding shaped how they lived. This issue is also raised by Peter Phillips: 'how might an improvement in our biblical literacy impact the way we follow Jesus? Can we be better Christians by engaging more with the Bible?' (2017, p. 7). This developed into an interest in how people engaged with the Bible and how the Bible initiated theological reflection. While my first thought was to consider how theological reflection might be reshaped to begin with the Bible rather than experience, it became clear that this is already practised by many Christians on a weekly basis, though not necessarily described as such, in their small groups or Bible study groups. Groups meet together to read the Bible and use it as a source of challenge, encouragement, information, inspiration. Thus, my two interests were brought together: what impact does reading the Bible in a small group have on people? However, this needed to become more nuanced, and this is when an interest in the concept of transformation emerged. The word 'transformation' is used frequently in the Church – by church leaders, Christian writers and speakers, and so-called 'ordinary' Christians themselves (the use of the term 'ordinary' is explored further below). Indeed, Elaine Graham's work on reconstructing Christian practice for a postmodern age is entitled *Transforming Practice* (1996). But what does transformation mean? What does it look like? How does it happen? What stops it happening? And how might the Bible and small groups be involved in transformation? This is what I set out to find out: *What factors in small groups might hinder or facilitate transformative biblical engagement?*[2]

As Hans de Wit (2004a) notes, there appears to be a general consensus that reading the Bible can be transformative. Indeed, Anthony Thiselton suggests the Bible 'may be read and understood with transforming effects' (1992, p. 2). Also, Peter Phillips states, 'We open ourselves to the transformative power of the Word only to find the Word transforming us to see the Bible in new ways' (2017, p. 49). However, as de Wit notes in a later work, 'immediate transformation' represents an 'ideal description' of the consequence of biblical engagement (2015, p. 55). Nevertheless, this immediate transformation does not appear to be the norm. Paul Ballard is therefore correct to assert that 'greater attention be paid to how the Bible actually functions and how it acts as Scripture' (2014, p. 171). This book seeks to pay greater attention to how the Bible might become a transformative text as it is read by 'ordinary' Christians.

The context of this biblical engagement is small groups. Small groups are a model of church that has grown significantly during the twentieth century (Croft, 2002). Small groups are seen to offer opportunities for 'concrete experiences of community' (Kleisser et al., 1991, p. 2), 'to become present in the environment of the workaday world' (Hopewell, 1988, p. 21), and 'discipleship within structures of mutual accountability' (Croft, 2002, p. 72). Christian small groups exist for a variety of purposes and thus are referred to by a range of different names: house groups, cell groups, Bible-study groups, formation groups, to name a few. It is suggested that approximately 40% of church members are part of a small group (Heywood, 2017), and while this is often presented as a low figure, this still represents a significant group that is under-researched. In the British context, a limited number of studies have been carried out into small groups, and in the Church of England context, which is the focus this research, this is even more limited.

This research, which is based on data drawn from three small groups associated with Church of England churches, seeks to explore in depth how the processes and dynamics at work in small groups might hinder or facilitate transformative biblical engagement. From the data, it is possible to gain a much deeper understanding of how 'ordinary' Christians understand the concept of transformation, and also to identify a number of themes that relate to the facilitation *and* hindrance of transformative biblical engagement. These themes are *expert, challenge* and *use of materials*.

The rest of this chapter will offer an introduction to the wider field in which this research is situated. This includes the 'turn to the reader' within hermeneutics, and the increasing interest in the context of the reader. Following this, attention will be paid to the emergence of 'ordinary theology' as a field of study, and the growth of research with 'ordinary readers'. The term 'ordinary reader' will also be explored, as this is seen by some to be a pejorative term. The final part of this introductory chapter will consist of an overview of the rest of the chapters that make up this book.

Biblical hermeneutics: 'the turn to the reader'

The so-called turn to the reader in biblical hermeneutics developed out of the emergence of reader-response criticism in the 1970s and 1980s (Fowler, 2008). This was the result of a shift of emphasis away from the text and towards the reader that had been propelled by the work of writers such as Paul Ricoeur. Ricoeur prompted a movement in interpretation by suggesting that 'the meaning of a text lies not behind the text but in front of it' (1981, p. 177). By this, Ricoeur meant that the meaning of a text was not something to be excavated but to be experienced: 'The meaning is not something hidden but something disclosed' (1981, p. 177). Ricoeur referred to the 'world' that was created by the text, and into which readers might step: 'Beyond my situation as reader, beyond the situation of the author, I offer myself to the possible mode of being-in-the-world which the text opens up and discloses to me' (1981, p. 177). Ricoeur emphasized the effect of the text on a reader as a key part of the process of interpretation. George Steiner puts this well when he says that 'interpretation' is 'that which gives language life beyond the moment and place of immediate utterance or transcription' (1975, p. 27). Indeed, Ricoeur suggested that it was the response of the readers that determined the value of a text: 'it is the response of the audience which makes the text important and therefore significant' (1976, p. 31) – hence the term 'reader-response' criticism. Terry Eagleton, writing at a similar time to Ricoeur, argued for a return to the use of rhetoric to analyse the way that literature is formed in order to create a particular outcome or response (1983). Thus, a common view in reader-response criticism is that 'literature *is* what happens when we read' (Tompkins, 1988, p. xvi, emphasis in original). In biblical studies, this meant that there was a shift away from considering texts as composed of various sources, and instead focusing on the text as a whole (Firth and Grant, 2008), and the effect that the text had on the reader. Indeed, Mark Bowald suggests there should be greater recognition that reading the Bible 'is always a response to the free and gracious speech action of God' (2015, p. 2).

With the shift of focus from the text to the reader, interesting questions emerge about the meaning of biblical texts. Kevin Vanhoozer summarizes one of these questions when he asks, 'Is there something in the text that reflects a reality independent of the reader's interpretive activity, or does the text only reflect the reality of the reader?' (1998, p. 15). For some, texts, including biblical texts, hold no inherent meaning beyond the meaning ascribed to them in the process of reading and interpretation (Tompkins, 1988). Whereas others, those who Vanhoozer would describe as a 'hermeneutical realist', maintain that there is meaning inherent in the text; there is 'something "there" in the text' (Vanhoozer, 1998, p. 26). Stanley Fish wrestled with the question of whether meaning lay with the text or with the reader, and over the course of his career developed the concept of interpretive communities: 'it is interpretive communities, rather than either the text or the reader, that produce meanings' (Fish, 1980, p. 14). For Fish, communities are responsible for both the writing and the interpretation of texts, because even though an individual may write a text, they are still a 'product' of an interpretive community (1980). Indeed, Gerard Loughlin expresses this in a compelling way: 'It is said that each individual is now his or her own storyteller, his or her own source of legitimacy: I author myself. But this is a delusion, for no one stands alone' (1999, p. 32). By focusing on the role of interpretive communities, Fish (1980) sought to move the emphasis away from a dichotomy between seeing meaning as either being somehow objectively inherent in the text or being subjectively created by the reader. Instead, the interpretive community both constructs the meaning in the text and interprets the meaning of the text.

Reader-response criticism often refers to the 'implied reader', which is a term popularized by Wolfsgang Iser, to refer to the reader that the original author intended to read their work (Fowler, 2008). However, due in part to the influence of the Enlightenment, there emerged an ideal of the 'singular unaffected reader' (Bowald, 2015, p. 2), despite the work of those such as Fish (1980) who focused on the role of communities in the process of interpretation. As well as this, biblical hermeneutics generally 'works with ideal, rather than real, readers' (Todd, 2009, p. 24). This ideal or 'normal' reader has tended to be presumed in modern times to be a 'white European or North American male' (Kessler, 2004, p. 453). However, this has been challenged by work that has sought to focus on 'how flesh-and-blood readers deal with texts' (de Wit, 2012, p. 17), which has been termed by some 'the turn to the empirical reader' (de Wit, 2012, p. 9). Indeed, Hans de Wit states that since the 1970s there has been a growth of interest in real readers emerging, and this has been acknowledged more fully in the Southern Hemisphere than in the West (de Wit, 2004a). These readers have come to be commonly referred to as 'ordinary readers', and it is to this area of research that we now turn our attention.

Ordinary readers

The term 'ordinary reader' originally emerged in the work of Gerald West (1993), who developed an approach to small group Bible study known as Contextual Bible Study (CBS). In West's *The Academy of the Poor: Towards a Dialogical Reading of the Bible* he offers a detailed definition of what he means by 'ordinary reader':

> The term 'reader' alludes to the well-chartered shift in hermeneutics towards the reader. However, I place the term in inverted commas to signal that my use of the term 'reader' is both literal and metaphoric in that it *includes* the many who are illiterate, but who listen to, retell and remake the Bible. The other term in the phrase, the term 'ordinary', is used in a general and a specific sense. The general usage includes all readers who read the Bible pre-critically. But I also use the term 'ordinary' to designate a particular sector of pre-critical readers, those readers who are poor and marginalized. (1999, p. 10, emphasis in original)

West acknowledges that many ordinary readers will often *hear* the Bible, rather than necessarily read it for themselves; this is the case even in more literate contexts, where the Bible is commonly read aloud by one individual as part of Sunday worship. That not all those who engage with the Bible read it has led some to suggest that another term might be helpful, such as 'interpreter' (Kahl, 2007, p. 148). The second part of West's definition focuses on the designation 'ordinary', which is used to suggest that these individuals read the Bible in an 'untrained' or 'pre-critical' way, which is in contrast to 'trained' readers (1993, pp. 8–9), or biblical scholars: 'Biblical scholars are those readers who have been trained in the use of the tools and resources of biblical scholarship and who read the Bible "critically"' (West, 1999, pp.10–11). While comfortable with the designation of biblical scholars as 'critical' readers, Kahl suggests that rather than 'ordinary' the term 'intuitive' might be used instead (2007, p. 148). Some have specified that ordinary readers are only those in 'situations of poverty, exclusion, persecution, illness and apartheid' (de Wit, 2004a, p. 6), but the term has been used more widely.

In the British context, Jeff Astley defines ordinary theology as 'the theological beliefs and processes of believing that find expression in the God-talk of those believers who have received no scholarly theological education' (2002, p. 1). Similarly, Andrew Village, also in the British context, has defined ordinary readers as those 'who encounter the Bible through the practice of their faith' (2013a, p. 145). In critique of both of these conceptions of ordinary theology, as well as that of West, is Pete Ward and Sarah Dunlop's recognition that this creates a dualistic view of theology and posits ordinary theology against a theological 'other':

> This 'other' serves as a reference point and it is variously seen as formal, or academic, or of the institution, or elitist. Thus the popular, common, ordinary, or local is defined in contrast to a reference that is often conceived as negative or requiring a corrective. (Ward and Dunlop, 2011, p. 296)

Village (2013a) has also acknowledged that while many so-called ordinary readers may not have received formal training in biblical studies, they may well hold a degree-level qualification in another discipline, so he has questioned to what extent these people are ordinary readers. Indeed, Andrew Rogers (2015) has suggested that it may be more helpful to speak of 'congregational hermeneutics', as this recognizes the potential variety of experience and knowledge possessed by a congregation.

Stanley Grenz and Roger Olson suggest that key to theology is reflection, and that theologies 'lie along a spectrum of reflection' (1996, p. 26). They suggest that this spectrum includes the following forms of theology: 'folk theology', 'lay theology', 'ministerial theology', 'professional theology' to 'academic theology' (Grenz and Olson, 1996, p. 26), with folk theology being seen as the least reflective and academic theology being seen as the most reflective. They define folk theology as 'unreflective believing based on blind faith in a tradition of some kind' (1996, p. 27), and suggest that lay theology develops as Christians question this folk theology and begin to become more reflective about their faith. The next stage on from this is ministerial theology, which is 'reflective faith as practiced by trained ministers and teachers in Christian churches' (1996, p. 31). After this is professional theology, and professional theologians are those who teach lay people and ministers; therefore they are there to 'aid lay and ministerial theologians in their journeys of reflection' (1996, p. 33). But Grenz and Olson describe this as a 'servant role and not a lordly role' (1996, p. 33). Finally, academic theology 'is a highly speculative, virtually philosophical theology aimed primarily at other theologians. It is often disconnected from the church and has little to do with concrete Christian living' (1996, p. 33). As they do envisage the five forms as part of a spectrum, it is reasonable to assume that an individual may exhibit traits of a number of forms of theology, with even highly academic theologians perhaps holding to certain traditions with so-called 'blind faith'. For Grenz and Olson, reflection is key to moving from one form of theology to another, but they are less clear about what might prompt this reflection. While

Grenz and Olson are critical of both folk theology and academic theology, they see the middle three forms as 'interdependent theologies' (1996, p. 34) which should be mutually beneficial to one another. Similarly, West (1993) emphasizes that both ordinary readers and biblical scholars have something to offer and something to learn from one another.

A further alternative to Grenz and Olson's spectrum of theology is the Four Voices of Theology model which was developed by Helen Cameron, Deborah Bhatti, Catherine Duce, James Sweeney and Clare Watkins as part of the Action Research: Church and Society project (ARCS). Cameron and her colleagues developed the four voices model in order to offer a framework for understanding how different and yet interrelated forms of theology may be conceived (2010). The four voices are normative theology, formal theology, espoused theology and operant theology. Normative theology is what a 'practising group names as its theological authority' (Cameron et al., 2010, p. 54), which might include the Bible or creeds. Formal theology is 'the theology of the academy, of the "professional" theologian' (Cameron et al., 2010, p. 55), and therefore includes academic works of theology, and is what Grenz and Olson refer to as academic theology (1996, p. 33). Espoused theology is 'the theology embedded within a group's articulation of its beliefs' (Cameron et al., 2010, p. 54), such as a church's statement of beliefs or a mission statement. Operant theology consists of '[t]he faith-carrying words and actions of believers' (p. 14) and is the theology 'embedded within the actual practices of a group' (Cameron, et al., 2010, p. 54). Cameron and her colleagues are aware of the work of Jeff Astley and his understanding of ordinary theology (2002), and present operant theology as an alternative to his conception of ordinary theology (Cameron et al., 2010, p. 14, fn. 14). Rather than seeing these voices as being points on a spectrum, where some forms of theology are seen as more valuable than others, they are instead seen as expressing equally valid forms of theology. Espoused and operant theologies have a role in not simply learning from normative and formal theologies, but also in challenging them. The authors develop an approach to practical theology that is influenced by action research and thus called Theological Action Research (TAR). They state, 'What becomes essential in this task is a practical and attitudinal commitment to a complex theology disclosed through a conversation method' (Cameron, et al., 2010, p. 56). This approach takes seriously so-called ordinary theology as a dialogue partner with so-called academic theology. Indeed, Pete Ward has suggested that all Christians are in a sense practical theologians: he notes, 'just by being active in the life of the church and by seeking to express a faithful Christian life in communities and the wider society, Christians are doing practical theology' (2017,

p. 14). Nevertheless, it must also be recognized that there does exist an academic discipline known as theology, and that this is in many ways distinct from the operant theology of many Christians. We will return to how practical theology should be conceived in section 4.1. Thus, while the terms 'ordinary reader' or 'ordinary theology' may be in some senses problematic, they will be used heuristically in this research in order to maintain continuity with the wider literature, but recognizing, as the work of Helen Cameron and her colleagues does, that ordinary theology has much to offer to more academic forms of theology.

Returning to focus particularly on how ordinary readers engage with the Bible, it is helpful to briefly consider some of the common features between ordinary readers' approaches to the Bible, as ordinary readers account for the majority of all Bible readers (Village, 2013b). A key feature that appears to influence the readings of ordinary readers is *context*. Speaking particularly of Contextual Bible Study, Louise Lawrence notes, 'contextual interpretations prioritize the local folk consciousness of readers and encourage explicit engagement between texts and contexts of the present' (Lawrence, 2009, p. 23). This feature, of connecting the text with the context of the reader, has been found by a number of researchers working with ordinary readers (Perrin, 2016; Todd, 2009; Village, 2013b). Indeed, Stevens offers a summary of this perspective when he says, 'The theological task is not only to exegete Scripture but to exegete life, and to do these together' (1999, p. 17). However, as Village (2013b) notes, this focus on the relevance of the Bible for everyday life and in addressing the context of the reader is not common in the work of biblical scholars. Some have raised concerns about the potential for misconstruing the text if too much weight is given to the context of the reader; Richard Briggs suggests that if we come to the biblical text simply in order to get answers to our preconceived questions, 'then we shall assuredly miss the ways in which the biblical witness ... seeks to reshape our concerns around an agenda which we do not naturally possess' (Briggs, 2007, p. 172). Indeed, Briggs might be concerned by Lawrence's comment that 'biblical texts find new meanings in encounters with different contexts' (2009, p. 125). Nevertheless, Todd noted that in small group discussions different 'voices' emerged: 'The "canonical" voice tends to offer inherited interpretations; the "contingent" voice tends to offer questions drawn from the participants' experience' (Todd, 2009, p. 15, see also Todd, 2005). This corresponds to the four voices model, perhaps with the 'canonical' voice representing normative theology, whereas the 'contingent' voice comes from the operant theology of the participants. Perhaps in the dialogue between existing interpretations (normative theology), that may have been handed down, and the challenges posed by current contexts (operant theology), ordinary readers can find meaning for themselves from the biblical texts, and may yet be challenged to 'reshape' their thinking in response to the biblical text (Briggs, 2007, p. 172).

In summary, the turn to the reader in biblical hermeneutics has led to the recognition of the role of the reader in the process of interpretation and in constructing meaning. In particular, greater recognition has been given to the impact of biblical texts, and other texts, on the reader, which can be seen in the development of reader-response criticism. However, the recognition of the role played by the reader in the process of interpretation has also led to certain issues being raised about where meaning is found: in the text, in the reader, or in and as a result of an 'interpretive community' (Fish, 1980). This is an ongoing discussion in biblical hermeneutics, and literary theory more widely. We have also explored the meaning and application of the term 'ordinary reader' and considered the fact that context appears to be a key feature of the readings of 'ordinary readers'.

In the rest of this chapter I will offer an overview of the rest of the chapters that make up this book.

Overview of chapters

In Chapter 2 I consider the concept of transformation from a biblical perspective, finding it to be *an ongoing process of change whereby individuals and communities come to more fully resemble Jesus Christ and glorify God by the power of the Holy Spirit, in anticipation of the future transformation of the whole of creation.* Consideration is then given to a number of potential approaches to transformative biblical engagement. Finally, in the third part of the chapter I consider how transformation might occur: What is the process of transformation? The work of Jack Mezirow, Walter Brueggemann, James Loder, Daniel Schipani and Laurie Green are explored. All of this enables a greater understanding of what transformation is and how the process of transformation might actually occur.

Given that this research is situated in the field of practical theology, in Chapter 3 I examine small groups from the perspective of both social psychology and education in order to develop a greater understanding of the nature of small groups. Some of the key characteristics of small groups that may lead them to be an ideal context for transformation are considered, before some prior research into small groups is presented, some of which illustrates the potential for transformative biblical engagement in small groups.

In Chapter 4 I identify the methodological assumptions underlying this research, showing how this fits with broader understandings of practical theology and the relationship between theology and other disciplines. A critical realist perspective underlies this work, thus the tenets of critical realism – ontological realism, epistemic relativism and judgmental rationality – will be examined. In this chapter I offer an exploration of reflexivity and the importance of recognizing the influence of the researcher upon the process of data production. I also introduce the methods used in this research (ethnographic observation, questionnaires, and focus groups), along with a justification for their usage despite any potential limitations. The results of the pilot study are presented, along with some reflections on this. The process of data analysis is explained, specifically how the key themes that emerged from the data were identified. Finally, this chapter also introduces the small groups that participated in this research and places them in the wider context of the Church of England and the different church traditions that constitute it.

Chapter 5 is the first chapter to include data from the research and in it I return to the concept of transformation, in order to develop a deeper understanding of how ordinary Christians understand this concept. The majority of the data is drawn from the focus group discussions.

This is followed by three chapters in which I focus on the key themes that emerged from the data, which are expert (Chapter 6), challenge (Chapter 7), and the use of materials (Chapter 8). In each of these chapters I make extensive use of data in order to unpack the importance of these themes in relation to their potential to hinder or facilitate transformative biblical engagement. As the focus of this research is *biblical* engagement, each chapter also encompasses a biblical case study in order to explore how this theme is addressed in the biblical context.

In Chapter 9 I draw together the three main themes of expertise, challenge and the use of materials and highlight some practical and theological implications of this research, namely the purpose of small groups and the leadership of small groups.

In the conclusion, Chapter 10, I draw together the whole book and identify the contribution that this research makes and some of its implications. Finally, the limitations of the research are highlighted, along with the suggestion of some possible avenues for further research.

Given the centrality of the concept of transformation to this research, it is to this area that we now turn our attention.

INTRODUCTION

Notes

1 In *Through the Eyes of Another* (2004), Hans de Wit and his colleagues present their research on a model of inter-cultural Bible-reading. The research sought to explore what would happen when groups of Christians from different cultures and situations were exposed to one another's interpretations. The method involved groups from all over the world reading the story of Jesus and the Samaritan woman (John 4), recording and then sharing their perspectives (along with information about their context) with a group from another culture, in order for the groups to then re-read the passage 'through the eyes of another'. De Wit and his colleagues wished to establish if reading the Bible from a new perspective might lead to transformed thinking and acting. This research, while not focused specifically on the cultural dynamics of Bible reading, is also concerned with what makes Bible reading transformative.

2 This book is a development of my doctoral thesis (Creedon, 2019).

2

Transformation

This chapter falls into three main parts: first, we will explore the concept of transformation, especially as it occurs in the Bible. Then we will assess how transformation is related to biblical engagement, specifically, in what sense biblical engagement can be said to lead to transformation. Third, we will consider the *process* of transformation, and how transformation actually occurs.

Transformation in the Bible

We will begin by exploring some examples of transformation in the Old Testament, before moving on to consider transformation in the life and teachings of Jesus, and finally, looking at references to transformation in Paul's writings. While in Western culture we might tend towards seeing transformation from an individual perspective, the Bible primarily sees transformation from a communal, societal or even eschatological perspective. And when transformation occurs in the life of an individual, this transformation is expected to affect others.

In the Old Testament, both the Exodus and the Exile can be understood as sources of transformation. The Exodus (Ex. 12) and the Exile (2 Kings 24) are both instances of the people of God facing a 'disorientating dilemma' (Mezirow, 1994, p. 224). As the Israelites first go through the disorientating dilemma of leaving Egypt, and then, much later, the disorientating dilemma of leaving the Promised Land, they go through a process of reflection, leading to a transformed perspective on what it means to be the people of God:

> By the rivers of Babylon—
>   there we sat down and there we wept
>   when we remembered Zion.
> On the willows there
>   we hung up our harps.
> For there our captors
>   asked us for songs,

TRANSFORMATION

and our tormentors asked for mirth, saying,
  'Sing us one of the songs of Zion!'
How could we sing the Lord's song
  in a foreign land? (Ps. 137.1–4)

Bennett and Rowland argue that in the Bible there is a 'powerful tradition' of exile – either spiritual or physical – leading to a transformed perspective (2016, p. 103). While the Israelites may go through a process of transformation during the Exile, a further transformation is necessary for them to return to the Promised Land. Ezekiel 36.16–38 prophesies about 'The Renewal of Israel', and Iain Dugud states that, 'a total transformation was required if the regathering and return were to be a success' (1999, p. 413). Not only was there a physical change – the return of the people to the Promised Land – but there also needed to be a 'number of moral and spiritual changes' (Taylor, 1969, p. 231), as can be seen in verses 25–26:

> I will sprinkle clean water upon you, and you shall be clean from all your uncleannesses, and from all your idols I will cleanse you. A new heart I will give you, and a new spirit I will put within you; and I will remove from your body the heart of stone and give you a heart of flesh.

They must go through a process of purification and then renovation in order to be sanctified (Dugud, 1999). Following the renewal of their spirits and hearts, changed behaviour is expected of the Israelites: 'the implanting of God's Spirit within them will transform their motives and empower them to live according to God's statutes and judgments' (Taylor, 1969, p. 232). The whole community is to go through a process of transformation.

Having briefly considered the notion of transformation in the Exodus, Exile and the return from Exile, we will now consider the life and teachings of Jesus. It has been suggested that Jesus' call – 'The time is fulfilled, and the kingdom of God is at hand; repent and believe in the gospel' (Mark 1.15) – was a call to transformation (Fleischer, 2006). John Dominic Crossan (1988) has considered the role of Jesus' parables in challenging people's worldviews; he suggests that parables 'shatter the deep structure of our accepted world' (p. 100) and 'give God room' (p. 99). Parables therefore make us vulnerable and open to God and the arrival of the Kingdom of God. We can see the transformative power of Jesus within the lives of the individuals that he encountered; indeed, John Riches has observed that change often follows such an encounter (2010). For example, Zacchaeus, having met Jesus, has his attitude transformed and acts to remedy the wrong he has done: 'Look, half of my possessions, Lord, I will give to the poor; and if I have defrauded anyone of anything, I will pay back four times as much.' (Luke 19.8). Zacchaeus' transformation leads to changed attitudes and actions.

The story of Saul's encounter with Jesus on the road to Damascus is even more dramatic than Zacchaeus' and so is the transformation that takes place; Saul goes from someone who wishes to imprison or kill Christians (Acts 9.1–2), to become Paul – someone who is willing to die to share the good news of Jesus (Phil. 1.20–21). Paul's transformation takes a particular form: conversion. Bernard Lonergan has described conversion as 'a decision about whom and what you are for' (1971, p. 268) and James Loder describes coming to know Christ as the 'decisive transformation' (1989, p. 64), and suggests that whenever an account is offered of Saul's conversion, it is always the transformation that is emphasized. Loder wanted to avoid conversion being viewed as a merely personal, emotional event, and instead argued, with Niebhur, that conversion is part of 'the ongoing transformation of human life under divine initiative' (1989, p. 19). Thus, an encounter with Jesus, either during his earthly ministry or following his resurrection, can be transformative, though we must remember that there were people who met Jesus and were not transformed (as far as we know), such as the religious leaders.

The resurrection could easily be argued to be the most significant instance of transformation in the Bible – what greater transformation can be imagined than the movement from death to life? When the women go to the tomb they are greeted by an angel, who tells them,

> 'Do not be afraid; I know that you are looking for Jesus who was crucified. He is not here; for he has been raised, as he said. Come, see the place where he lay. Then go quickly and tell his disciples, "He has been raised from the dead, and indeed he is going ahead of you to Galilee; there you will see him." This is my message for you.' (Matt. 28.5–7)

Jesus' resurrection is not only a singular historical event, but also points beyond itself as it changes history; a new reality has emerged (Kerr, 2009). As we will see below, Jesus' resurrection points towards the ultimate transformation of our resurrection bodies (Phil. 3.21); it also points towards the future transformation of the whole of creation. In Revelation 21 we are told, 'Then I saw a new heaven and a new earth; for the first heaven and the first earth had passed away, and the sea was no more' (21.1), and 'the one who was seated on the throne said, "See, I am making all things new."' (21.5a). Transformation is not to be understood merely at an individual or societal level, but at an eschatological level. We look toward

TRANSFORMATION

the future transformation, but we also recognize that the transformation has already begun, and that in Jesus the Kingdom of God has come (van Daalen, 1986). We are in the 'now' but look towards the 'not yet' of the future and ultimate eschatological transformation (Rogers, 2009).

It is worthy of mention that the actual term that we translate into English as 'transformation' occurs very rarely in the Bible; however, as Joanna Collicutt notes, that does not mean the theme of transformation is absent from the Bible:

> The actual word 'transformation' doesn't occur very often in the New Testament. Perhaps this is because it is so fundamental to its message, so deeply embedded, so woven into its narrative that it doesn't need to be voiced explicitly. But the idea, if not the word, is everywhere. (2015, p. 4)

The term 'transformation', or its derivatives, is used only three times in the New Testament (though it also occurs three times within the deutero-canonical literature): Romans 12.2, 2 Corinthians 3.18 and Philippians 3.21, and it will be helpful to explore each of these passages. The Greek term translated as 'transform' is *metamorphoō* (from where we get the English word 'metamorphosis') which is used to describe a change in form. It is also translated as 'transfigure', such as in the transfiguration of Jesus, so it appears in Matthew 17.2 and Mark 9.2 (Liefeld, 1978). Romans 12.2 states, 'Do not be conformed to this world, but be *transformed* by the renewing of your minds, so that you may discern what is the will of God – what is good and acceptable and perfect'. Some attempts have been made to suggest that conformation refers only to 'outward form' whereas transformation refers to 'inward being', but this view has been challenged (Barrett, 1991, p. 214; Ziesler, 1989). Indeed, while the 'essential change' may be inward, this change is then 'worked out in ordinary living' as believers strive to live according to the 'New Age' rather being conformed to the current culture (Ziesler, 1989, p. 294). Again, the transformation here will affect a whole community; Paul refers to the renewing of your *minds* (plural) not the renewing of your *mind* (singular). The rest of Romans 12 offers instructions for how Christians should live, so even after our minds are renewed we are still in need of guidance as to how to live (Barrett, 1991). There are parallels with Ephesians 4.22–24, where the theme of renewal is also found:

> You were taught to put away your former way of life, your old self, corrupt and deluded by its lusts, and to be *renewed* in the spirit of your minds, and to clothe yourselves with the new self, created according to the likeness of God in true righteousness and holiness.

The Christians in Ephesus are instructed to reject the influences of their old life and accept the 'radical change' that comes from following Jesus (Stott, 1989, p. 181). As in Romans 12, this exhortation is followed with ethical instructions, referred to in the NRSV as 'Rules for the New Life' (Eph. 4.25–32).

Both 2 Corinthians 3.18 and Philippians 3.21 take up the theme of reflecting God's glory:

> And all of us, with unveiled faces, seeing the glory of the Lord as though reflected in a mirror, are being *transformed* into the same image from one degree of glory to another; for this comes from the Lord, the Spirit. (2 Cor. 3.18)

> He will *transform* the body of our humiliation that it may be conformed to the body of his glory, by the power that also enables him to make all things subject to himself. (Phil. 3.21)

2 Corinthians 3 refers back to the story of Moses (Ex. 34.29–35), whose face shone when he had been speaking with God, so that he covered his face with a veil. However, here Paul is suggesting that we can all reflect God's glory: indeed, transformation occurs in order that we might better reflect his glory (Keener, 2005). Paul also identifies the role of the Spirit in bringing about transformation, but appears to identify Jesus and the Holy Spirit as the same (Barclay, 1975), though, given the Trinitarian nature of God and our expectation that the persons of the Trinity would work in unity, this is not overly problematic. There are also parallels between 2 Corinthians 3.1–18 and Ezekiel 36 (Keener, 2005): just as the renewal of Israel was seen to reflect God's glory, so the Corinthians were to be transformed to reflect God's glory. Philippians 3.21 looks towards Christ's return when we will reach 'full conformity to his resurrection body' (Thielman, 1995, p. 200). So while the transformation spoken of in Romans 12.2 is seen to be for the present ('*be* transformed'), the transformation of 2 Corinthians 3.18 is seen to be ongoing ('we are *being* transformed'), and the transformation of Philippians 3.21 is for the future ('He *will* transform).

In the Bible, we can see that the purpose of transformation is to glorify God by conforming us to his Son, Jesus Christ, through the work of the Holy Spirit. Transformation should therefore be understood in Trinitarian terms. We have also seen that transformation is not only individual, but also societal and cosmic: while Saul experienced an individual transformation, he went on to desire transformation for others (Loder, 1989), and we saw in Ezekiel that the whole people of Israel were to go through a process of transformation. Finally, Revelation points towards the transformation of the whole of creation. Indeed, transformation is primarily seen as occurring within the community of the people of God and as affecting the whole community. We have also seen that transformation is a process that begins now but is ongoing, and will be brought to fulfillment in the future resurrection. Therefore, within this work, transformation is understood as *an ongoing process of change whereby individuals and communities come to more fully resemble Jesus Christ and glorify God by the power of the Holy Spirit, in anticipation of the future transformation of the whole of creation*. That transformation is envisioned as *ongoing* in the Bible is clear from the way that it is spoken of in the present (Rom. 12.2) and future (Phil. 3.21) tenses, as well as references to *being* transformed (2 Cor. 3.18). We will consider this process of transformation in more detail below. That this transformation is understood both individually and communally is clear from the fact that the biblical texts are not addressed to individuals, but to communities, and emerged from communities. This is not to say that individuals are not transformed, but that individuals are transformed *in community* into the body of Christ: 'Now you are the body of Christ and individually members of it' (1 Cor. 12.27). We are not to be transformed into something unknown; our transformation is to lead us to become more like Jesus: 'He will transform the body of our humiliation that it may be conformed to the body of his glory' (Phil. 3.21). As we are transformed to become more like Jesus, we bring glory to God, as we become more the people he intended us to be. This is only possible through the work of the Holy Spirit (2 Cor. 3.18), who enables us to be transformed. And we look toward the final future transformation of the whole of creation:

> Then I saw a new heaven and a new earth; for the first heaven and the first earth had passed away, and the sea was no more ... And I heard a loud voice from the throne saying,
> 'See, the home of God is among mortals.
> He will dwell with them;
> they will be his peoples,
> and God himself will be with them;
> he will wipe every tear from their eyes.
> Death will be no more;
> mourning and crying and pain will be no more,
> for the first things have passed away.' (Rev. 21.1, 3–4)

Thus, from a biblical perspective, transformation is seen to be *an ongoing process of change whereby individuals and communities come to more fully resemble Jesus Christ and glorify God by the power of the Holy Spirit, in anticipation of the future transformation of the whole of creation.*

Before we move on, a brief comment on the relationship between transformation and *formation*. Richard Briggs (2007) appears to treat formation and transformation almost indistinguishably and suggests it would be a mistake to draw a distinction between them. Instead, he suggests that both lead to our 'conformation' to Jesus Christ (Briggs, 2007, p. 178), as seen in Philippians 3.21. Rosemary Haughton sees formation as a natural process of development, but sees transformation as something more radical, though she sees formation as underlying transformation: 'without the long process of formation there could be no transformation, yet no amount of careful formation can transform' (1967, p. 32). Like Loder, Haughton sees transformation as resulting from conversion, and describes the 'salvation event' as 'the point of transformation' (1967, p. 32). Similarly, Beverly Johnson-Miller (2005) sees formation as underlying transformation and understands transformation to be the 'reshaping of formation' (p. 32), and suggests that the factors that affect one's formation will also affect one's transformation. For both Haughton and Johnson-Miller, formation has a foundational role in transformation. Alan Le Grys (2010) differentiates between the normative, formative and transformative role of the Bible, which he developed from the work of Sandra Schneiders (1991). Le Grys suggests that the Bible has both a clear normative (regulatory) role and a formative role, whilst its transformative role is less clear, and there is less evidence for its ability to lead to changed readers. While Le Grys' work has wider relevance to this study, when considering the relationship between transformation and formation, it is clear that for Le Grys, transformation is something distinct from formation. Thus, while Briggs treats formation and transformation in unison, Haughton and Johnson-Miller see a strong relationship between formation and transformation, and Le Grys sees the two as separate processes. There is a risk in becoming mired in semantics, as clearly transformation and formation are closely linked, with only a prefix separating them. However, I would suggest that transformation has a stronger meaning than formation, as it implies a *change* from one state to another, rather than simply a *development* from one state to another, which is implied by formation. Romans 12.2 states we should 'be *transformed* by the renewing of your minds' not '*formed* by the renewing of your minds'. Therefore, while I would agree that they are closely related, I would suggest that transformation has a stronger meaning.

We will now move on to consider how biblical engagement might lead to transformation.

Transformative biblical engagement

In *New Horizons in Hermeneutics: The Theology and Practice of Transforming Biblical Readings*, Anthony Thiselton argues for the 'urgency' of asking 'how the language of the biblical writings may speak creatively, and may be read and understood with transforming effects' (1992, p. 2). In this section, we will consider some different approaches to the Bible and biblical engagement which could be said to be transformative. Before we explore some different approaches to the Bible and biblical engagement, it is important to note the role of the Holy Spirit in biblical engagement. Thiselton has traced the role of the Holy Spirit throughout the Bible and asserts that from the Old Testament onwards the Spirit of God is seen as an 'Agent of God' who brings 'renewal of the heart' (2013, p. 3). Similarly, Amos Yong asserts that the emphasis on the role of Holy Spirit in bringing transformation is an 'old theme' (2002, p. 256). As early as Augustine, and continued in the thinking of Luther, is the idea that 'the Bible conveys the living Word of God to us only as the Spirit makes us able to hear it' (Heron, 1983, p. 105). It is through the work of the Holy Spirit that the Bible ceases to be simply a text and becomes the Word of God. And it is through the work of the Holy Spirit that the Bible becomes transformative, as it 'calls us beyond ourselves, lays claim to our lives, demands our response, and, in the end, transforms our inabilities' (Yong, 2002, p. 256). The Holy Spirit therefore has a key role in transformative biblical engagement. However, John Stackhouse has cautioned against what he refers to as 'intuition', when individuals claim to have been inspired by the Holy Spirit to interpret or apply a passage of the Bible in a particular way, even where this is highly contradictory to what others determine the passage to mean (2015, p. 24). Stackhouse does not wish to reject the role of the Holy Spirit in the process of biblical engagement, but he would affirm the importance of the role of community in the process of interpretation. Loder also emphasizes the role of community in determining 'whether God has spoken' (1989, p. 23). Interestingly, Kahl (2007) has noted that ordinary readers are more likely to acknowledge and prioritize the role of the Holy Spirit in the process of biblical interpretation when compared with academic interpretations. This could be considered an example of the separation between spirituality and theology, which Daniel Hardy has highlighted (2001), and it could be suggested that ordinary readers are more likely to prioritize the spiritual, and academic readers are more likely to prioritize the theological. Hardy notes: 'Large numbers of people now treat spirituality as central to human concerns, where theology often now appears to have lost its position as normative for human life' (2001, p. 95).

One reason for viewing the Bible as a text with the power to transform is related to its status as divine revelation. For Karl Barth, the Bible is the product of God's action – 'God's own address to us' (2010 [originally published 1932], p. 106) – in written form. Key to understanding Barth's view of the Bible is understanding that for Barth the Bible is a witness to God's revelation in Jesus: 'revelation in fact does not differ from the person of Jesus Christ' (2010, p. 117). For Barth, the fullest revelation of God is found in the person of Jesus, to the extent that to speak of divine revelation is to speak of Jesus. Indeed, the New Testament appears to 'designate Jesus as the supreme revelation of God' (Dulles, 1983, p. 155). This leads Barth to argue that, 'to the extent that the Bible really attests revelation it is no less the Word of God than revelation itself' (2010, p. 118) – so in the sense that the Bible reveals God by witnessing to Jesus, it is considered to be revelation. Therefore, the Bible is divine revelation as it bears witness to the historical revelation of God in Jesus Christ, who is the fullest revelation of God. Richard Briggs has argued that 'wrestling' with God's revelation in the Bible is transformational, as it is a 'self-involving concept which reconstitutes the recipient' (2007, p. 177). By this Briggs is suggesting that when one encounters God in the Bible, one cannot help but be changed as a result. Briggs refers to this process of transformation as a 'reshaping' or 're-schematizing' (2011, p. 135); as we grapple with God's self-revelation in Jesus Christ our minds are renewed – or changed – so that we might live more closely in accordance with God's will. Briggs' use of the term 'wrestling' recalls Jacob's wrestling at Peniel, meaning 'the face of God': as Jacob declared, 'I have seen God face to face' (Gen. 32.30). Jacob is changed by this encounter: 'You shall no longer be called Jacob, but Israel, for you have striven with God and with humans, and have prevailed.' (Gen. 32.28). To use Briggs' language, Jacob is reconstituted by this encounter, this revelation of God, face to face, and this suggests that we might be similarly reconstituted as we encounter God's revelation in the Bible. Avery Dulles suggests that revelation is transformative as 'it introduces us into a new spiritual world, shifts our horizons, our perspectives, our point of view' (Dulles, 1983, p. 138). For Barth, Briggs and Dulles, the Bible's revelatory character makes it a transformative text. However, Sandra Schneiders has suggested that in order to experience the transformative power of the Bible, one first needs to have faith (1991). Schneiders summarizes her position on this issue as follows:

> Faith as a fundamental openness to the religious truth claims of the text is a requirement for even minimally valid interpretation of the text as *text*; faith as thematic Christian commitment is necessary for interpretation of the Bible as *scripture*. (1991, p. 61, emphasis in original)

Schneiders suggests that some level of faith is necessary not only for correctly interpreting the biblical text, but also for the biblical text to be transformative. In support of this assertion is the work of Andrew Village, who carried out research into the factors affecting the biblical interpretations of ordinary readers, finding that those with a higher view of the Bible tended to be more shaped by the text (2007, p. 160), thus suggesting that beliefs about the Bible do have some effect on how influential the text is. Interestingly David G. Ford found that even those who did not identify as Christian saw the Bible as a transformative text, and were concerned that the text would 'convert' them (2015, p. 13). It appears that even amongst those who are non-religious, the Bible is still seen by some to hold some form of transformative influence or power. Indeed, it has been described as possessing 'agent-like properties' (Engelke, 2013, p. xv)

Hans-Georg Gadamer's *Truth and Method* (originally published 1960) has become a landmark piece for understanding the relationship between the reader and the biblical text, but it also has relevance for understanding the transformative potential of the biblical text. Gadamer argues that 'the meaning of a text goes beyond its author', as it is 'always co-determined' by the reader (2013, p. 307), who is herself influenced by her own situation and horizon. Bowald has referred to the influence of the reader in the process of interpretation as 'human agency' (2015, p. 2). Gadamer also refers to the 'temporal distance' between the authors and events of the biblical texts and the modern-day reader; however, he does not view the temporal distance between the text and the reader negatively, but sees it as a positive factor that endows the reader with the knowledge that history, custom and tradition provide (2013, p. 308). Indeed, the distance between the horizon of the text and the horizon of the reader can help to identify the reader's prejudices, which Gadamer identifies as either 'true prejudices' that help us understand or 'false prejudices' that lead to misunderstanding (2013, p. 309). The process of interpretation can challenge our false prejudices, rather than simply leaving them unrecognized or reinforced. The potential fusion of horizons brings together the horizon of the text and the horizon of the reader so that 'a higher universality that overcomes not only our own particularity but also that of the other' emerges (2013, p. 316). Thiselton (1992) emphasizes the importance within Gadamer's work of recognizing the 'distinctiveness' of both the horizon of the text and the horizon of the reader, and that is only when this distinctiveness is acknowledged that a 'creative and productive' fusion of horizons occurs (p. 8). Within Gadamer's framework, transformation ensues when the fusion of horizons occurs to create 'something of living value' (2013, p. 317).

Andrew Rogers (2009; 2015) sought to explore the process by which congregations' horizons were transformed through biblical engagement, but noted that biblical engagement could also lead to the affirmation of existing horizons. Thus, Rogers distinguished between 'affirmative' and 'disruptive' readings, noting that both might lead to the transformation of congregational horizons (2015, p. 39). Indeed, this corresponds with Bernard Lonergan's use of Joseph de Finance's model of horizontal and vertical exercises of freedom: horizontal exercises are decisions or choices made within our current horizon, whereas vertical exercises are decisions or choices that move us beyond our current horizon to a new horizon (1971, p. 237). It is perfectly possible for the horizon of the text and the horizon of the reader to correspond prior to a fusion of horizons, and in such a situation, the reading would not be seen to be as transformative.

The last fifty years have seen a growth in approaches that set out to read the text from a particular context, often referred to as a 'social location', such as one's gender, race, class, sexual orientation, age, and so on (Ehrensperger, 2008, p. 136). Liberationist and feminist criticism or readings are two such approaches, which form part of 'a family of contextual theologies' (Grey, 2007, p. 105) that we will briefly explore here due to their relevance to transformative reading. It has been suggested that within both liberation and feminist theology, 'transformation means social change that brings equality, freedom, and justice to people' (Kim, 2013, p. 6). Within liberation theology, a three-stage approach is used to discern appropriate action, comprising of seeing, judging and acting (Boff and Boff, 1987). At the first stage – seeing – the situation of the poor and oppressed is analysed to determine the causes of poverty and oppression, making use of any methods that are appropriate for exploring this question. At the second stage – judging – the question is: 'What has the word of God to say about this?' (Boff and Boff, 1987, p. 32); how does the Bible inform our understanding of poverty and oppression and what should the Christian response be. The final stage is action: following a detailed analysis of the experience of the poor and oppressed, and after engaging with the Bible, a definite action is decided upon. In the words of Carlos Mesters, 'criticism can be derived from the Word of God to foster transforming action' (1993, p. 16).

Similarly, feminist theology aims to challenge the oppression faced by women, and opposes androcentric and patriarchal readings of the Bible in favour of those that pursue 'equality and justice for women and all humanity' (Kim, 2011, p. 2). There is significant variety in the way that feminist scholars have engaged with the Bible, but one approach, offered by Elisabeth Schüssler Fiorenza (1994), attempts to reclaim the history of women in early Christianity, which she claims has been forgotten due to the androcentric nature of the biblical texts. She argues that Christianity began with 'the discipleship community of equals' brought together by Jesus, which included both men and women (Fiorenza, 1994, p. 34). Fiorenza thus makes use of a 'hermeneutics of suspicion' to challenge traditional readings of biblical texts in order to highlight the way texts have been used to oppress women, and instead attempts to read texts in ways that are empowering (1994, p. liii).

Both liberationist and feminist readings seek to challenge the oppression faced by particular groups within society and lead to transformed perspectives as well as transformed actions. However, Anthony Thiselton has questioned whether liberationist and feminist readings, along with other contextually-driven approaches, are so concerned with the perspective, or horizon, of one particular social location that they may 'filter out' aspects of the biblical text that do not share this concern (1992, p. 410). This can be seen in the way that liberation theology has favoured certain biblical texts over others (Boff and Boff, 1987, p. 34), and in Fiorenza's claim that only those biblical texts that 'critically break through patriarchal culture … have the theological authority of revelation' (1994, p. 33). Therefore, while they may lead to transformed action, it may only represent a very particular form of transformation.

Yung Suk Kim is editor of the *Journal of Bible and Human Transformation* and has sought to develop a holistic model of human transformation in response to reading the Bible. The *Journal of Bible and Human Transformation* (JBHT) is concerned with the role of the Bible in the various dimensions of personal and societal change. To date, it has published five articles between 2011 and 2016. Kim argues that we need to move from an understanding of transformation that sees it as a 'static, linear change to a dynamic, circular change' (2013, p. xvi). Kim suggests there are three modes of being: 'I am no-body', 'I am some-body', and 'I am one-for-others' (2011, p. 13), and three 'subjects of transformation': self, neighbour and God (2013, p. xvi). Kim (2013) uses various examples of how these modes and subjects arise in various biblical texts; here we will focus on Psalm 13.

According to Kim, Psalm 13 begins with a state of 'I am no-one' (or no-body) due to the feeling of abandonment and powerlessness: 'How long, O Lord? Will you forget me forever?' (v.1). From verse 3, a state of 'I am some-one' (or some-body) emerges as a sense of relation develops: 'Consider and answer me, O Lord my God!', and then in verse 5 the psalmist moves to a state of 'I am one-for-others', as he develops a sense of 'commitment and determination' (Kim, 2013, p. 56): 'I will sing to the Lord, because he has dealt bountifully with me' (v.6). In Psalm 13, the transformation occurs as we realize that we still need to engage with our enemies, or 'difficult neighbours' (Kim, 2013, p. 57), but remembering that God's steadfast loves remains with us as we do so. Kim observes that we do not always start in the place of 'nothingness', but that the experience of 'nothingness' – the state of 'I am no-one' – is crucial for the process of transformation (2013, p. 22). This is perhaps akin to Mezirow's understanding of the role of a 'disorientating dilemma' (1994, p. 224). The concept of the process of transformation is one we will consider in more detail below.

Kim's model has further aspects that cannot be explored here, but a key feature of holistic transformation is the way it affects our sense of self, our relation to our neighbours and our relation to God (2011). The emphasis on the way that transformation affects our relationships with others is key, as it prevents us seeing transformation from a purely individual perspective, which Kim critiques as inherently leading to a focus on the 'recovery of individuality' (2013, p. 4). Nevertheless, while the three modes of being provide a helpful lens through which to consider biblical texts, it appears problematic to assume that each mode is to be found in every biblical text, or that reading biblical texts through such a lens will necessarily privilege transformative readings. However, the emphasis on 'I am one-for-others' certainly has strong biblical support: 'No one has greater love than this, to lay down one's life for one's friends' (John 15.13). Empirical research into this model of transformative reading in practice would be a valuable addition to further developing and refining this approach.

David G. Ford has identified six different types of transformation that Christians experience when they read the Bible. These are: encountering Jesus; encountering God; hearing God speak; gaining a new perspective; access to magical powers; or bringing about social change (Ford, 2019). Ford's types of transformation emerged from research carried out amongst a group of Catholics who did not normally engage with the Bible outside of Mass, but spent a year engaging with it, including participating in group discussions led by Ford. Ford identified two main findings, first, that the participants became more interested in the Bible, and second, that they gained a new perspective that positively impacted their spiritual lives. However, Ford notes that these two findings are not unrelated: 'As more is known about the Bible, so new information is gleaned which when reflected upon by the participants resulted in their spiritual nourishment' (2019, p. 9). Ford reflected that this suggests that the form of transformation that was most commonly experienced by the group was the fourth type: gaining a new perspective. We will see in due course that this is understood by a number of writers to be a key part of the process of transformation.

We have already noted that Thiselton views the Bible as a transformative text, but he also points out that Bible-reading in the Christian community can often appear 'uneventful, bland, routine, and entirely unremarkable' (1992, p. 8). This may be due to the fact that readers participate in what David Ford has termed 'counter-reading' to prevent themselves being transformed (2015). Ford observed that some of his participants deliberately engaged with the biblical text in a skeptical manner to 'disempower the assumed threat posed by its reading' (2015, p. 13). But if transformation is viewed as an ongoing process, then it is not necessarily to be expected that dramatic and immediate results should appear as soon as one opens the Bible. This potentially challenges the view that the Bible possesses 'agent-like properties' (Engelke, 2013, p. xv). Despite Thiselton's critique of the non-transformative nature of much Bible-reading that takes place within the Christian community, he also emphasizes the fact that we should not deliberately pursue 'destructive iconoclastic critiques' that relentlessly challenge our horizons (1992, p. 9). It should be expected that where individuals and communities are participating in the ongoing process of transformation, that they may be affirmed as well as challenged in their reading of the Bible.

Having explored the theme of transformation in the Bible, we defined transformation as the *ongoing process of change whereby individuals and communities come to more fully resemble Jesus Christ and glorify God by the power of the Holy Spirit, in anticipation of the future transformation of the whole of creation*. We then considered how biblical engagement might lead to transformation, first considering the role of the Holy Spirit and then examining the concept of revelation, the fusion of horizons, liberationist and feminist readings and holistic transformation. Each of these can lead to transformative readings, involving changed understandings, horizons and actions, but none of them should be seen as a way of guaranteeing transformation. Having defined transformation as an ongoing process, we will now consider how the process of transformation might take place, and will consider the work of a number of writers who have sought to identify distinct stages in the process of transformation.

The process of transformation

A key question for this research is, 'What does transformation look like?' As Makonen Getu points out, not all aspects of transformation can be 'quantified'; it is an 'inside-out phenomenon' (2002, pp. 97, 92), which means that while transformation may have taken place, it may be difficult to identify in some instances. The concept of change is key to understanding transformation, indeed, the following definitions of transformation all emphasize change:

> A *change* in the forms or structures of one's religious being ... Religious transformation involves a change or complex series of changes that enable movement from one state of being to another. (Johnson-Miller, 2005, p. 33, emphasis added)
>
> [The church] needs to help adults see that discipleship is not just about 'understanding the faith' but about learning how to live it, and that *learning* is concerned with *change* and that will lead to *growth*. (Baumohl, 1984, p. 10, emphasis added)
>
> A deeply rooted *change* in people's economic, social, political, spiritual and behavioural conditions resulting in their enjoyment of wholeness of life under God's ordinances. (Getu, 2002, p. 92, emphasis added)

And some have even pointed out that transformation may not only describe 'positive' changes, but any change that leads to a reordering of our understanding (Loder, 1989, p. 4). Therefore, we can say that transformation looks like change. As well as change, a key feature of transformation is that it is an ongoing *process*: in the words of Walter Wink, 'It is a process, not an arriving; we are "transforming", not "transformed"' (1989, p. 77). Therefore there may be recognizable steps or phases to transformation that we can identify. In what follows, I consider the process of transformation in order to answer the question, 'What does transformation look like?'

A number of writers have sought to identify distinct stages or steps in the process of transformation. Here I summarize the work of Jack Mezirow, Walter Brueggemann, James Loder, Daniel Schipani and Laurie Green before providing an evaluation of their models.

Jack Mezirow

Jack Mezirow is an educationalist who developed an approach to adult learning known as transformative learning theory. Mezirow posits that in our day-to-day lives we are guided by meaning structures, which are comprised of *meaning perspectives* and *meaning schemes*. A *meaning perspective* is 'the structure of cultural assumptions within which new experience is assimilated to – and transformed by – one's past experience' (1978, p. 101); a meaning perspective can be understood as a specific worldview one might hold, and so meaning perspectives influence how we see the world and understand our experiences within it. A *meaning scheme* is a 'specific manifestation' of a meaning perspective (1994, p. 223); this would be a particular view or attitude we hold due to our meaning perspective, for example, our view on abortion or euthanasia. For Mezirow, transformation occurs when our meaning structures are challenged and we are forced to re-examine them, often in the light of some form of dilemma, challenge or life crisis (1978) – for example, the loss of a job, a relationship breakdown or other 'disorientating dilemma' (1994, p. 224). This process is called *perspective transformation*. Mezirow identifies ten 'phases' of perspective transformation, beginning with a 'disorientating dilemma' (1991, p. 168). The second phase leads to 'self-examination with feelings of guilt or shame' and this is then followed by a 'critical assessment of epistemic, sociocultural, or psychic assumptions', and then the fourth phase of 'recognition that one's discontent and the process of transformation are shared and that others have negotiated a similar change' (1991, p. 168). This is particularly the case within Mezirow's original research, which focused on re-entry programmes for women returning to education or employment after a gap (1978). Mezirow found that in the context of small groups, women had the opportunity to critically reflect on their own meaning perspectives, particularly cultural expectations about women, and were able to challenge these. The next four phases (phases five to nine) all focus on developing a new perspective, which leads to new actions; the phases are: 'exploration of options for new roles, relationships, and actions', 'planning of a course of action', 'acquisition of knowledge and skills for implementing one's plans', 'provisional trying of new roles', and 'building competence and self-confidence in new roles and relationships' (1991, pp. 168–169). Mezirow (1978) was influenced by the work of Paulo Freire and his work on 'conscientization': Freire was working with Latin American peasants in order to help them become conscious of the fact that the status quo under which they lived was not the only possible way in which they might live (Freire, 1972). For Freire, conscientization should lead to challenging unjust societal structures, as well as personal change. Freire's influence on Mezirow can be seen in Mezirow's concern for 'consciousness raising' (1991, p. 186) and the importance of action following transformation, which will lead to more 'socially-responsible, clear-thinking decision makers' (2000, p. 8) – though clearly there is no universally accepted understanding of what constitutes 'socially-responsible' actions or behaviours. The final phase of perspective transformation is 'a reintegration into one's life on the basis of conditions dictated by one's new perspective' (Mezirow, 1991, p. 169). In summary, according to Mezirow's transformative learning theory, perspective transformation takes place when we face a disorientating dilemma which forces us to critically examine our meaning perspectives, which, when accompanied by constructive discourse, can lead to 'perspective taking' (1978, p. 104) that ultimately leads to the construction of a new meaning perspective.

Walter Brueggemann

We will explore the work of Walter Brueggemann on orientation, disorientation and reorientation. Brueggemann's work is not intended to offer a model of the process of transformation, however, I believe it does so implicitly. In *Praying the Psalms*, Brueggemann suggests that the psalms reflect the common human experience of orientation, disorientation and reorientation, with the latter two being the most common (2007). *Orientation* is understood as a 'situation of equilibrium' (2007, p. 3), which Brueggemann suggests is more commonly expressed within Proverbs but can be found in a select number of psalms, such as 37 and 145. Verses three and four of Psalm 37 state, 'Trust in the Lord, and do good; so you will live in the land, and enjoy security. Take delight in the Lord, and he will give you the desires of your heart'. Brueggemann describes the state of orientation as being one 'we all yearn for': 'It consists in being well-settled, knowing that life makes sense and God is well-placed in heaven, presiding but not bothering. This is the mood of much of the middle-class Church' (2007, p. 3). As is clear from Brueggemann's description of the state of orientation, this may be a comfortable state to be in, but it is not a state that is especially open to or welcoming of transformation. Nevertheless, we often pretend to be a in a place of orientation when we are really in a place of disorientation, due to societal pressures to behave in certain ways, hence Brueggemann's comment about the middle-class Church representing a state of orientation. *Disorientation* comes about from an 'awareness that life is not whole' (p. 9), and could be said to be a state of disorder or chaos, which leads to the psalms of complaint or supplication, for example, 22, 13 or 88. The psalmist cries out in Psalm 88, 'But I, O Lord, cry out to you; in the morning my prayer comes before you. O Lord, why do you cast me off? Why do you hide your face from me?' (v. 13–14). This state of being 'painfully disorientated' (2007, p. 2) comes as we recognize the difficult, frightening, harmful, and damaging aspects of life. The language of disorientation is also used by Mezirow when he refers to the role of the 'disorientating dilemma' (1994, p. 224) in precipitating the process of perspective transformation, and Brueggemann also suggests that a life event, such as a marriage failure or job loss, may lead us to recognize the experience of disorientation. This state of disorientation could also be said to be similar to Kim's first mode of being: 'I am no-body' or 'I am no-one' (2011, p. 13). Brueggemann suggests that as we bring this sense of disorientation to the psalms of complaint and lamentation, not only do we discover a new understanding of the psalms, but we discover a new understanding of our situation. These psalms are 'disorientation addressed to God. And in that address, something happens to the disorientation' (2007, p. 11). *Reorientation* emerges as a new situation:

> This is not an automatic movement that can be presumed upon or predicted. Nor is it a return to the old form, a return to normalcy as though nothing had happened. It is rather 'all things new'. And when it happens, it is always a surprise, always a gift of graciousness, and always an experience that evokes gratitude. (p. 11)

This reorientation is not something we achieve, but is a gift from God, and is expressed in Psalms 103, 30 and 96, along with others. Psalm 30 begins, 'I will extol you, O Lord, for you have drawn me up, and did not let my foes rejoice over me. O Lord my God, I cried to you for help, and you have healed me' (v. 1–2). In the state of reorientation there is still an 'awareness that life is not whole' (p. 9), nevertheless, 'We dare to say in our existence there is richness of life along with the reality of death. We experience the power of resurrection as well as the inescapabilty of crucifixion' (2007, p. 11). In contrast to some other writers (Browning, 1996; Loder, 1989), Brueggemann presents reorientation in entirely positive terms, as an experience that evokes gratitude, whereas others have noted that change or transformation are not always positive. This movement from a state of orientation, to disorientation, to reorientation, points towards how perspectives can be transformed through engagement with the Bible, especially the psalms, and how the Bible can give voice to common human experience. While Brueggemann does not offer this as a model of transformation, he does suggest that it allows us 'to speak of "passages", the life-cycle, stages of growth, and identity crises' (2007, p. 3). So it could be said to offer a biblical framework for considering how the process of transformation occurs.

James Loder

We will now consider the work of James E. Loder, which is explored in *The Transforming Moment* (1989, originally published in 1981). Loder refers to the 'logic of transformation' as consisting of five steps, beginning with 'conflict-in-context' (1989, p. 3), which, much like Mezirow's (1991) approach, refers to some form of disorientation that disrupts our desire for constancy. Others, such as Stephen Brookfield, have also suggested that some kind of 'trigger event' can lead to transformation (1987, p. 26), though Brookfield emphasizes the fact that these trigger events can be positive events: perhaps starting a new job or getting married may lead to a process of critical reflection, leading to transformation. Similarly, Fowler speaks of the way different crises can lead to development (1995), and Browning has suggested that crisis is an essential 'condition' for transformation (1996, p. 281). Following this conflict-in-context comes the next stage: 'interlude for scanning' (Loder, 1989, p. 3). This is the point at which alternative ways of resolving the conflict are considered, much like Mezirow's (1991) idea of exploring new roles. This is then followed by 'insight felt with intuitive force', at which point a resolution to the conflict emerges that 'reconstellates the elements of the incoherence and creates a new, more comprehensive context of meaning' (Loder, 1989, p. 3). This has echoes of Brueggemann's state of 'reorientation' (2007, p. 11). An example of this could be gaining a broader understanding on a particular issue, much as Mezirow's work emphasizes 'consciousness raising' (1991, p. 186) as a desired outcome of transformation. Stage four consists of 'release and repatterning' (1989, p. 4); Loder suggests that the 'Eureka moment' of finding a resolution leads to a release of energy to analyse and modify the original situation in response to the new resolution (1989, p. 4). The final stage, 'interpretation and verification', emerges out of the desire to have the resolution confirmed so that constancy can be returned (Loder, 1989, p. 4); we do not wish to live with conflict-in-context and are therefore working towards a resolution that leads to balance being restored. Thus, as for Mezirow, for Loder transformation results initially from some form of conflict that upsets our existing patterns of thought or action, and because we are not comfortable we search for a solution to the conflict, and in the process, our existing patterns of thought and/or action are transformed.

Daniel Schipani

Fourthly, we turn to the work of the practical theologian Daniel Schipani, and in particular his reflections on the transformative potential of intercultural Bible-reading, which came out of the 'Through the Eyes of Another' project (see de Wit et al., 2004; de Wit and Dyk, 2015). Schipani suggests that intercultural Bible readings can be seen as a 'special way of generating a *creative process*' that has five recognizable steps

(2015, p. 105, emphasis in original). While both Mezirow and Loder start their models with some form of dilemma or conflict, Schipani sees the first step as forming a community in which 'trust and mutual respect are key', including 'trust in the text', as well as 'receptive expectation' (2015, p. 105). The emphasis within small groups on mutual support and fellowship has been noted by a number of researchers (Todd, 2009, 2013; Walton, 2011, 2014; Wuthnow, 1994). This emphasis on 'receptive expectation' highlights the importance of members being open to transformation, whereas within Mezirow's and Loder's work, there may not have been an initial desire for transformation. Schipani's second step involves 'a search for understanding, consolation, reorientation and resolution' (2015, p. 106); we have already heard the language of reorientation in Brueggemann's work and the language of resolution within Loder's work. For Mezirow, Loder and Schipani, some form of exploration stage is essential. Step three, as within Loder's work, involves new ideas emerging; indeed, while Loder speaks of 'insight felt with intuitive force' (1989, p. 3), Schipani speaks of 'new insights, intuitions, and meanings' (2015, p. 106). Within Schipani's model, however, emphasis is placed on the relationship between the text and the group process as being significant in generating new ideas. Step four, which is again very similar to Loder's model, encompasses a release of energy and a 'kind of "eureka effect"', which may lead to 'catharsis and lamentation as well as celebration and motivation for new action' (Schipani, 2015, pp. 106–107). Much as Mezirow's original participants were empowered through the process of perspective transformation (1978), Schipani suggests that step four also brings with it a 'sense of empowerment' (2015, p. 107). Step five, the final step, involves validation and confirmation:

> validation and confirmation take place in two ways: both retrospectively, that is, how the new insights or changed views effectively connect with the critical or conflicting situation that the participants face, as well as prospectively and praxeologically, which can also generate further praxis. (Schipani, 2015, p. 107)

Schipani notes that the 'transformation process' is not accomplished until this has occurred (2015, p. 107). While for Schipani the 'creative process' of transformation is a group process, for Loder, it is more individual, with confirmation coming about through the internal reordering and acceptance of an individual's thinking. For Schipani, a key factor in the process of transformation is the interaction between the text and the group members in generating new insights which lead to transformed thinking, and, crucially, action or praxis. This can be seen in

Brueggemann's work, where it is in the interaction with the psalms that the reorientation occurs.

Laurie Green

I wish to introduce one further way of articulating the process of transformation: the Let's Do Theology Spiral as found in the work of Laurie Green (1990; 2009). The Let's Do Theology Spiral is more commonly referred to as 'The Pastoral Cycle' (Ballard and Pritchard, 2006) and is influenced by Kolb's Experiential Learning Cycle (Kolb, 1984). The cycle can be followed by individuals or used by groups, but given the focus of this research, the explanation that follows will focus on its use in a group, which is also how Green presents it as being used. Those who are familiar with the cycle, which is used in theological reflection, will probably have already noted some similarities between it and the models explored above. The model begins with an *experience*, which an individual shares with a group, and the focus is particularly on how the experience makes them feel – what is their emotional response? This is akin to the Mezirow's or Loder's dilemma or conflict. After this, the experience is *explored*, which is when the experience is analysed, and Green suggests making use of historical, geographical, social, economic, cultural and religious information in order to fully analyse the experience (2009, p. 63). Once a thorough analysis of the experience has been produced, the next stage is to *reflect* on the experience. At the reflection stage, theological learning is brought to bear on the experience; the Bible, hymns, the creeds, theological doctrines, 'the great themes of the faith', can all be used in the process of reflecting theologically on the experience and exploration (Green, 2009, p. 21). Following the reflection stage the group should ask the following question: 'in light of all the Experience, Exploration and Reflection about this issue, how does God want us to Respond?' (Green, 2009, p. 23). This takes us to the *response* stage, as the group determines the appropriate way forward in light of the discussion that has occurred. This response should 'derive from a hunger to see God's will done' (Green, 2009, p. 24). Finally, and even if a group's response does not lead to a specific action but to a greater awareness, a new situation has emerged, which will ultimately lend itself to a *new experience*, so that the cycle begins again. This model of theological reflection owes much to Liberation Theology, and the Base Ecclesial Communities that emerged in Latin America (Green, 2009), in particular the See-Judge-Act model (Boff and Boff, 1987). While Green's model offers a process whereby individuals and communities are transformed, Green also sought to transform the way theology was done (2009, especially pp. 3–16). This is an ongoing consideration within the field of practical theology, which will be explored in more detail in Chapter 4.

There are some clear points of similarity between the five writers as well as some clear points where they diverge. Mezirow, Brueggemann and Loder see some form of dilemma or disorientation or conflict as the start of the process of transformation. Green's model starts with an experience, which is not necessarily a negative experience. Schipani emphasizes the importance of a situation of trust and openness at the start of his model. And all five writers diverge in regards to the extent that transformation is viewed as either an individual or group process, or combination of the two. Loder presents transformation as being highly individualistic, whereas for Schipani and Green the group context is key. Mezirow emphasizes both: the transformation may initially impact an individual, but the transformation takes place within the context of dialogue with others; Mezirow envisages the transformation will not lead to merely individualistic outcomes (2000). Brueggemann, who did not set out to develop a model of transformation, understands the movement from orientation to disorientation occurring naturally as part of the human experience. The transformative aspect of his work is the process of reorientation, which happens when individuals bring their experience of disorientation to the Bible, specifically the psalms, and a reorientation takes place. Loder, Mezirow and Schipani see a necessity to explore alternative solutions, and all three also identify some kind of process whereby possible solutions are tested. In Green's model, we assume that during the 'response' stage various possible responses are considered. And particularly for Mezirow and Schipani, transformation will lead to transformed action as well as transformed thinking. Bringing together the work of an educationalist (Mezirow), a biblical scholar (Brueggemann), and three theologians (Loder, Schipani and Green), two of whom are practical theologians (Schipani and Green), has enabled an exploration of the process of transformation from a variety of perspectives.

I firmly support the idea that transformation often involves challenges, moments of crisis, or disorientating dilemmas that lead to periods of upheaval of one's previous perspectives; this may lead to a period of continued uncertainty or a new perspective may emerge quite swiftly. This period of challenge occurs as we realize that our perspective is not necessarily God's perspective, or in the words of Terry Veling, 'Is my current reality the "lens" through which I search the scriptures, or does my searching of the scriptures provide the "lens" through which I view my current reality?' (2005, p. 25). As we realize perhaps that our perspective, or lens, is not 'correct', we are forced to consider solutions to this challenge: what is the 'correct' perspective on this issue or concern? I put 'correct' in inverted commas to make clear that I am aware of the problems of using this term, but I use it here heuristically. As various solutions emerge, a process of reconsideration occurs, as these are considered in light of both the Bible, as well as other Christian teaching, and in light of experience, both individual and communal. Once a clear solution emerges a 'eureka moment' may occur, and it will seem almost inevitable that change will take place as a result. A new perspective has emerged, and while this may not necessarily lead to action, it will have certainly led to changed views, attitudes, feelings or concerns. The process of transformation is never complete, but it could be said that one 'cycle' of transformation is complete until the next cycle begins. This is why Green uses the idea of a spiral – the Let's Do Theology *Spiral* – to represent the ongoing nature of the process (2009).

It is important to note that I am not suggesting that this is the only way of understanding the process of transformation. While I have affirmed here the role of challenge in the process of transformation, I also acknowledge that others have seen the role of affirmation as part of the process of transformation (Rogers, 2015). And while I support the view that affirmative readings of the Bible can reinforce the process of transformation and would not wish to go as far as Browning in seeing crisis as 'necessary' for transformation (1996, p. 282), I would assert that some form of challenge is often necessary for transformation to take place. And I would wish to affirm that transformation, ultimately, is the result of God's agency (Browning, 1996) in our lives and not 'an achievement coming from us' (Brueggemann, 2007, p. 23).

In this chapter we have considered the concept of transformation, first from a biblical perspective, which led to the development of a definition of transformation as *an ongoing process of change whereby individuals and communities come to more fully resemble Jesus Christ and glorify God by the power of the Holy Spirit, in anticipation of the future transformation of the whole of creation.* We then considered how the Bible might be considered to be a transformative text and ended by exploring the process of transformation, beginning with a consideration of the concept of change, which is a key concept when considering transformation. We then explored how five different writers (Jack Mezirow, Walter Brueggemann, James Loder, Daniel Schipani and Laurie Green) have sought to understand the process of transformation.

3

Small Groups

Hans de Wit has claimed that 'a lot has been written about transforming reading but very little about the conditions that reading (the Bible) must meet if change is intended' (2004a, p. 30). Here the focus is on whether small groups provide the 'conditions' or context within which biblical engagement can take place, and whether the conditions within a small group will lead to biblical engagement which is more likely to have transformative outcomes. We will begin by exploring the development of small groups in order to provide some background to our later discussion of the transformative characteristics of small groups, and the transformative potential of biblical engagement in small groups.

The development of small groups

Humans are inclined towards forming relationships and groups – at birth, most people enter into a family group and, during their lifetimes, people will engage with a huge range of different groups: friends, colleagues, neighbours, and so on. The experience of being in groups has been described as 'fundamental' (Benson, 1991, p. 3). Some of these groupings are unintentional; however, individuals may also intentionally join a group for a specific purpose. This brings us to a principal distinction between 'natural' and 'created' or 'artificial' groups (Douglas, 1983). A 'natural' group is generally considered to have arisen organically, for example, a family or friendship group. A 'created' or 'artificial' group arises for a specific purpose, for example, a focus group or a bird-watching group. Yet the difference between the two is not always clear: one might join a bird-watching group, become good friends with the other members, and then socialize with them beyond the time they spend bird-watching – is the group still a 'created' or 'artificial' group? Douglas recognizes this difficulty, and suggest that these labels apply primarily to the 'origin' of the group, because in all other ways artificial and created groups may function comparably in terms of the group processes at work (1983, p. 35). However it could be argued that some groups, such as counselling groups, will not function comparably, as there is often a clear leader – a trained counsellor or therapist – who takes responsibility for guiding the group (Aveline and Dryden, 1988).

We have already identified that there are different forms of group – 'natural' and 'created' or 'artificial' – and we shall now specify the *forms* of small group that are being considered here. The focus will be on 'created' or 'artificial' groups, so it is valuable to explore what Douglas (1983) meant by these terms, and how they have been developed. Douglas defines 'natural' groups as 'groups that arise out of the everyday needs of human beings', whereas an 'artificial' group is 'specifically and consciously generated' (1989, p. 38, 39). He recognizes that all groups are in some sense 'created' and argues that groups appear more 'natural' the further one is from their creation. Thus, while the terms are in some ways unhelpful, the definition of 'artificial' groups as those that are 'specifically and consciously generated' points to a key feature of 'artificial' groups in general: that of purpose.

Groups that are deliberately formed are often done so for a specific purpose. It is thought that the first usage of small groups within social psychology occurred in 1898 (Tindale and Anderson, 1998), and their usage within social work emerged during the 1930s (Younghusband, 1976). Today, small groups are used in a huge variety of settings. Tindale and Anderson identify seven common 'domains' or 'applied settings' of small groups: learning and education settings; community/healthcare settings; international relations; legal/jury relations; organization/performance settings; military teams; and focus groups (1998, pp. 3–4). Yet spiritual or religious groups are not included within their domains and nor are common interest groups (such as book clubs, for example). In spite of these limitations, Tindale and Anderson do indicate that there is a breadth of ways of using small groups.

Roger Walton (2014) uses the phrase 'church-related small groups' to refer to small groups that are affiliated with a church, to delineate them from secular small groups or Christian small groups that are independent from a church. Church-related small groups exist for a variety of purposes and thus are referred to by a range of different names: house groups, cell groups, Bible study groups, formation groups, and so on. This is not including other forms of small group, such as choirs, Parochial Church Councils, or youth groups, which are also affiliated to churches. Roger Walton (2014) has tracked the development of church-related small groups since 1900, suggesting there has been a development from *study groups* (1900–1940s), to *house groups* (1940–1970s), and then on to *mission and discipleship groups* (1960–2000s). The primary aim of study groups was to educate people in and about Christianity; the primary aim of house groups was to support people pastorally; and the primary aim of mission and discipleship groups – as the name suggests – was to impact the wider community. However it is worth noting that a given small group may aspire to fulfil all three of these aims.

We need now to briefly consider what constitutes a 'small' group, as there is a range of opinion here. Hare (1995) argues that a group consisting of anywhere between 2 and 30 members can be considered a 'small' group, but others suggests a much lower maximum, such as 15 (Whitaker, 1987) or even 7 (Fink, 2004). Johnson and Johnson suggest that members must be involved in 'face-to-face interaction' (1982, p. 7), which indicates that the size should enable members to be able to converse with one another as fellow participants, without feeling as if they are speaking to an audience. Whitaker (1987) claims that a size of 6–15 allows enough interaction for creative and helpful discussions, but beyond that size, direct interaction between members becomes limited. Thus a useful measure of whether or not a group is considered small might be whether or not a single conversation or discussion can take place, in which all members are able to contribute – though often a group leader or arbiter will be necessary to facilitate the conversation.

The transformative characteristics of small groups

We will now consider the potential of the small group context to effect transformation amongst small group members. First, we will examine the literature that suggests that the small group context provides a means by which to achieve transformation, and secondly, we will consider a specific example of a small group leading to transformation among its members. It is not possible to consider all the different means by which small groups might lead to transformation, but a selection of examples will be examined. Here, transformation is not seen in terms of our definition (*the ongoing process of change whereby individuals and communities come to more fully resemble Jesus Christ and glorify God by the power of the Holy Spirit, in anticipation of the future transformation of the whole of creation*), but from an educational or psychological perspective and generally in terms of personal development – though the two understandings of transformation are not necessarily mutually exclusive.

David Johnson and Frank Johnson refer to the 'unique powers of group experiences' to lead to personal growth (1982, p. 441). So what is it about (small) group experiences that gives them this unique power? The term 'group dynamics' is used to refer to the processes at work in a group, and acknowledges the fact that groups are not static, but are dynamic organisms (Jaques, 1991). While not everything that one experiences in a group falls under the title of 'group processes', it is a helpful way of distinguishing some common experiences that people within a group are likely to undergo. Benson defines group processes as 'changes over time in the internal structures, organizations, and culture of the whole group, part of the group or an individual member' (1991, p. 74), and it is the existence of and interaction between these different group processes that can lead to transformation.

Johnson and Johnson (1982) identify the unique functions of groups in leading to growth or change (or transformation), above and beyond individual reflection or paired discussion. They identify a list of nine 'events' that take place in groups that may lead to change, but we will focus on one particular event here: 'change is promoted by other group members modelling constructive behaviour and attitude patterns the participants wish to master' (1982, p. 445). Johnson and Johnson are by no means alone in referring to the role of the group in shaping the behaviour of its members; Douglas (1983) identified the role of groups in leading to conformity among members, and the development of 'group norms', which are shared or expected behaviours and attitudes that regulate the behaviours and attitudes of members (Whitaker, 1987, p. 37). These are a common feature identified within group processes. In some contexts, it would be exceptionally unhelpful to simply imitate the behaviours or attitudes of others, particularly if the behaviours and attitudes being modelled were dysfunctional or damaging. However, speaking in the context of growth groups, Johnson and Johnson (1982) highlight the positive impact of observing and then internalizing effective means of solving problems or addressing issues. For example, if someone found handling public criticism difficult, they may find it immensely helpful to see how others handle public criticism in order to be better equipped for future instances. As the authors point out, in a group there are more people to observe and thus more opportunities to see a variety of positive models to consider emulating. This could be linked with Mezirow's concept of 'perspective taking' (1978, p. 104), as individuals have an opportunity to observe and then experiment with alternative attitudes and behaviours (Whitaker, 1987). However, as noted above, if an unhelpful response to public criticism were being offered, this may have a detrimental effect upon the member for whom this was already a problematic issue.

Thus, if group norms are being utilized in order to effect a positive change in members' behaviours or attitudes, it is crucial that these norms do not remain implicit, as they often are (Whitaker, 1987), but are considered and assessed for their helpfulness in promoting growth and change. A key feature of Johnson and Johnson's explanation of change taking place rests on the fact that the group member wishes to master a new behaviour or attitude; they desire change. This supports the emphasis on the voluntary and self-directed nature of much adult learning (Cranton, 2016) – transformation is unlikely to occur or be permanent if someone is reluctant or unwilling to change. Nevertheless, it has been found that group discussion can bring about changes that have been resisted when attempted via alternative methods (Younghusband, 1976), so even when an individual is initially resistant to change, it may still be possible for change to occur. However, this raises serious questions about the ethical implications of such an approach. For example, is it acceptable to endeavour to bring about a change in someone else if they are opposed to such a change?

We have already noted that 'created' or 'artificial' small groups are often formed for a purpose (Douglas, 1983). Whitaker suggests that groups can be used to help participants move from a 'current state' to a 'preferred state', but that this is only possible if one has a clear idea of what this 'preferred state' is (1987, p. 8). Jarlath Benson (1991) suggests that one possible way of understanding the 'current state' or needs of a group is by utilizing Abraham Maslow's hierarchy of needs. Based on clinical experience, Maslow suggested that the key motivating factor amongst people was perceived needs, and he identified a range of different types of needs which, when met, would then lead to another type of need emerging (1970). A 'perceived' or 'felt' need is a want or desire experienced by an individual, which may not be considered a necessity by all (Bradshaw, 1994). While Maslow acknowledged that not everyone experiences these needs to the same degree and within the hierarchical order shown below, the norm was that once the lower needs had been met, higher needs emerged. Table 1 offers Maslow's hierarchy in the left column and my own suggestion of how this might apply in a group context in the right column.

Maslow's model is focused on the individual and developed from a psychological perspective, so it does not seek to offer a corporate understanding of these needs. From a theological perspective, we might consider 'self-actualization' to refer to Jesus' promise, 'I came that they may have life, and have it abundantly' (John 10.10). Benson (1991) argues that behaviour in a group can be understood in terms of the interaction between the different perceived needs of different members of the group. He also suggests that identifying needs forms a key part in identifying the purpose of the group and in motivating people towards that purpose, leading to transformation. It has been noted that if an individual's needs are not being met, they may wish to leave the group and potentially join another group where they feel their needs will be

Maslow's (1970) hierarchy of needs (starting with the lowest)	Examples of how these needs *might* be met in a group context ...
Physical needs	The group might act if one of their members was struggling financially, to ensure that they had food and money to pay bills.
Safety needs	The group might meet in a location that was safe but also comfortable.
Love needs	The group might enable its members to feel part of a community and loved.
Esteem needs	The group might encourage members to recognize the things they are gifted at.
Intellectual needs	The group might enable members to learn new ideas and skills.
Aesthetic needs	The group might encourage members to recognize the higher principles that governed their ideas and actions.
Self-actualization needs	The group might enable members to become everything that they are capable of.

Table 1: How Maslow's hierarchy of needs could be applied to the group context.

met more effectively (Thompson and Kahn, 1976). Clearly this means that groups will be most likely to meet the needs of their members, and effect transformation, when the members have shared needs and thus are all motivated towards meeting common needs. However, a group may become dysfunctional if one individual's needs are allowed to dominate, or the fulfilment of their needs are in conflict with those of another. This is why it is also helpful to consider whether a 'perceived' or 'felt' need is also a 'normative' need; a 'normative' need is defined by experts (such as doctors, psychologists or church leaders) as a 'desirable' need (Bradshaw, 1994, p. 46). For example, someone might be encouraged to join a small group if their psychologist considered them to need help with their interpersonal skills (Johnson and Johnson, 1982). So a small group may lead to transformation if it motivates people to get their needs met – leading to change – but not if the needs of one individual come into conflict with needs of another in such a way that neither set of needs is fulfilled, and change does not occur.

Leadership is a key factor that might affect the transformative potential of a small group, as both group processes and the influence of needs can be shaped by a leader. Even in a 'mature' and well-established group, the leader still maintains ultimate responsibility for maintaining the group (Aveline and Dryden, 1988, p. 8). The fact that the leader maintains some level of authority may lead group members to transfer childhood responses, such as dependency or disobedience, onto the leader (Jaques, 1991). Harris' (1995) work on transactional analysis highlighted the different ways that individuals can relate to one another, either as Adults, Parents or Children. Small group leaders should encourage members to relate to them, and to the rest of the group, as adults and equals, rather than reverting either to Parent or Child mode. Heron identifies three kinds of authority that facilitators and group leaders, can possess: tutelary (the leader is 'competent' in a certain capacity to be passed on to the group), political (the leader has the authority to make decisions that affect the group), and charismatic (the leader influences members simply by 'their way of being and behaving') (1999, pp. 19, 20). In any given group, it is important to consider what form of leadership may be most effective and most likely to lead to transformation, as well as taking responsibility for other factors that might affect the transformative potential of the group, such as group processes or perceived needs.

We will now move on to consider a specific example of a small group leading to transformation within an education setting.

Jack Mezirow's transformative learning theory, which we considered in Chapter 2, grew out of his research on re-entry programmes for women returning to education or employment after a gap (1978). We have already considered his model of transformation, but we will now focus specifically on how this takes place in the context of a small group. Mezirow found that in the context of small groups, women had the opportunity to critically reflect on their own meaning perspectives, particularly cultural expectations about women, and were able to challenge these. According to transformative learning theory, the 'disorientating dilemma' can be seen as the experience of returning to education or employment, but it is only in the context of the small group that women start to challenge their existing meaning perspectives.

One of the nine factors that Johnson and Johnson (1982) identify within small groups as promoting change is the process of revealing one's experiences and feelings, followed by the realization that others share these experiences and feelings, leading to greater understanding of one's own situation. Without the context of the small group this realization would be unlikely, as the women would not be given the opportunity for 'intensive self-examination' (Mezirow, 1978, p. 102). Thus while

Cranton (2016) argues that small groups, or more generally, collaboration, are not a crucial feature of perspective transformation, there is evidence that without a context for self-examination, constructive discourse and perspective-taking, it would be unlikely that transformation would occur. As we participate in dialogue with others, we are able to assess our own 'meaning perspectives'. As we engage with the meaning perspectives of others we begin to assess our own meaning perspectives. Mezirow refers to the 'trying of new roles' (1991, p. 169) or 'perspective taking' (1978, p. 104), which occurs when we consider the world from someone else's perspective, specifically, someone who is more aware than ourselves.

However, it is not simply at the stage of perspective transformation that small groups are valuable; Mezirow emphasized the fact that sustaining a new perspective was only possible in association with others who also share the new perspective (1978). Indeed, Heron (1999) has argued that it is only through being in relationships with others who are working towards autonomy and wholeness that one can become whole. Jean Vanier also suggests that as individuals grow, the whole community can grow (2010), so transformation should be understood at group level. Mezirow (1978) found that the women involved in his research went on to see themselves and society differently, often leading to personal changes – such as a sense of independence – and social action. It appears that small groups can provide a context for intensive self-examination, which may otherwise not occur, and that they can thereby facilitate transformation, by transforming people's perspectives in a way which leads to action.

There are many other factors both within and beyond small groups that may have an influence upon whether or not they lead to transformation, and not all of these are observable. For example, the length of time a group has been running may have an impact on group processes, especially on how comfortable members feel in sharing their experiences or feelings, which has been found to lead to transformation (Johnson and Johnson, 1982). Alternatively, the state of mind of each individual member will also play a significant role, but this is not necessarily determinable. As well as this, outside factors may have an influence, such as current events that are going on in the community, country or world. And, perhaps most difficult to measure or observe, is the role of the Holy Spirit in bringing about transformation. There are various other factors that may be influential, however, not all of these will be observable or measurable.

The transformative potential of biblical engagement in small groups

In this final section, we will consider the transformative potential of biblical engagement within small groups. Is there something about the context of and conditions within a small group, when compared to other contexts, which will lead to biblical engagement that is more likely to have transformative outcomes?

Greg Ogden has suggested that there are three features necessary for transformation to occur: 'transparent trust', 'the truth of God's Word', and 'mutual accountability' (2003, pp. 154, 162, 168). He therefore suggests that the Bible is most likely to have a transformative impact when a group of two to four, who are committed to trust and accountability, read it together. Unfortunately, Ogden does not provide any research to support this: he merely offers anecdotal experience. He suggests that larger groups dilute the level of trust and accountability, potentially reducing the probability of transformation. However, as we have seen from the literature on small groups, there is a range of advice about the appropriate size of a small group (Hare, 1995). Research carried out by Wuthnow (1994) also found that small groups have a propensity for becoming inward-looking, and this propensity may well be heightened in smaller groups. Depending on the desired outcome of the group, it would not necessarily be a negative occurrence for the group to be inward-looking, though if the aim was to reach out to the local community, an outward focus would be essential. Thus, while trust and accountability will be significant factors in enabling individuals to feel safe and comfortable in a small group, these are not conditional upon the group having fewer than four members. So there is no reason to assume that a smaller group size is necessary in order for biblical engagement to be transformative. In any small group care should be taken, particularly during the early stages of the group (Whitaker, 1987), to ensure that trust and accountability emerge amongst the group members. It may be helpful to use Bruce Tuckman's model of group development, which recognizes the stages of 'forming', 'storming', 'norming', 'performing' and 'adjourning' (Tuckman and Jensen, 1977). John Heron offers an alternative model of 'wintertime', 'springtime', 'summertime' and 'autumn' (1999); either would enable an analysis of the likely levels of trust and accountability that might be present, as well as the presence of other group processes.

We will now consider the contributions of Walter Wink and E. H. Robertson to the question of transformative biblical engagement, before considering some recent research in this field.

Walter Wink's (1981) approach to biblical engagement within small groups is influenced by insights from psychotherapy, in particular split-brain theory, which posits that we over-use the left side of our brain – the logical, analytic side – and under-use the right side of our brain – the emotional, creative side – which prevents transformation occurring. Wink argued that the two sides of the brain must be brought back together, so that 'critical study' and 'personal encounter' can be unified within the process of biblical engagement (1981, p. 14). While Wink is wary of saying that any approach or context leads to transformation – 'transformation, when it occurs, is a profound mystery' (1981, p. 81) – he does suggest that transformation can be facilitated or impeded by the approach and context used. He did, however, emphasize that transformation should be the goal of biblical engagement within small groups, and suggested three methods that should be used to facilitate transformation: effective questions, contributions from scholarship, and right-brain activities, such as mime, painting or writing. Wink's belief was that in unifying the right and left sides of the brain, people would be able to integrate the insights gained during biblical engagement into their everyday lives. It could be argued that a small group is not necessary for this to occur, but Wink sees the small group context as providing the means by which insights are generated and then applied. In summary, according to Wink, biblical engagement within small groups can be transformative, especially when consideration is given to how individuals will incorporate the understanding gained from biblical engagement into their everyday lives.

E.H. Robertson (1961) was convinced that biblical engagement must empower people to participate in the world in which they lived. He was concerned that Pietist perspectives lead people to see the Bible as 'belonging to another world' (1961, p. 9) and to seek to live in this other world, and therefore not to engage with the world in which they live. He was equally concerned that liberal perspectives saw the Bible as a source of illustrations but not as authoritative. He wished to offer an alternative, which he saw in the lives of pastors meeting together in Nazi Germany, as well as in a number of other contexts. From analysing these contexts, Robertson developed three principles of effective biblical engagement: it must be deep, contextual and group-based (1961). Biblical engagement should be *deep:* it should engage with the insights that have come from scholars who have studied the passage under consideration in order to discern its meaning – though some would argue that a text does not have a fixed, permanent meaning, and would therefore reject the idea that it is possible to discover any passage's ultimate meaning (Loughlin, 1999). Biblical engagement should be *contextual:* following a deep engagement with the passage, one should then ask what the passage means for the present specific context. Finally, biblical engagement should be *group-*

based: while acknowledging that one can engage meaningfully with the Bible alone, Robertson suggests that in a group there is less danger of individuals merely interpreting a passage in a way that supports their own beliefs and there is greater opportunity for exploring the meaning of the passage from alternative perspectives. For Robertson, it was only in the context of a small group that biblical engagement could be both deep and contextual, in order to enable people to participate in the world in which they lived in a way that took seriously the authority of the Bible.

More recently, in *Through the Eyes of Another* (2004), Hans de Wit and his colleagues developed a model of inter-cultural Bible-reading in order to explore what would happen when groups of Christians from different cultures and situations were exposed to one another's interpretations. The method involved groups from all over the world reading the story of Jesus and the Samaritan woman (John 4), recording and then sharing their perspectives (along with information about their context) with a group from another culture, in order for the groups to then re-read the passage 'through the eyes of another' (de Wit et al., 2004). This has similarities with Mezirow's concept of 'perspective taking' (1978), whereby individuals try to take on the perspective of another person. Hearing interpretations from other cultures led to one group's traditional (cultural) interpretations being challenged by interpretations from another culture, and also challenged assumptions that a text 'accords with our dominant worldview'; this was particularly the case for individuals from privileged and wealthy cultures and backgrounds (Schipani and Schertz, 2004, p. 442). In his later work, de Wit refers to the fact that we are 'prisoners of dominant reading traditions', which inter-cultural reading can help us to escape from, leading to transformation (2012, p. 46). This relates to Gadamer's (2013) argument for the importance of recognizing our prejudices and identifying those which lead to misunderstanding. In some cases, the process of inter-cultural reading did lead to transformation, both of people's interpretations of John 4 and of their attitudes and actions; however, this was not true for all the participants and some were merely pleased to have participated in the process (Miranda-Feliciano, 2004). And despite the great potential of intercultural Bible-reading, it is beyond the capacity of the average small group.

Other relevant research includes the method of Contextual Bible Study (CBS), which has its roots in liberation theology and was pioneered by Gerald West in South Africa. It involves ordinary readers and 'socially engaged biblical scholars' reading the Bible together (West, 2007); this approach supports E. H. Robertson's (1961) contention that both depth and context are key for transformative biblical engagement. The focus was on the context in which the readers were involved, and they read together in order to bring out 'community-based action' and 'particular projects of transformation' (West, 2007, p. 5). The aim is to empower ordinary readers to interpret biblical texts for themselves, and each session ends with the question: 'What actions will you plan in response to this Bible study?' (West, 2011, p. 444). CBS has been hailed by some as a means of facilitating transformation, as it enables participants to engage with the Bible in a contextually appropriate way, which in turn leads to potentially transformed praxis within their context. Within the British context, three studies of CBS have been conducted: by Janet Lees (2007), Louise Lawrence (2009) and John Riches (2010). Janet Lees (2007) made use of CBS amongst those with communication difficulties and those living in inner-city communities in Britain. She developed an approach called 'remembering the Bible', as members of the community who had dyslexia, hearing impairments, learning difficulties and speech difficulties struggled to 'read' the Bible. Instead, they 'remembered' stories from the Bible together and reflected upon their meaning for their everyday lives. Louise Lawrence (2009) focused on the theme of 'place' in order to explore how CBS might be used to combat the increasing sense of 'displacement' that has occurred in response to our 'increasingly transitory ways of living' (p. xvii). The communities included a group from a city regeneration area, a rural village, a fishing village, a group of deaf people, and groups of clergy. Lawrence then selected a number of biblical texts in order to look at the issues of 'home', 'those out of place', 'sustainability', and 'displacement' (2009, p. xix). She was interested to discern a 'hermeneutics of place' and to identify how groups, through the process of CBS, might respond to the needs their communities. Finally, John Riches, along with colleagues (2010), used the CBS method in Scotland and sought to identify who the 'poor and marginalized' were in this context, which led to an emphasis on social transformation. They describe the outcome of CBS as 'the story of the power of Scripture, mediated through a uniquely enabling process [CBS], working to transform people's lives, individually and communally' (2010, p. 22).

In the previous chapter, we noted the relationship between formation and transformation, and the role of small groups in formation has also been noted. Both Donahue (2002) and Walton (2014) have noted the potential of Bible study groups in forming individuals in their Christian identity. Donahue notes that 'Christian community is the body of Christ expressing the life and message of Christ' (2002, p. 27); in this sense, small groups could be said to be an embodiment of the Gospel. Walton (2014) focused on the formational role of small groups, and asserted that communities have a key role in affirming and expressing the Christian story. James Bielo (2009) noted the role of Bible study groups in helping to distinguish American Evangelical identity, and thus in initiating individuals into this identity. Bielo noted a preoccupation amongst some groups with the group's identity as Lutheran, and members were recorded as frequently referring to other groups, generally in order to highlight the superiority of their own Lutheran position.

Alongside the above research, which has highlighted the transformative potential of biblical engagement in small groups, other research has not found transformation to be an outcome of participating in biblical engagement in small groups. Both Roger Walton (2011, 2014) and Andrew Todd (2009, 2013) have identified the importance of mutual support, relationships and fellowship as key outcomes of small groups. Walton's research into 56 church communities in North East England found that the groups were 'primarily acting as a form of mutual support' (2011, p. 99), which supports the findings of Robert Wuthnow's (1994) research in the American context. While Walton (2014) focused on the formational role of small groups, and asserted that communities have a key role in affirming and expressing the Christian story in order to engender change, he did not find that small groups lead to transformed praxis. His concern was that we have primarily turned Bible study groups and other forms of Christian small group into simply self-help groups, leading to inward-looking attitudes (2011). While Todd was less critical of the emphasis on mutual support, he also found this to be a key outcome of the three Bible study groups he researched in East Anglia (2009). Todd observed that an 'alignment' had to take place between what a text appeared to be saying and the members' 'concern for people' (2013, p. 81), with their concern for people often leading to a reinterpretation of the text. Mutual support is not a negative outcome of biblical engagement within small groups; on the contrary, one would hope that mutual support is always found within Christian communities. However, one might rightly suggest that mutual support should not be the only or *primary* outcome of group Bible study. As well as this, care needs to be taken that mutual support does not lead to collusion in resisting change. As Donahue notes, 'Christian community is the body of Christ expressing the life and message of Christ to build up one another and redeem the world for God's glory' (2002, p. 27). Thus mutual support is key, but largely in order to enable Christians to accomplish other outcomes.

We have already considered the role of small groups in enabling individuals to make connections between the biblical texts and their own contexts, but when this is reduced to searching for a prescription for a specific issue or concern, it can become problematic. Ruth Perrin (2016) researched some Bible study groups of young evangelicals (those considered to be part of 'Generation Y') and found that the key concern of most groups was what they could learn from the Bible in order to apply that knowledge to their everyday lives. In principle, this is a highly commendable aim, however, Perrin (2016) found that this could lead to highly 'individualistic' and 'personal' applications (p. 49) with the potential to distort biblical texts. Wuthnow has referred to this approach as resting on the belief that 'the Bible is true because it works in everyday life' (1994, p. 5). Richard Briggs (2007) has critiqued this justification for reading the Bible, as he argues that if we simply bring our own concerns and questions to the Bible we risk misinterpreting and misunderstanding the biblical texts, rather than engaging with the concerns found in the Bible. Andrew Todd's finding of the 'alignment' that took place when groups were faced with a biblical text that challenged their contemporary experience and privileged contemporary experiences over textual authority (2013), may be an example of what Briggs is concerned about. If small groups become too focused on the individual, then, in Wuthnow's words, 'these communities can be manipulated for personal ends, and the sacred can be reduced to a magical formula for alleviating anxiety' (1994, p. 4). When this happens, transformation is unlikely to take place.

Having identified the broad context in which this research fits, and considered the concept and process of transformation, and explored the potential of small groups to be transformative, we will now move to look at the methodological assumptions underlying this research.

4

Methodology and Methods

In this chapter I identify the methodological assumptions underlying this research as well as the research methods used to gather data. I begin by showing how my methodological assumptions fit within broader understandings of practical theology and the relationship between theology and other disciplines. I then outline the critical realist perspective that underlies this work, including the tenets of critical realism – ontological realism, epistemic relativism and judgmental rationality. Thirdly, I include a section on reflexivity, where due attention is paid to the impact that the researcher has on the research process. Following from this, more detail is offered about the specific methods used in this research – ethnographic observation, a questionnaire and focus groups – as well as the results of the pilot study, the process of data analysis and the small groups who participated in this research.

Practical theology

Any work of practical theology must address how the relationship between theology and other disciplines is understood and worked out in the practice of the research process. In order to do so, it is important to identify the *purpose* of practical theology.

I follow the outlook of practical theologians such as Pete Ward (2017), and John Swinton and Harriet Mowat (2016), who see practical theology as seeking to enable more faithful Christian practice. Swinton and Mowat offer the following summary of the purpose of practical theology: 'the knowledge generated by practical-theological research is intended to increase our knowledge and understanding of God and to enable us to live more loving and faith-filled lives' (2016, p. xiii). In common with Ward's conception of practical theology (2017), Swinton and Mowat focus on the potential impact of practical theology for the practices of the Christian community. So how does envisaging practical theology as a discipline that seeks to enable more faithful Christian practice impact upon the relationship between theology and other disciplines? Are theology and the other disciplines seen as equal dialogue partners, or is greater weight given to one discipline? Is one discipline considered to be normative?

There is an ongoing discussion in practical theology as to whether theology should hold a normative role, or whether other disciplines – such as sociology, anthropology, psychology, education, or history – should be considered as equal dialogue partners, with no one discipline being considered to represent the normative perspective or position (Cameron et al., 2010, pp. 25–27). I consider theology to hold the normative perspective or position, and thus to be considered more authoritative than the other disciplines that are utilized. Indeed, I am in agreement with Alister McGrath's assertion that,

> Christian theology should use or appropriate as many world-views and forms of language [and other disciplines] as are appropriate to explicate the truth of God's Word *without* allowing itself to enter into a relation of dependence upon them. (McGrath, 2002, p. 201, emphasis in original)

Practical theology should make use of other disciplines in order to carry out the 'faithful pursuit of understanding' (Ward, 2017, p. 167), which will 'enable us to live more loving and faith-filled lives' (Swinton and Mowat, 2016, p. xiii). In other words, practical theology, in utilizing other disciplines, can offer a great level of understanding about the practices of Christian individuals and communities, in order to enable these practices to become more faithful expressions of Christian living.

Key to the theological task of practical theology is the Bible. Andrew Purves, in arguing for an approach to practical theology that is grounded in the doctrine of the Trinity, makes the following statement,

> Because of the work of the Holy Spirit, God is active through the Scriptures but also surely in situations of human experience. The basis for the interpretation of the latter is given by the former, and the meaning of the former is found as a lived reality in the latter. (2004, p. 12)

Purves is suggesting that human experience must be interpreted, in response to the Bible and within a biblical framework, as an outliving of biblical teachings. The emphasis is on the way that the Bible informs practice, though this is not straightforward, as Swinton and Mowat have acknowledged:

> Practical Theology therefore finds itself located within the uneasy but critical tension between the text and the script of revelation given to us in and through Jesus and formulated historically within scripture,

doctrine and tradition, and the continuing innovative performance of the gospel as it is embodied and enacted within the life and practices of the Church as they interact with the life and practices of the world. (2016, p. 5)

So, if theology – understood as the Bible, doctrine and tradition – is given priority, how does it relate to the other disciplines? Richard Osmer identifies four key questions that practical theology should ask:

1 What is going on?
2 Why is this going on?
3 What ought to be going on?
4 How might we respond? (2008, p. 4)

Osmer sees these four questions as relating to four tasks in theological interpretation, the first being *the descriptive-empirical task* and the second being *the interpretive task*, which makes particular use of other disciplines. The third question relates to *the normative task*: 'Using theological concepts to interpret particular episodes, situations, or contexts, constructing good ethical norms to guide our responses, and learning from "good practice"' (Osmer, 2008, p. 4). This is very similar to Laurie Green's Let's Do Theology Spiral (2009), and sees theology as having a key role in interpreting practices and potentially critiquing practices. It is not enough to simply say what *is* going on, but what *ought* to be going on. Hence, the fourth task – *the pragmatic task* – leads to the development of 'strategies of action' (Osmer, 2008, p. 4). Other disciplines cannot be allowed to have the final say about what ought to be going on or how we should respond. In order for practical theology to be *theology*, the normative task must rest with theology, and if we see human experience as a 'lived reality' of the Bible (Purves, 2004, p. 12), then every stage of the process of practical theology is essentially a theological task. Thus, while Osmer's questions provide a helpful framework and are valid questions for practical theology to ask, I would wish to see each question as theological. Indeed, as Helen Cameron and her colleagues have argued, practical theology should be 'theological all the way through' (2010, p. 51). They critique the idea that theology is 'the icing on the cake already baked in the oven of social sciences' (Cameron et al., 2010, p. 51). Therefore, if we ask Osmer's first question, 'What is going on?', we might look to see what the practices that we are observing tell us about people's operant theologies (Cameron et al., 2010), rather than purely focusing on a more sociological or psychological explanation of what is happening.

In summary, I see practical theology as being a primarily theological task that seeks to better understand the realities of Christian practice in order to reflect on this practice to enable more faithful Christian practice in the future.

Critical realism

Having considered broadly how theology relates to the other disciplines that are utilized in this research, it is now important to identify the particular philosophical and theological perspective underlying this research – that of critical realism.

Critical realism, which was originally developed by Roy Bhaskar (2008), rests upon three key principles: ontological realism, epistemic relativism and judgmental rationality (Owens, 2011). *Ontological realism* refers to the fact that reality exists beyond our experience of it (from a Christian perspective, the ultimate reality is God); *epistemic relativism* maintains that our understanding and experience of reality is partial and limited; yet *judgmental rationality* upholds that it is still possible to judge between alternative perspectives on reality. Put simply, there is a 'real world', but people will understand the world differently depending on their own worldview, beliefs, and values (Cameron and Duce, 2013, p. 29); however, some understandings of reality can be said to be more accurate or more true than others. Critical realism challenges the so-called 'epistemic fallacy' of conflating epistemology and ontology (Wright, A., 2013, p. 10), or in the words of Margaret Archer and her colleagues: 'The epistemic fallacy involves the fallacious inference that because there is no epistemologically objective view of the world, there is also no objective world ontologically' (Archer et al., 2004, p. 2). The lack of objective knowledge of the world does not mean that the world does not objectively exist. In Bhaskar's words, 'the object is the real structure or mechanism that exists and acts quite independently of men [sic] and the conditions which allow men access to it' (2008, p. 17). This is the basis of ontological realism, challenging social constructivist accounts of reality that suggest that there is no reality beyond that which we can experience and thus construct (Swinton and Mowat, 2016). Indeed, Helen Collins has suggested that a social constructivist account is 'not entirely compatible with an evangelical framework which asserts that there is a reality 'out there' which can be known through revelation' (2016, p. 73). By contrast, critical realism posits that there are two dimensions, a 'transitive dimension' and an 'intransitive dimension'; the former is how we experience and believe reality to be, and the latter is how reality actually is (Archer et al., 2004, p. 2). In considering critical realism, and in particular how critical realism might enable practical theologians to reconsider their use of empirical methods, Andrew Root offers the following reflection: empirical methods can 'never possess the fullness of reality, for reality will always escape any humanly constructed method of observation' (2016, p. 56). In research, this means that we must be humble about the fact that even the most effective means of data collection cannot claim to fully present the realities of the people and situations that are researched. There is an acknowledgment that we are limited in our ability to grasp and define reality.

We have already noted that McGrath encourages theologians to make use of other disciplines, but warns against becoming dependent upon them, and he applies this also to critical realism, suggesting it should be 'deployed in an ancillary, not foundational' manner (2002, p. 200). Critical realism must not be allowed to take on the 'normative task', to use Osmer's (2008) terminology, but instead must also be used, like other disciplines, to allow us 'to increase our knowledge and understanding of God and to enable us to live more loving and faith-filled lives' (Swinton and Mowat, 2016, p. xiii). Indeed, in the words of John Mansford Prior, 'I am committed to searching for a greater truth beyond the truth elicited by myself, my group, and my ecclesial tradition' (John Mansford Prior, 2015, p. 78). Critical realism enables a recognition of the relative nature of our knowledge, while maintaining 'the ideals of truth, objectivity and rationality' (McGrath, 2002, p. 195). Therefore, while I consider theology to have a normative role in practical theology, I also believe that our theology must remain open to acknowledging that we have misinterpreted or misunderstood, and therefore developed a poor or incorrect theology. Thus, our theology must especially acknowledge epistemic relativism and judgmental rationality. To use the four voices model, operant and espoused theologies must be enabled to challenge formal and normative theologies, as well as themselves being challenged (Cameron et al., 2010).

The different research methods used in this research offer multiple perspectives on reality (epistemic relativism), in the hope that by bringing them together in dialogue and critique (judgmental rationality), greater understanding can be gained about reality (ontological realism). This fits with Clifford Geertz's conception of 'thick description', which he developed from the work of Gilbert Ryle, to describe the process of producing an account which reflects the 'multiplicity of complex conceptual structures' that make up reality (Geertz, 1973, p. 10). This also links the idea developed in Bhaskar's work on the stratification of reality – 'reality is multilayered' – meaning that whilst we might engage with only one strata of reality, this will have a relationship with other strata of reality (McGrath, 2002, p. 219). This would therefore produce a 'multiplicity' of perceptions and responses to reality, which it is necessary to try and articulate. It is therefore not surprising that Swinton and Mowat identify the importance of engaging in a 'process of complexification' in order to address the 'multifaceted entities' with which practical theology is concerned (2016, p. 15). Practical theology, in the process of seeking to understand the realities of Christian practice, must not seek to overly simplify or reduce the multiplicity of these practices, but instead must engage with them as they are in reality, and seek as much as possible to present them as 'complex, multifaceted entities' (Swinton and Mowat, 2016, p. 15).

As explored above, epistemic relativism leads us to acknowledge that our perspective on reality is only one perspective and is thus limited, which is why it is important in any piece of research to acknowledge the role played by the researcher, which is the focus of the next section of this chapter.

Reflexivity

Swinton and Mowat suggest that reflexivity is the 'most crucial' aspect of the research process (2006, p. 59). They define reflexivity as, 'the process of critical self-reflection carried out by the researcher throughout the research process that enables her to monitor and respond to her contribution to the proceedings' (Swinton and Mowat, 2006, p. 59). Reflexivity is essential in recognizing that it is impossible to remove oneself from the process of research; instead, it recognizes the role and significance of the researcher in every aspect of the research process. This goes beyond simply acknowledging that the presence of the researcher will inevitably have an impact upon those being researched, even if only to a limited extent (Cameron and Duce, 2013), unless the research is undertaken covertly. Reflexivity involves acknowledging how who one is shapes the whole research process – so it is important to acknowledge those factors that may be of particular significance in relation to a given research area. I will seek to do this below.

Given the focus of this research, it is important that I am open about the fact that I do believe that engaging with the Bible can be transformative. However, my desire in this research was not to *prove* that engaging with the Bible leads to transformation, but to consider whether engaging with the Bible *in a small group* might be transformative, and to consider the factors that may hinder or facilitate transformative engagement. And certainly, it is important to acknowledge that not all biblical engagement leads to transformation.

A common concern in research in the church context is how much to reveal about one's own faith (Cameron and Duce, 2013). Indeed, Bielo (2009) found that his participants wanted to know about his faith commitments, and that they were reassured to discover that he was a Christian – perhaps because he was then viewed as an 'insider' (Cameron and Duce, 2013, p. 91). As an ordinand, it was immediately clear to the participants that I was an 'insider' to the Christian faith. Louise Lawrence (2009) has suggested that clergy often take on the dual role of insider and outsider, as they are part of the church community (insider) but, at times, seek to critically reflect upon the community (outsider). However, despite any insider status I may have held as an ordinand when I first arrived at each group, I was essentially a stranger and most certainly an outsider to the small groups, and as my primary role was one of observation, I never ceased to be an outsider. My outsider status was probably also accentuated by the fact that I only visited each group on three occasions. Nevertheless, each group made me feel very welcome: for example, one group always asked if I had any prayer requests when they were sharing requests, and on another occasion, I was specifically asked to participate in the discussion.

Other factors, such as my age, gender and race, will also have had an influence, both as to how I experienced the research process and as to how the participants responded to me. Based on the questionnaire responses, I was one year younger than the youngest participant and sixty-one years younger than the oldest; in fact, one small group had been running for almost my entire lifetime. This meant that on occasion, due perhaps to my age and being from a different generation from those I was researching, I disagreed with the views being expressed. For example, during a discussion about why there might be a lack of prayer in our culture, one participant responded,

> I'd like to add two points to what's been said, on why is prayer so neglected. One is that Christian mothers are not teaching their children to pray [general agreement]. I think it's easy to neglect, with all the pressures of life, but my mother, who was a great Mothers Union person, insists in her talks, 'Mothers, you must teach your children to pray and set an example and pray yourself'. And the other reason is, I think our culture is not good at quietness and silence [agreement]. How often do you see young people on bicycles or even running with music earphones and music? This whole business of shutting out silence (SGA – 3).

Both these points may have validity, but my initial response, as a young woman, was to react against this comment and to be tempted to reject it on principle, due to it seeming *to me*, a little sexist – do not Christian fathers have a role in teaching their children to pray? – and a little ageist – is it only young people who struggle with silence? Indeed, this was an occasion when I struggled not to intervene and challenge the above statement.

As a white British person, I also experienced the research from a 'white' perspective. One of the key features of whiteness is often said to be its 'invisibility' to those who are white (Whitmore, 2011, p. 187), or alternatively, referring specifically to white privilege, 'as an absence of the negative consequences of racism' (Eddo-Lodge, 2018, p.86). For example, I chose not to include a question about race or ethnicity on the questionnaire, but did include one on age and gender. I decided not to include a question about race as previous research had not done so, for example, Village (2007) asked about gender and age, but not about race, and also because I felt given the small sample size, it would be difficult to determine the impact of race. However, does this indicate an assumption, on my part, that race does not matter, which may have come out of my experience of being white, and therefore experiencing white privilege? While it is not possible for me to know what impact being from another race or ethnicity would have had upon the research, it is important to acknowledge that my whiteness will have had an impact upon the research, along with my age and gender.

Here I have sought to highlight the role of the researcher in the research process and to identify some of specific characteristics of myself as researcher that will have shaped this research. The intention of this is to honestly acknowledge that, 'Nothing happens within the research project that is not filtered through the researcher's own experiences, interpretations, and agendas' (Collins, 2016, p. 65).

Methods

This research utilized mixed-methods research in order to gain the greatest possible insight into the area of biblical engagement in small groups. The use of a mixed-method approach is seen as a useful approach for research within practical theology, as it offers a means of taking what is best from the available methods in order to produce richer data and a deeper understanding (Swinton and Mowat, 2006, pp. 50–51). Walton (2014) notes that questionnaires, interviews and case studies have become the primary means of researching small groups. Interestingly, focus groups are not included in his list, perhaps because he sees them as 'an artificial simulation' if created purely for the purpose of researching small groups (Walton, 2014, p. 109). The use of observation, questionnaires and focus groups allows for triangulation, and when combined, produced a greater depth of data than using only one of these methods, and also meant that the data produced by one method could be used as a check against another. Like Rogers (2009, p. 89), I see this as in keeping with a critical realist research methodology: using one form of data to critique another can be seen as a means of enabling judgmental rationality, in the hope of gaining a clearer sense of reality. It is also hoped that by using a range of methods that the data produced will be more likely to reflect the 'complex, multifaceted entities' that are presented in the research (Swinton and Mowat, 2016, p. 15).

The final choice of data collection methods used in this research was the culmination of a process of continual critical reflection in order to develop the most appropriate means of collecting data to address the question: *What factors in small groups might hinder or facilitate transformative biblical engagement?* The research methods (ethnographic observation, questionnaires and focus groups) used in this research are explained in detail below. First however, I explain the process by which the participants were identified.

Identifying participants and gaining access to small groups

Identifying and gaining access to participants was more difficult than I had originally anticipated. Like some previous research (Bielo, 2009), I initially used church websites to try to identify churches that ran small groups, and to ascertain what church tradition the church broadly fell within. I then made contact with the church leader (the vicar or priest-in-charge), or with the individual identified on the church website as being responsible for small groups, by email. This individual was the first of two gatekeepers, the second being the small group leader (Creswell, 2013). In total I contacted thirteen churches, of whom one was unable to assist with the research, one was unwilling to pass on information about the research to their small groups for fear of overburdening them, and two of whom I never heard back from. The other church leaders or small group co-ordinators passed on information to a small group leader or to multiple small group leaders. Out of these nine churches, the small group(s) at five of the churches did not wish to participate, but three small groups were willing to do so (and one responded after the selection of small groups had been made). The most common reason given for small groups not wishing to participate was because they did not wish to be recorded or because they were concerned that the knowledge that they were being recorded would prevent them from being themselves.

Once permission had been granted for me to carry out my research with a small group, I arranged a time to visit the small group. As in all instances this was the first time I had met the groups, I began by introducing myself and what my research was about. While this varied slightly with each group, it included the same key information:

- My name.
- The college I was studying at.
- The fact that I was conducting research into small groups and the use of the Bible in small groups.

I then distributed printed copies of the Information Sheet and Consent Form, both of which had been sent to the group leader with the request that they be distributed to the group in order to aid the group's decision on whether or not they would like to consider participating in the research. No-one raised any objection to my presence in any of the groups at this stage (or at any other stage), so I then asked the group members to complete the consent form and at this point I began observation (and audio-recording).

Ethnographic observation

Ethnography is defined as 'the study of people in naturally occurring settings or "fields" by means of methods which capture their social meanings and ordinary activities' (Brewer, 2000, p. 10). We have already seen, that small groups would not necessarily be considered 'natural' groups, but 'created' or 'artificial' groups (Douglas, 1983), however, small groups are a common feature of church life, and thus a legitimate area or 'field' of research. And, as Douglas (1983) recognizes, 'created' or 'artificial' groups have much in common with 'natural' groups. When constructing an ethnographic account, the researcher is concerned with accurately representing the beliefs, behaviours, rituals, symbols, and other features of a given group of people. However, this is not a straightforward exercise in reporting the activities of a group, as these activities need to be interpreted, and this means that the researcher has a significant role to play in how the group being observed is represented, which highlights the importance of reflexivity. Van Maanen refers to the 'rhetorical appeals' (2011, p. xix) made within ethnographic accounts, as researchers attempt to convince the reader that their representation of the group is authoritative. Despite the potential challenges associated with ethnographic research, it has become an increasingly popular way of researching aspects of church life (Ward, 2012).

My research involved only three small groups (and a pilot study), so the focus was on in-depth knowledge, which is often the case with qualitative research (Ward, 2017). While some existing research has looked at a large number of small groups and churches (Walton, 2014; Wuthnow, 1994), others have involved much smaller numbers; both Perrin (2016) and Todd (2009) researched three small groups. Thus, there was an existing precedent for limiting the study to this size.

I visited each small group on three occasions between May and July 2018. A key factor to consider when carrying out observation is the level of involvement of the researcher: much ethnographic research involves participant observation, which means that the researcher joins in with the activities being studied (Scott and Morrison, 2006). However, there is a wide range of different levels of participation, from 'complete participation' to 'complete observer' (Creswell, 2013, pp. 166–167). Given that my research was concerned with how group processes impact upon the transformative potential of small groups, it was vital that any participation from myself did not interfere with these processes – though of course, as already mentioned, the presence of an observer will have almost certainly altered the processes in some way (Cameron and Duce, 2013). I took more of an observer role during the research, similar to what Bielo referred to as a 'silent observer' or 'nonparticipant' (2009, p. 42). Nevertheless, while being generally 'silent', I sat amongst the groups, followed the reading of Bible passages or reading from study notes, and, obviously, laughed when amusing things occurred or funny comments were made. Like Bielo (2009), I participated if someone asked me a direct question, but aimed to avoid changing the focus or direction of the discussion with my response.

As mentioned above, I audio-recorded the small group discussions, beginning the recording just before the formal Bible study took place and ending the recording as it ended or after a time of prayer. All of small groups met around coffee tables or other low tables, which provided the perfect place for the recording device to be placed centrally, while being as unobtrusive as possible. I supplemented the audio-recordings with field notes, which provided further details not picked up by the audio-recording. I mentioned to each group that I would be making notes during their discussions, and deliberately chose a notebook that did not look like a journalist's notepad but had a colourful hard cover, as I was mainly writing with the notebook on my lap. These notes included details such as what occurred before and after the recording, how the room was arranged, where participants sat, who was speaking, details about how participants were connected (for example, married couples), and, crucially, my own thoughts during and immediately after each meeting.

Questionnaires

A questionnaire was distributed to all members of the small groups who were present during my second visit. This research made use of a self-administered or self-completion questionnaire that was completed while I was present, which meant that I could provide clarification about any aspect of the questionnaire. There is always a risk, if the researcher is present, that participants may feel slightly pressurized (Cohen et al., 2011) or that the researcher may unintentionally steer their answers, perhaps by giving leading examples. However, this pressure was minimized as much as possible by ensuring I did not rush participants in any way, by placing completed questionnaires straight into an envelope (so they remained anonymous), and having the participants complete the questionnaire after I had already attended two meetings, so they had started to get to know me a bit.

There have already been a number of uses of questionnaires to carry out research within the area of biblical engagement and/or small groups (Village, 2007; Walton, 2011, 2014), the most significant on small groups is the work of Robert Wuthnow. Over three years, Wuthnow (1994) and his team of researchers across the USA surveyed 1021 people who were in small groups, and 962 who were not in small groups. They made use of a face-to-face questionnaire, which consisted of 87 questions focused on the role that small groups played in the lives of participants, or, for those who were not in a small group, the reasons they were not in a small group. Despite the fact that the survey was not conducted in the UK, many of the questions are still highly relevant to the UK context. As such, a number of the questions from Wuthnow's questionnaire were used, though adapted significantly, in this research (see Appendix A for those questions used in Wuthnow's research that were influential, and Appendix B for the full questionnaire used in this research).

It has been suggested that it is best to start questionnaires with generic, simple questions to 'warm people up' rather than starting with more in-depth questions (Cameron and Duce, 2013, p. 21). This can also provide an opportunity to collect demographic data. Therefore, the questionnaire began by collecting this demographic data, including the length of attendance at the small group. The next part of the questionnaire included a question about what had led the participants to join their small group, followed by a question on what they saw as the purpose of a church-related small group, as well as whether the participants felt their small group was fulfilling this purpose. This offered an indication about whether or not individuals join small groups with the goal of transformation, change or development in mind. This is important as individuals will rarely experience ongoing transformation if they do not wish to (Mezirow, 1978). As well as this, prior research has found that individuals will leave small groups if they are not fulfilling an individual's expectations (Wuthnow, 1994). The next question focused on the various features that may have been present in the small group, and how important these were to participants. One feature was 'Studying and discussing the meaning of biblical passages', which, when compared with the relative importance given to other features, gave an indication of how important participants considered biblical engagement to be. The penultimate question offered a list of possible outcomes which may be the result of attending a small group. Walton found that 87% of respondents to his questionnaire stated they had become closer to God as a result of participating in a small group, whereas only 18% had become more involved in 'local issues' (e.g. loneliness or poverty) (2014, p. 113). Wuthnow (1994), however, found that 62% of small group members had worked alongside other members of the group to help people in need who were not group members. He also found that they became more involved in their communities and were prompted to 'think more deeply about pressing social and political issues' (Wuthnow, 1994, p. 346). The final question asked participants whether or not they thought they had changed as result of being in a small group, and if so, what they believed to have caused this change. As is customary, there was space left at the bottom for any other comments participants wished to make, and the questionnaire ended with a note of thanks.

Focus groups

During my final visit to the small groups, I led each in a focus group discussion. I originally considered using individual interviews, but given that the focus of this research is small groups, I decided that focus groups were a more appropriate means of data collection, especially as interaction between participants is a key feature of focus groups (Kitzinger, 1994). While group composition and venue (Cohen et al., 2011) are often concerns when organizing a focus group, within this research both these factors were predetermined. This is highly beneficial as the groups already knew one another and were meeting in their normal location;

they had also had the opportunity to grow accustomed to my presence at their meetings.

While during previous visits I had been observing, during the focus group I led the discussion and each focus group discussion was audio-recorded. The questions asked during the focus group focused on transformation, and as the focus group took place during my final visit, there was no longer a risk in skewing the research by revealing my focus on transformation. Each question was asked in order to build upon the responses of the previous question and to narrow down the focus of the discussion (the full set of questions can be seen in Appendix C). At times, the discussion developed in such a way that a question was answered before I asked it. Sometimes I still asked the question, to ensure that everyone who wished to comment had done so; at other times, when the topic has already been discussed at length, I did not ask it. Cameron and Duce (2013) recommend ending with a question that allows participants to reflect on the overall discussion. Ruth Perrin (2016), in her research on the biblical interpretation of young evangelicals, ended each focus group with the question, 'Why do you think this passage is in the Bible?' (p. 36). This would have enabled groups to draw all their thinking on the current Bible passage together. The final question I asked each focus group was, 'Do you find engaging with the Bible in this group to be transformative? Why?'. This question addressed the absolute heart of my research and also allowed the participants to draw together their reflections from the whole discussion. I ended each focus group by asking if any of the participants wished to add anything further.

At the end of my final visit, I thanked the group for allowing me to attend their meetings and for participating in my research. Some groups asked to pray for me and my research, which I was touched by.

The pilot study

The small group that participated in the pilot study included four women and two men – including two married couples, one of which hosted and coordinated the group. The group meeting began with prayer and sung worship before a Bible study based on Matthew 18, following the Bible study the group completed the questionnaire and then participated in the focus group. Following the pilot study, I made some small changes to the questionnaire. Some of these involved formatting or slightly rephrasing questions, and I removed one question, which it became clear was superfluous. In relation to the focus group, I noted that a number of questions were closed as opposed to open, and while this helped provide a definite 'yes' or 'no' response, it meant I continually asked follow-up questions. So, for example, I rephrased 'Does the Bible have anything to say about transformation?' to 'What, if anything, does the Bible say about transformation?'. Other than this, the questions worked well and provided a good level of insight into how the members saw the relationship between being in a small group, engaging with the Bible, and being transformed.

Prior to conducting the pilot study, I had intended to ask the groups to work through set questions on a biblical text or texts over the course of three meetings, which I would have observed. Prior research has taken this more interventionist approach, for example, Ruth Perrin's (2016) work used three set texts and questions, and de Wit and colleagues also made use of set texts (de Wit et al., 2004; de Wit and Dyk, 2015). However, having conducted my pilot study I was aware that even being present for the meetings felt intrusive, and my presence will likely have affected the behaviour of the participants, however marginally (Cameron and Duce, 2013). Therefore, I felt apprehensive about also requesting that groups use a set text and questions for three weeks. Within existing research on small groups, some have used set texts (de Wit et al., 2004; Lawrence, 2009; Perrin, 2016), but others have simply observed the groups carrying out their normal practices (Bielo, 2009; Rogers, 2015). There is therefore a precedent for either approach, and having observed the normal practices of the pilot study group I was able to learn a lot from the choice of text, style of questions and how the leader led the discussion of the text. I therefore decided not to use a set text and questions, and instead observed the normal practices of the groups in the main study.

Data analysis

As Rogers notes, data analysis is not a discrete stage in the research process, but is 'ongoing before, during, and after the fieldwork process' (2009, p. 92). This is why reflexivity at every stage of the research process is essential in order to be aware of the role of the researcher in the continual process of data analysis. However, following the collection of all the data, there is a formal process of data analysis as well as the continual process of data analysis that takes place during the data collection stage.

This section will the describe the process by which the themes that are addressed in the following chapters were identified. This process involved a number of stages: first, familiarization with the data; secondly, identifying as many emerging themes as possible; thirdly, identifying which of these themes were most central; and finally, selecting those themes that were most pertinent to the research question (*What factors in small groups might hinder or facilitate transformative biblical engagement?*), meaning those that related most closely to transformative biblical engagement. These stages will be discussed in more detail below.

Stage one: familiarization with the data

As the researcher, I was not unfamiliar with the data prior to the process of analysis; as Collins notes: 'Nothing happens within the research project that is not filtered through the researcher's own experiences, interpretations, and agendas' (2016, p. 65). Nevertheless, it was still necessary to refamiliarize myself with all of the data in order to be able to identify recurring patterns and themes. Therefore, I read back over all of my field notes, which included my initial reflections after each small group meeting and my ongoing reflections between meetings. I also went back over all of the audio-recordings of each meeting in order to make detailed notes about the key discussions that took place, any notable events or comments, and anything that related directly to the research question (*What factors in small groups might hinder or facilitate transformative biblical engagement?*). Once I had refamiliarized myself with all of the data, stage two could begin.

Stage two: identifying emerging themes

This stage began with creating a mind-map that included all the themes that I had identified while refamiliarizing myself with the data. I noted from which group(s) the themes emerged from and during which meeting or which focus group. At this stage, the aim was not to focus too closely on how the emergent themes related to the research question, but to remain open to the various themes that emerged from the data. Once this initial mind-map had been constructed it was then possible to reflect further on the themes, and to consider if any other themes were present but had been overlooked in the initial identification. Following the identification of a large number of themes, the next stage began.

Stage three: identifying key themes

Once the initial themes had been identified, it was then possible to reconsider all of the themes in the light of the data and consider which themes were most key, in particular, which themes emerged from all the groups and appeared to have a significant bearing on how the groups operated. At this stage, a large number of themes were excluded. For example, one theme that was initially identified as a key theme – age – actually turned out not to be as significant as originally predicted. When further analysis was carried out, it was seen to be a factor that had an impact upon various aspects of the groups, but this impact was difficult to isolate from other demographic factors, and was not seen to be significant enough to warrant an in-depth analysis. Thus, in the chapters that follow, age is referred to where it is seen to be relevant, but it is subsumed under the other, more central themes. It is not possible to offer an in-depth analysis of every theme that emerges from the data, indeed, as Ford notes, a choice must be made between 'narrow and deep' or 'broad and shallow' (2015, p. 43). The choice made here, in keeping with much qualitative research (Cohen et al., 2011), was to opt for a narrow and deep analysis that enabled a full treatment of each theme.

Stage four: selecting themes

The final three themes that were selected were: expert, challenge and use of materials. These were selected on the basis of two main criteria. First, these themes emerged from all three groups, even if that meant they were present by their absence – so while one of the themes is expert, there was not an identifiable expert in one group, but this absence was significant. It was important that there was enough data available that related to the theme in order for a full analysis to take place. Secondly, the theme had to be of direct relevance to the research question. This does not mean that it was possible to discern at this stage whether the theme *would* be significant in facilitating or hindering transformative biblical engagement, but that there was evidence to suggest that it *might* be significant. While there were many fascinating themes that emerged from the data, the focus of this research was what small group processes hinder or facilitate transformative biblical engagement, therefore, each theme had to be considered in light of this. As has already been said, the use of these criteria led to the selection of three key themes: expert, challenge and use of materials. Once these themes had been selected, all the data that related directly to each theme was collated and then analysed. This process allowed for the identification of sub-themes. This approach can be seen in the work of other researchers, such as Jan Grimell, who researched the transition from military to civilian life, and identified five main themes, each of which had between three and eight sub-themes (2018). One example of the emergence of a sub-theme occurred in analysing the data relating to the use of materials, where it became clear that there were two key factors or questions to consider: *what* materials were used and *how* were they being used? The sub-themes relating to each of the key themes can be seen below, and are explored in detail in the chapter relating to each key theme.

Key theme	Sub-theme
Expert	Internal experts
	External experts
Challenge	Challenge as a desired practice
	Text-generated challenge
	Group-generated challenge
Use of materials	What materials were used?
	How were materials used?

Table 2: Themes and sub-themes of the research

After selecting these themes – expert, challenge, and use of materials – it became clear that each of them related to the leadership of the group. This is therefore discussed in Chapter 9 in order to draw all the themes together in a consideration of their role in hindering or facilitating transformative biblical engagement.

As has already been recognized, the researcher is highly influential in every stage of the research process (Collins, 2016), and therefore another researcher *may* have elected to focus on different themes. Nevertheless, the process described above aimed to ensure that the themes that were selected were representative of the data, and significant portions of data are included in the following analysis to ensure the groups that were involved in this research are presented as accurately as possible.

We will now move on to a brief introduction to each of the small groups that participated in this research.

The participants

This section includes some background information about the participants (which they provided as part of the questionnaire responses) and a brief description of the routine activities of the small group meetings.

Much existing research into small groups, and in particular Bible study groups, has focused on evangelical churches (e.g. Bielo, 2009; Perrin,

2016), but I tried to draw from a wider range of churches. My initial hope was to include an Anglo-Catholic, an evangelical and a broad church in my research, while of course acknowledging that no church will perfectly exemplify a whole tradition, and that there is a breadth of theological positions and spiritualties in every tradition. Even had I found three 'ideal' churches that did exemplify their traditions, there would no doubt have been members of those churches that would not have identified themselves as being of the same tradition as the church they attended. Instead, they may have attended it due to proximity to their home, due to knowing existing members of the congregation, or for a whole variety of other reasons.

The groups are referred to as Small Group A, Small Group B and Small Group C. The order of the designation is based purely on the order in which I began visiting each group. The pseudonyms used have been randomly selected in order to protect the identity of the participants, and any identifying comments have been removed from the data that follows.

Small Group A

Small Group A met fortnightly on Friday evenings from 7.15pm and generally finished between 9 and 9.30pm. They met in the communal area of a sheltered housing residence, as one of the members of the group lived in the residence with her husband, though he did not attend the group. The general pattern of the meeting was a short period of socializing from about 7.15 to 7.30, followed by the Bible study, which was prefaced by a prayer. The Bible study generally lasted an hour, and then there was a chance for prayer requests and a period of silent prayer, which was brought together with the Grace. Then at about 9pm there was tea, coffee and biscuits and a chance for a chat. When I started observing the group, they had been using Tom Wright's (2012) *James* Bible study guide – part of the 'For Everyone Bible Study Guides' series – for six weeks, and were on the seventh study at my first observation. There was an expectation that members would have read the study before the meeting and would have considered the questions that Wright poses.

The group had been running for a significant length of time, and some members had been in the group for roughly 26 years, though some had only joined the group 18 months ago. During the time I was observing the group, the numbers attending ranged from 6 to 10. Roger organized the group, but members took it in turns to lead the Bible study, so each meeting I observed was led by a different individual, with one being led by Roger himself. The age range of members was 55–88, with an average

age of 75, based on those who completed the questionnaire. There were three married couples within the group – Jessica and Adam, Julia and Roger, and Joan and Keith – and then four other women who attended: Louise, Beth, Sarah and Jane. The group members were predominantly retired, but prior to their retirement their occupations included teaching, nursing, and church ministry, and some had been homemakers and the primary caregiver to children.

As part of the questionnaire, participants were asked to select the church tradition(s) that they most identified with from a list of options: Anglo-Catholic, Broad Church, Central, Conservative, Charismatic, Evangelical, Liberal, Open, Traditional and Other. Formal definitions of these different traditions were not provided, as this may have been off-putting for some participants and appeared overly academic, instead participants were able to interpret the traditions as they wished. In Small Group A, two identified as Anglo-Catholic, two as Broad Church, two as Evangelical, two as Liberal, one as Open and one as Traditional. There were also some people who selected two options: these combinations were Broad Church and Liberal, which was selected by two people, and Anglo-Catholic and Traditional. One person also commented, 'I enjoy all types of tradition'. The group therefore included individuals who identified with a range of church traditions, though no-one identified as Charismatic or Conservative. Of all the churches, the church associated with Small Group A was the most traditional, and although there were various Sunday services, the small group participants tended to attend the two morning services, which were the two more traditional services. Therefore, the responses to the questionnaire appear to be reflective of the style of worship that the small group members experienced on a Sunday.

Small Group B

Small Group B started about eighteen months before I started observing the group (May 2018) and was led and hosted by an ordained minister, Caleb, and his wife, Stephanie, at their home. Most members had been part of the group since it had begun, though some had joined only six to nine months ago, and one couple attended for the first time on the occasion of my final visit. The group met fortnightly on Monday evenings from about 7.45pm (with the aim to start at 8pm) until about 9.45pm. The general pattern of the meetings was that the members gathered in the living room of Caleb and Stephanie's house from about 7.45pm, and there were drinks and snacks available (which different members of the group often brought). There was a brief period of chatting until about

8pm, which was also when any information was shared, for example, the dates for the next few meetings. Then the Bible study section of the meeting would begin, which would last until approximately 9pm. Like Small Group A, members took it in turns to lead. The group were using Brian McLaren's (2015) *We Make the Road by Walking* as the basis for their discussions – and had been using this since starting to meet together. Then from about 9pm until about 9.45pm, there was a period of sharing prayer requests and praying aloud, before a final period of chatting at the end.

During the time I was there, thirteen different people attended meetings, though the number in attendance ranged from seven to eleven. Four married couples were part of the group – Caleb and Stephanie, John and Juliet, Robert and Tessa, and Nathan and Erin, as well as three other women – Sally, Martha and Tabitha, and two men – Alex and Aaron. Based on the questionnaire results, the age range was between 48 and 80, with an average age of 59. However, on my final visit a couple attended who appeared to be in their late twenties or early thirties. Again, based on the questionnaires, which were not completed by every member of the group, there were a mix of occupations amongst group members, including a teacher, legal adviser, nurse, administrator, ordained minister, and two members who were retired, one of whom specified they used to be an architect.

When asked to select the church tradition(s) that they most identified with from a list of options (see above for full list), one chose Broad Church, one chose Central, three chose Liberal and two chose Open. One individual did not choose from any of the options and two chose Other. The person who did not select any option commented, 'Christian (Try and avoid labels!)'. And the two who selected Other commented 'Generously orthodox (but I don't like labels!)' and 'An individual searching for understanding'. The final comment, suggesting a desire for greater understanding, is a reflection of the values document that was created when Small Group B started, which identified the following three values: 'A safe and supportive setting', 'A place for growth' and 'A place for discerning God's will'. All of these indicate an openness to growing and learning. This document was developed by those in leadership at the two churches associated with Small Group B, and it appeared that the group were in support of these values.

Small Group C

Small Group C had been running just less than a year when I first visited (June 2018), and met weekly on Wednesday evenings at Philip and Gabi's house. The group met at 7.30pm with a time of chat as people arrived and drinks were made; this was then followed by the Bible study part of the evening that began at about 7.45pm. The group were following small group material produced by the church and, like both Small Group A and B, members took it in turns to lead the group. After the Bible study, which would last approximately an hour, there was a period of sharing prayer requests and a time of extemporary prayer. There was then also another period of socializing afterwards for about a quarter of an hour before members left.

While I was there eleven different people attended, with the weekly attendance ranging from seven to nine. Based on the questionnaire results, the age range was 28–72, though only one person was in their twenties, with everyone else being in their fifties, sixties or seventies, and the average age was 58. Occupations included a number of roles related to healthcare and medicine, as well as a full-time mum and volunteer, upholsterer, accountant, public servant, counsellor, and teacher. There were four married couples in the group – Philip and Gabi, Clive and Debs, Joanna and Paul, and Stephen and Joy – as well as three women – Samantha, Tamara and Olivia.

When asked to select the church tradition(s) that they most identified with from a list of options (see above for full list), eight chose Evangelical, two chose Traditional and one chose Charismatic. One individual selected both Charismatic and Evangelical, and one individual selected both Traditional and Evangelical. One individual also added 'Reformed' to their response. No-one self-identified as Anglo-Catholic, Broad Church, Central, Conservative, Liberal or Open. Unlike Small Group A and B, where there was quite a range of different options, the majority of Small Group C identified as Evangelical. The church associated with Small Group C is known in the area as an Evangelical church, and therefore it is perhaps unsurprising that those who would self-define as Evangelical had chosen to attend this church on the basis of its perceived tradition. This is supported by the fact that the hosts did not live in parish of the church they attended and with which Small Group C was associated. The fact that this may also have been true of other members of the group may be why there was a high level of uniformity in the responses of Small Group C in self-identifying as Evangelical.

In summary, the small groups involved in this study reflected a range of different church traditions, and each group included members from a range of traditions. Despite this, the practices of each group were very similar, with each following a pattern of Bible study followed by prayer, though some had social time before the Bible study and some afterwards. The duration of the small groups varied, with one having been running for twenty-six years and the other two having been running for less than two years. Two groups had a very similar average age of 59 (SGB) and 58 (SGC), whereas one group had a much higher average age of 75 (SGA). All of this is intended to provide some background information about each group in order to situate the findings of the research.

5

An 'Ordinary' Understanding of Transformation

In this chapter we will consider how the participants involved in this research viewed transformation, the data being drawn primarily from the focus group discussions, when an in-depth exploration of transformation took place. The structure of the chapter follows the order of the focus group questions (see Appendix C).[1]

Transformation as a process of change

One of the key ideas that came out of all three groups' discussions of transformation was *change*. Often this was accompanied by other terms to describe the change: 'complete' (SGA), 'miraculous' (SGA), 'significant' (SGB), 'dramatic' (SGB), 'obvious' (SGC), and 'massive' (SGC). One member of Small Group C said that transformation was 'A change of attitude, behaviour, thinking, feelings'. The concept of change being key to transformation is an idea that we have already considered and can be seen in the work of a number of writers (Baumohl, 1984, p. 10; Getu, 2002, p. 92; Johnson-Miller, 2005, p. 33).

During Small Group C's discussion, there was some reflection on the relationship between change and transformation:

Debs: 'Yes, I think you can have a massive change, can't you? Which, maybe that's the beginning of your journey, but then I think that continues, and as you say, it is a continual, it is a continuum.'

Olivia: 'And, I think that's where the word for me is misleading. For me, the first part is a rapid change, something quick, something so obvious, yet you are talking about the change that's much more slow, that's transformation, at a different pace isn't it.'

...

Debs: '... In fact, transformation is stronger than change, isn't it? Really it is much stronger than change.'

AN 'ORDINARY' UNDERSTANDING OF TRANSFORMATION

Gabi: 'Even longer lasting.'
Debs: 'Yeah.'
Gabi: 'Change brings transformation.'
Debs: 'Yes, that's better isn't it, if it is a continual, in the, in the right direction maybe.'
Philip: 'Transformation brings change, yes.'
Clive: 'Is it reversal or transformation?'
Joy: 'Mmm, it is ever moving isn't it, so you could transform from one thing into another, into another, it doesn't mean that you have transferred, er transformed in one direction, you could transform into this and then you could do this and then you could, so you can change direction …'
(SGC – Focus Group)

The group were trying to ascertain how change relates to transformation, or even whether change is a helpful way of understanding transformation. There seemed to be agreement that while change might be something rapid, transformation was something slower; it was a process. Indeed, this is an idea that has also been acknowledged previously, as in the work of Walter Wink: '[transformation] is a process, not an arriving; we are 'transforming', not 'transformed'" (1989, p. 77). Or, as de Wit puts it, 'transformation is defined in theology as a profound, durable process of change' (2015, p. 60). It was interesting that Gabi said, 'Change brings transformation', whereas Philip said, 'Transformation brings change'. This perhaps highlights the complicated nature of the relationship between change and transformation.

In response to question two – What does transformation look like? – Jessica in Small Group A said: 'When you get old.' Seeing a connection between ageing and transformation is one that Donald Capps would almost certainly support, stating that, 'the ageing process, which begins at birth, is *growth-oriented* from beginning to end' (2014, p. 85). This certainly supports the idea that transformation is more of a gradual process of change than a dramatic change – though this is in some ways counter to other comments made about transformation being 'miraculous' (SGA) or 'dramatic' (SGB). It might be argued that ageing was one kind of transformation, but it might be more appropriate to suggest that the ageing process may be a possible stimulus for transformation. Woolf has referred to middle age as a 'transitional life experience' as people move from younger adulthood to older adulthood (Woolf, 2011, p. 45), but this could equally apply to those transitioning from adulthood to older adulthood, or from one stage of older adulthood to another (Capps, 2014). These transitions may provide a stimulus for transformation.

Small Group A also referred to how someone's appearance might change and that they might 'glow':

Louise: 'Okay, if that person has been transformed, you see a change in their appearance and in their ways that change.'

...

Jessica: 'They glow.'
AC: 'Glow. OK.'
Jessica: 'Yes, glowing.'
(SGA – Focus Group)

There was also a comment in Small Group C that transformation would mean people 'Would look different.' The references in Small Group A to a 'change in their appearance' and 'glowing' could evoke images of Moses' face shining with the glory of God (Exodus 34.29–35) or Jesus' transfiguration, when 'his face shone like the sun' (Matthew 17.1–2). This could also link to 2 Corinthians 3.18:

> And all of us, with unveiled faces, seeing the glory of the Lord as though reflected in a mirror, are being transformed into the same image from one degree of glory to another; for this comes from the Lord, the Spirit.

This is a passage that was mentioned later during the focus group when reflecting on what the Bible says about transformation.

During Small Group B's discussion, there was an interesting link made between transformation and evolution:

Stephanie: 'I was looking at, maybe slightly random, but I was looking at the stages of the damselfly today. There have been mating damselflies in our pond, and that, when you said transformation, is what I thought of, just then, because that metaphorically applies to Christians, larva, like things coming round too, but just that this blob turns into something beautiful.'

Caleb: 'For me transformation, I am trying to think isolated, but you said growth and change so far haven't we? Um it's, it's quite significant change …'

Nathan: 'It is more dramatic.'

Caleb: '… it's more dramatic than evolutionary change, yes. Something might be transformed over millions of years and evolution and to be what can be a different thing that would be transformed, but it is not a trans … Do you see what I am saying?'

(SGB – Focus Group)

AN 'ORDINARY' UNDERSTANDING OF TRANSFORMATION

Stephanie uses the analogy of the development of a damselfly to describe transformation, though Caleb and Nathan then suggest that transformation is more 'dramatic' than development or evolution, and that it is more 'significant'. Throughout their discussion, Small Group B made reference to scientific analogies and terminology, and here there is reference to the stages of a damselfly and the process of evolution. We have seen that Loder (1989), Mezirow (1991) and Schipani (2015) have all been able to identify stages in transformation, and though akin to the process of evolution, there is a need for some form of external influence in order for transformation to occur. And, unlike in the development of a damselfly, transformation is not inevitable.

Stephen in Small Group C identified different kinds of transformation:

Stephen: 'I think for me there is like two different transformations, so I think it is great when somebody's life is transformed from say, like we had a friend he is just back, he was a drug addict and he found Jesus and his life was transformed.'

Joy: 'That was just what I was going to say.'

Stephen: '... which was amazing but then I think my transforming, transformation is going to take a lifetime. I think I am being transformed but it is a long, long process.'

Gabi: 'Process yes.'

(SGC – Focus Group)

Stephen suggests that some people may go through a dramatic transformation, perhaps particularly due to the circumstances of their life when they became a Christian, but for others, transformation is more of a long-term process. This links with an earlier comment made by Philip:

Philip: 'I think, I think, you know, the transformation that I, I suppose we look at in the Christian life is, is coming, coming to faith in the first instance and there can be big changes that we see when that happens but now there is this, you know, the theological word, it is the sanctification which is the ongoing change ... and to becoming, because it is about becoming more Christlike that is what sanctification is about and, you know, we can never plateau because there is, there is always more of Christ than we can find.'

(SGC – Focus Group)

Here the focus is less on the circumstances of someone's life, and the distinction is between an initial transformation at conversion, and the more long-term transformation process of sanctification. In *The Transforming Moment*, James Loder describes coming to know Christ, or conversion, as the 'decisive transformation' (1989, p. 64). Philip uses the word 'sanctification' to refer to ongoing change; indeed, David Peterson notes that sanctification has 'commonly' been used to refer to *'a process of moral and spiritual transformation, flowing from justification by faith'* (1995, p. 15). This understanding of sanctification is very much in keeping with how Philip uses the term to refer to an ongoing process of change. This discussion highlights the fact that transformation may take different forms, and this is one of the factors that makes it a complicated phenomenon to identify.

Small Group B's discussion highlighted the potential difficulty of identifying transformation:

Stephanie: 'It would have to be obvious, if it is transformation, then it's obvious, you don't miss it.'
Erin: 'Well, I suppose somebody might miss it, even if you felt transformed.'
Stephanie: 'But, I would, okay so my own, I would hope my own transformation would be obvious to me, but, yes.'
AC: 'Do you think it could happen the other way around, so someone else spots it but you miss it?'
General agreement.
Caleb: 'Yes, I think it normally, given that we are talking about positive change, it normally is a real change in energy of someone, which as you say might be obvious on the outside or it might just be an internal thing, which really you could say my attitude to this has been transformed by, you know, and what you mean, but it might not be that obvious, but your, your approach to something might be transformed as a result of transformation.'
(SGB – Focus Group)

The discussion begins with Stephanie asserting that one of the features of transformation is that it is obvious, but Erin challenges this, and suggests that while you may know you have been transformed, others may not be able to identify the transformation that has taken place. Caleb then helpfully suggests that whether or not the transformation is obvious will depend on what kind of change has taken place; has their attitude or approach been transformed? – with the implication being that it is only when this transformation is externally expressed that others will be able to identify the internal transformation that has taken place. This

AN 'ORDINARY' UNDERSTANDING OF TRANSFORMATION

has been noted by Makonen Getu, who points out that not all aspects of transformation can be 'quantified'; it is an 'inside-out phenomenon' (2002, pp. 97, 92), which means that while transformation may have taken place, it may be difficult to identify in some instances. And this is exactly the point made within the above discussion.

In summary, key to the groups' understanding of transformation was the concept of change and this was understood to be a process of change which, perhaps like the development of a damselfly, had stages. Ageing and glowing were both given as possible examples of what transformation might look like, and there was a recognition that transformation could take different forms, both dramatic and immediate and more long-term. There was also recognition that transformation could be difficult to identify.

Factors that promote or hinder transformation

Both Small Group A and C highlighted the role of choice in either enabling or preventing transformation. Small Group B did not specifically mention choice, but they referred to the role of resistance, as did Small Group A:

AC: 'How does transformation happen?'
 ...
Louise: 'Make a decision they, that you want to change.'
 (SGA – Focus Group)

Debs: 'It is choice, isn't it, it is a choice, I suppose.'
Gabi: 'Yes.'
Debs: 'So if we don't choose, to open ourselves and to look then we won't change.'
 (SGC – Focus Group)

AC: 'And then 4. What do you think prevents transformation happening?'
 ...
Louise: 'Being stubborn.'
Roger: 'State of mind.'
AC: 'What do you mean by that?'
Roger: 'Some people don't want to change anything.'
Julia: 'You mean resisting.'
Roger: 'Resisting, yes.'
 (SGA – Focus Group)

Sally: 'Being resistant to a new concept.'
(SGB – Focus Group)

In each of these cases, the emphasis is on the agency of the individual in either choosing to be changed or transformed, or being resistant and not choosing to be open to change or transformation. Daniel Schipani, when discussing the transformative potential of intercultural Bible-reading, suggests that 'receptive expectation' (2015, p. 105) is key for transformation to take place. Indeed, Johnson and Johnson (1982) assert that change will only take place if an individual wants to change. However, some research has found that group discussion in particular can bring about change even when this is not desired (Younghusband, 1976), though this is potentially ethically questionable and it seems unlikely that any change would be maintained. So openness to transformation is likely to be a key factor in creating the right conditions in which transformation can take place. Indeed, one member of Small Group C noted that 'fear' might be a factor preventing change, and this is supported by writers such as Anton Baumohl (1984) and John Hull (1985), who have recognized that learning and change can be painful.

Small Group B again focused on more scientific language and referred to the role of a catalyst:

AC: And how would you say transformation happens? There may not be one answer.'
Stephanie: 'I was about to say time, but that is not necessarily always true.'
Sally: 'There is something that happens that affects one and and you change back.'
Stephanie: 'As a catalyst.'
Sally: 'As a catalyst, yes.'
Caleb: 'There is a, normally.'
Aaron: 'Something that is a reaction.'
Nathan: 'A catalyst enables a reaction where it causes two other things that ordinarily wouldn't change something new comes in and suddenly kapow!'
Stephanie: 'It can be that, I don't know if all transformation is a reaction, that is one kind of transformation.'
(SGB – Focus Group)

The idea of a catalyst brings to mind Mezirow's concept of a 'disorientating dilemma' (1994, p. 224), which is some form of dilemma, challenge or life crisis (1978) that might lead an individual to reconsider their per-

AN 'ORDINARY' UNDERSTANDING OF TRANSFORMATION

spectives. Members of Small Group B are suggesting that some form of catalyst may provide the impetus for the process of transformation to occur, though Stephanie notes that not all forms of transformation will necessarily take place as the result of a catalyst.

Small Group A and B also brought up the role of God in the process of transformation:

Adam: 'It is the work of the Holy Spirit really.'
...
Keith: 'It is God, God and the Holy Spirit.'
Roger: 'Well, conversion.'
Julia: 'Through prayer.'
Jessica: 'We have done with our prayers.'
Louise: 'It's Jesus that makes the transformation.'
(SGA – Focus Group)

Caleb: 'I was going to say there is a precipitating event or series of events that will, that will have I think a part of transformation I think, which is a bit of a reaction. I think, I can't, I'm sorry, I can't help but say in a Christian sense I think the Holy Spirit is, is I do think, I believe that about the Holy Spirit, I think the Holy Spirit moves in people and transform, I think other things, well, oh well, I was going to say other things might be but I don't know I think all positive transformation is actually somehow founded in the Holy Spirit, yes.'
(SGB – Focus Group)

John: 'No I think, I think maybe Caleb gave quite good answer to that, that it is not so much down to us but God working through us can bring around transformation we may not even see that ourselves but be aware of it but I think I am aware of it when I see it in other people, definitely, I think.
(SGB – Focus Group)

On the whole, the responses emphasize the role of the Holy Spirit in particular in leading to transformation, though Small Group A makes reference to each person of the Trinity. The groups suggested that the Holy Spirit was at work in people to bring about transformation. Andrew Root (2014) and Andrew Purves (2004) have both critiqued practical theology for its over-emphasis on human agency at the expense of recognizing the role of divine agency. Root argues that practical theology should take seriously the 'real experiences of God's coming to people in concrete and lived ways' (2014, p. xi). More specifically, the above excerpts indicate the centrality of the role of the Holy Spirit in the process of transformation, which is in keeping with more Pentecostal or charismatic spiritualities, that give 'priority to an *encounter* with the person of the Holy Spirit ... and the personal and corporate *transformation* that results from such an encounter' (Cartledge, 2015, p. xii). Back in the 1980s, Anton Baumohl distinguished between the human and divine dimensions of discipleship: 'As we disciple adults we need to recognize the two dimensions to that process: one involving human agencies – teachers, group leaders, programme designers, communicators, trainers, pastors – and the other focused on the (sometimes mysterious) work of the Spirit' (1984, p. 19). Baumohl's comments apply equally well to the process of transformation, as it involves both human and divine agency. Indeed, Peterson has noted that different levels of emphasis have been placed on the role of human agency in the process of change (1995). Small Group A's responses offer a more Trinitarian approach to the process of transformation; they refer to the Holy Spirit, God and Jesus. As Purves has argued, 'the Trinity is the basis for Christian practical theology' (2004, p. xxv). For these groups it is clear that God, particularly in the person of the Holy Spirit, has a central role to play in the process of transformation: 'I think all positive transformation is actually somehow founded in the Holy Spirit' (Caleb, SGB).

The final factor that was emphasized, particularly by Small Group C, was the role of others in the process of transformation, though this was also picked up by other groups to a lesser extent:

Adam: 'Anna just going back to transformation, how it occurs, I think small groups like this can help transformation, they can help develop ones' faith through the Bible reading, through listening to other people's experiences and through obviously submitting to God in prayer.'
(SGA – Focus Group)

Olivia: 'I think out of what Joy was saying, it struck me, when she was speaking, that transformation must have, to be sustained, must have good support. So the Billy Graham conference I remember as a little girl in [place] going to, I think possibly his conference loads of people have faith and those people who prayed on their point but I think one of the things that was felt at the time by clergy in the city, there wasn't enough after support, so all these people that night got healed or come to God, come to God and then they were left without any church prepared to, to take them on.'

AN 'ORDINARY' UNDERSTANDING OF TRANSFORMATION

Debs: 'To follow up, no follow up.
Olivia: '... and to take them on, because they didn't have Alphas and things in those days when I was little so, so I think support is one word that comes to my mind, even for anything any transformation.'
Debs: 'It is a nurturing, it needs to be ...'
Philip: 'Nurture, yes.'
Debs: '... it needs to be a nurturing.'
Philip: 'A role model to follow, so I think the whole discipling and being discipled, I think is important and all these things. It is standard in relationship isn't it and we are, we are changed by having the, the rough edges knocked off us.'
(SGC – Focus Group)

While Adam's comment highlights some of the different activities that small groups might practice, and that might be enhanced by being practised together, the discussion in Small Group C focuses specifically on the support that is available from a small group, and the positive reinforcement that this can provide. Indeed, Olivia notes that if people do not receive support then they will not be transformed, and this is echoed by Debs and Philip, who speak of 'nurturing'.

When considering how transformation happens and what might prevent it happening, choice was a key factor, and therefore, choosing not to change was also seen as being a barrier to transformation. There was recognition that some form of catalyst may be necessary for transformation to take place. Emphasis was also placed on the role of divine agency in initiating transformation and the role of human agency in supporting transformation.

The Bible and transformation

When asked 'What, if anything, does the Bible say about transformation?' and 'What, if anything, does the Bible have to do with transformation?' there were a range of responses. Small Group A and C made reference to specific biblical verses or stories, whereas Small Group B took a slightly different approach and could be said to have focused on the meta-narrative of transformation throughout the Bible:

Caleb: 'So, the Bible, I think when the Bible talks about repentance, that is one of one sort of transformation that it is talking about.'

Erin: 'I guess the Bible has glimpses of different possibilities at different periods throughout it. So, within the context of the violence of the Old Testament there are glimpses of how things can be different so there are both transformations in how people think and transformations in the possibilities of how people can think, which are kind of weaved throughout the narrative of the Bible.'

Aaron: 'Yes, you are right, there is a lot of that actually isn't there, a lot of characters who get really transformed. In fact, a lot of it is about that, isn't it?'

Nathan: 'People who run off, their own way and don't want to do something and …'

Stephanie: 'Or they don't think they can do something and find themselves doing it.'

Sally: 'They would rather do anything but what they are supposed to be doing.'

Stephanie: 'But I think there is both, there are people who say, No I don't want to, but there are lots who are like, Really me? You want me to go talk to Pharaoh? Or, You want me to make this big decision?'

(SGB – Focus Group)

Caleb: 'I think as well as well as the characters that were all mentioned throughout and all the different angles we have on it I think the overall arc of the Bible is actually all about transformation in the bigger, in terms of, in a way creation at the start is about transformation of something out of nothing and then there is the whole trajectory of Israel and then Jesus transforms, transforms people's perspectives or tries to of Judaism and then there is a new community that is transformed by that teaching and then it ends up in Revelation with, with the talk of the new, a newly recreated heaven and earth with a renewed heaven and earth which is about transformation as well so I think there is a whole arc of transformation I think going through the Bible.'

(SGB – Focus Group)

While there were some specific references made to biblical characters or stories, such as Moses or Jonah, the overall discussion focused on the theme of transformation found across the Bible. The first excerpt focused on the fact that while some individuals mentioned in the Bible were initially reticent to fulfill what God was calling them to do, there are many examples of how they then go on to be transformed and carry out God's calling. Caleb then takes the idea even further and refers to the 'arc of transformation' that is present throughout the Bible, and begins with the creation story and then follows the biblical account to Revelation and the references to future transformation. Caleb's assertion is in keeping with the view espoused by Joanna Collicutt:

> The actual word 'transformation' doesn't occur very often in the New Testament. Perhaps this is because it is so fundamental to its message, so deeply embedded, so woven into its narrative that it doesn't need to be voiced explicitly. But the idea, if not the word, is everywhere. (2015, p. 4)

The idea of the Bible as providing a meta-narrative is one that has received support from a number of writers (Bauckham, 2003; Goheen, 2008; Wright, C., 2006; Wright, N. T., 1992), partly in response to the postmodern critique of the meta-narrative (Lyotard, 1992). Certainly, the suggestion that the Bible could be read through a lens of transformation, without distorting individual texts, seems a defensible claim.

When discussing 'What, if anything, does the Bible have to do with transformation?' there were two ways this question was addressed: one was to focus on the Bible as a text and the way it might provoke transformation, and the other was to focus on the way that God might use to the Bible to transform, though the two are not mutually exclusive. In relation to the first approach, the following two excerpts are relevant:

Julia: 'Well, it points us to ways in which transformation can take place doesn't it. It is endless possibilities isn't it that it, it, I think that it, through the different stories I mean who would have thought that Elijah would have, it is a bit of a bloody story in the end isn't it, but it certainly brought the Israelites back to God, you know, and who would have thought that would have happened? I mean that was an incredible transformation wasn't it, through his faith, you know, I think it does give you endless possibilities.'
(SGA – Focus Group)

Nathan: 'I think it is a complex insanely complex resource in a sense so it's always possible that, you know, every time we read a different translation or read something that you haven't read for years or, you know, read something maybe you have never picked up before like there was a, that's, that's in the you know can be the new thing adds in to you that suddenly

>   might provoke a change or provoke some kind of effect and so or even just things that are familiar but suddenly they are put together in a new way and I think that is very much that kind of a catalyst we are talking about something new coming in to, to provoke change I think is a kind of, you know, as I say it is such an amazing confusing complex, incredible thing, you know document that of course we have that potential to do.'
>
> Aaron: 'Yes can make you, I am dabbling in chemistry terms that I am way beyond my comfort zone here but can make you feel a little uncomfortable or even unstable and so that your state can be more amenable to being changed because you read stuff and you think, Oh I don't like that bit, but it is kind of too late it is in there.'
> (SGB – Focus Group)

Julia seems to be suggesting that the biblical text provides many possibilities, or examples, of how transformation has taken place in the past, and therefore, how it might take place in the future. In that sense, the Bible almost offers exemplars of transformation that we might seek to replicate. Alternatively, Nathan points towards the complexity of the text as a factor that enables multiple and varied responses, some of which might be transformative, and Aaron suggests that perhaps those texts that might be considered 'difficult' might provide a catalyst, or 'disorientating dilemma' (Mezirow, 1994), that may lead to transformation. David G. Ford, who carried out research amongst a group of individuals who considered themselves non-religious, found that even these individuals saw the Bible as a transformative text, and were concerned that the text would 'convert' them (2015, p. 13). While the above individuals do not make specific mention of the role of divine agency in this process, they may well also see this as a part of the process.

In relation to the second approach – how God might make use of the text to transform – the following two excerpts are relevant:

> Louise: 'It is the word of God it is the truth and it is that when we read it and know it is the word of God that should help us to change.'
> (SGA – Focus Group)
>
> Joy: 'Well it is the Holy and living word, so it can always, I find it speaks to me.'
>
> Debs: 'It speaks to everyone.'

Gabi: 'But obviously, that, that's in conjunction with the Holy Spirit I suppose the Trinitarian thing as well, so it not just Jesus it is the Holy Spirit and God above that is in Scriptures.'

Debs: 'I suppose it will actually lead, I think lead you to certain, certain parts of which is the one which you need at the time. If you actually go to Jesus, go to and ask then I think you will be, the Spirit will actually lead you to sections of the Bible which will speak to you at that time.'

(SGC – Focus Group)

The participants are suggesting that God uses the Bible in order to transform people, and that the Holy Spirit might lead you to certain biblical passages in order that you might be transformed. The above comments reflect what Kevin Vanhoozer has referred to as a belief in transcendence: 'The belief that there is something "in" the text, a presence not of the reader's own making, is a belief in transcendence' (1998, p. 455). The individuals express a belief in the idea that the Bible is God's Word, and therefore has a unique power to speak to them, and perhaps transform them, in a way that is not typical of other texts. Indeed, this is in keeping with Barth's assertion that the Bible should be understood as, 'a human word which has God's commission to us behind it … a human word in which God's own address to us is an event' (2010, p. 106). The above comments, especially those made by Debs, also suggest a belief in what Vanhoozer has termed 'Spirit-led exegesis' (1998, p. 411): the individuals trust that the Holy Spirit will guide them to specific texts and enable God to speak to them through those texts. It reflects a view found in the work of writers such as Augustine and Luther, that 'the Bible conveys the living Word of God to us only as the Spirit makes us able to hear it' (Heron, 1983, p. 105).

In summary, the Bible was seen by some as having transformative power because of its qualities as a text, but also because of the way it was used by God to speak to people through the text.

The transformative potential of small groups

The groups emphasized the value of relationships and fellowship and the value of hearing different perspectives in their small groups, though crucially they did not offer any examples of finding the groups transformative.

The main emphasis in Small Group A was on fellowship, and the importance and value of the relationships that had developed because of the group. However, one of the first responses to the question made an interesting distinction:

Julia: 'Well Keith and Joan, we have been together for 26 years.'
Keith: 'It certainly is very informative if not transformative.'
(SGA – Focus Group)

The distinction between being informed and transformed is potentially significant, and of course it would be possible to be both informed *and* transformed. Mezirow's transformative learning theory places emphasis on the role of becoming more informed in the process of transformation (1978). Sandra Schneiders (1991) has distinguished between reading the Bible to be informed and reading the Bible to be transformed. She suggests that while someone reading the Bible to be informed may not be interested in transformation, someone reading the Bible to be transformed must also be interested in being informed (1991, p. 14). In Timothy Gorringe's *Redeeming Time* (1986), he seeks to develop an educational model of salvation which, rather than seeing education as the removal of ignorance, sees it as the process of becoming fully human:

> Salvation means 'becoming like Christ' ... To become like him means therefore to become fully and truly human. But if this is the case the goal of education and the goal of salvation are the same: both are concerned with the realization of human fullness, with becoming human, the liberation of the whole wealth of human potential. (Gorringe, 1986, p. 8)

Gorringe would reject the dichotomy of being either informed or transformed, and instead sees the two as occurring simultaneously, or at least that would be his hope. Clearly, in this instance, Keith felt that while the group provided a context for learning, it had not necessarily provided a context for transformation. Nevertheless, given that Keith had attended the group for twenty-six years, it is reasonable to assume it was fulfilling some need or Keith may have stopped attending (Benson, 1991).

Small Group B emphasized the value of hearing different perspectives and providing space for transformation to potentially occur:

Sally: 'I think having people's different perspectives can make one think differently, see something totally differently to the way one had before or give, perhaps give you a sort of more definite views.'
Aaron: 'It can make you question yourself.'

AN 'ORDINARY' UNDERSTANDING OF TRANSFORMATION

Caleb: 'In a way I think you can't engineer it either in so far as if it happens it happens, I mean all you can do is read the Bible together and if some transformation happens for you or I tonight when we read the Bible brilliant but if it doesn't happen tonight then that's also fine sort of thing, do you know what I mean, there is something about you can't really control it, it just depends on what you brought and what is going on in our lives what is going on tonight but yes, it is for me it is a forum where it certainly can happen and I want to enable it to happen, and, yes.'

Nathan: 'Provides similar things we were talking about, provide space to, you know, safe space where you can engage with things and provides new ideas in other people, you know, the kind of time in our busyness you know it does some of those things we have talked about as being important, you know, it can give that opportunity and shape that.'
(SGB – Focus Group)

When completing the questionnaire, six out of the seven members of Small Group B who completed the questionnaire indicated that 'Hearing the views of others' was 'Very important' to them, and so the above comments are in accordance with the questionnaire results. Caleb's comment that you cannot engineer transformation is akin to a comment made by Walter Wink: 'transformation, when it occurs, is a profound mystery' (1981, p. 81). But, like Wink, both Caleb and Nathan suggest that certain contexts make transformation more or less likely.

Small Group C again highlighted the value of relationships and fellowship, but they have not found the group to be transformative thus far, and Gabi suggested this was not necessarily what she wanted from the group:

Gabi: 'I think yes, I think my response to the question is I don't find that word particularly helpful in terms of valuing the group, I value the group, I value the relationships and value the honesty and I, and I value that it has got many dimensions to it, so it has spiritual, it has got the emotional, it has got the physical, feeling, you know, so it is just yes it is fellowship in the broader sense for me which I think is, is really good, really good. And I like the different personalities and what each person has to bring, yes, that feeds me.'
(SGC – Focus Group)

The emphasis on the value of relationships and fellowship is something that has been identified by a number of researchers (Todd, 2009, 2013; Walton, 2011, 2014), though an emphasis on fellowship does not exclude an emphasis on transformation. However, Olivia and Philip both offer comments that suggest that they do want transformation to occur, but that the current practices of the group are not enabling this:

Olivia: '... I think the study hasn't helped me this term transform enough, it hasn't been, I haven't taken away enough from it because it is not just the relation level ...'
(SGC – Focus Group)

Philip: 'And I think as we have said the Bible is vital for transformation, and I think we aren't spending as much time in scripture as we might do, then we don't be in a transformational group, because I think the catalyst for transformation has to be, has to be scripture.'
(Small Group C – Focus Group)

Olivia felt that the Bible study questions the group were following had not facilitated transformation, and Philip felt that the group were not making enough use of the Bible for transformation to occur. These three comments, all made by participants in the same group, highlight the difficulty of balancing the needs and expectations of a group.

In summary, the participants valued the relationships and fellowship that their small groups provided, and some felt that the groups provided a safe place where transformation could take place, but others said that they valued their group for others reasons, for example, for learning or for relationships. However, one individual noted that their small group could be more transformative if more time was spent engaging with the Bible.

Is engaging with the Bible in a small group transformative?

When addressing the question 'Do you find engaging with the Bible in this group to be transformative? Why?', Small Group A picked up on the idea of challenge and a few members commented on finding the study questions challenging:

Julia: 'Oh I think it is quite challenging, isn't it? I think this Tom Wright one has been very challenging.'

Jane:	'Yes, it is very.'
Julia:	'Some of the things I didn't feel I could answer until we discussed.'
Jane:	'Very interesting.'
	(SGA – Focus Group)

Being challenged may well be considered a potential catalyst leading to transformation, and crisis, though not synonymous with challenge, has been deemed a 'necessary' condition for transformation, though an 'insufficient' condition in and of itself (Browning, 1996, p. 282). However, while there are some comments about the questions being challenging, there are no examples given as to how this challenge has led to any form of change or transformation. Instead, the challenge has been addressed when an answer to a difficult question has been provided. The challenge therefore remained at an intellectual level, rather than at a more personal level, which relates to the discussion in 6.5, where a dichotomy was set-up between informative and transformative.

As in Small Group B's responses to the previous question, here again the focus was on the role of others:

John:	'Sometimes in the group, I think a small group it is not so much the Bible if we can move away from the Bible as such, I mean, I think sometimes it is things that people say that really make you think that really kind of like you go away thinking even more rather than it necessarily being the Bible, I, I don't know, that's what I think sometimes.'
	(Small Group B – Focus Group)

Interestingly, John specifically notes that it is not the Bible but the group that provides the catalyst for transformation. This is akin to Mezirow's research, that indicated that constructive discourse was a key factor in enabling perspective transformation to take place (2000). This is also in accordance with Gorringe's view on the role of relationships in the process of education and salvation: 'God "dwells" in, and his education is conducted in and through relationships of friendship, kindness, mutual acceptance and forgiveness' (1986, p. 18). As we relate to others we are transformed, but this does not mean there is not a role for the Bible in this process; in Gorringe's words, the Bible is seen as 'constituting the fully harmony of the revelation of God's will' (1986, p. 25). Thus, it is in reading the Bible in relationship, such as in small groups, that we open ourselves up to be transformed.

Gabi in Small Group C suggests that at different times different people may be more or less likely to be transformed:

Gabi: 'Yes it is how we do it well in terms of, you know, some people have complained that this present study hasn't been particularly meaty although obviously what Debs said earlier about actually having to engage with our heart as well as our head with Scriptures you need both but for something maybe we need to meet before we have, you know, each person will respond differently in different seasons so in a way whatever we do, well our earlier, depending on what we are studying I will either get something out of it or not and that isn't necessary dependent on the group it is dependent possibly where I am at in my journey and I maybe helped in that by the other, the discussion we have in the group or, or not. So, I think there is many different ways of.'
(SGC – Focus Group)

Gabi's point, perhaps similar to that made by Caleb in Small Group B, is that it is difficult to create a context in which transformation can be guaranteed; people are different and will respond differently to different texts at different times and in different places.

In summary, none of the group members explicitly said that they found engaging with the Bible in their group to be transformative; however, there was acknowledgment of being challenged, of being led to think differently because of other peoples' contributions, and of the possibility for transformation when the circumstances were right.

Transformation Revisited

Having explored the data that related specifically to transformation, we will now consider how this data fits with our original definition of transformation and with the wider literature. How do the insights gained from some 'ordinary theologians' inform our understanding of transformation?

Following an overview of a selection of biblical material, I initially defined transformation as *an ongoing process of change whereby individuals and communities come to more fully resemble Jesus Christ and glorify God by the power of the Holy Spirit, in anticipation of the future transformation of the whole of creation*. The emphasis on the *ongoing process of change* reflected the perspective offered by texts such as 2 Corinthians 3.18 where the emphasis is on the ongoing nature of transformation, 'we are being transformed', but I also noted that there was further transformation still to come, as referred to in texts such as Philippians 3.21, 'He will transform'. This view of transformation as a process of change is echoed in the literature, as seen in the work of Walter Wink and Hans de Wit, who speak of transformation as 'a process, not an arriving; we are 'transforming', not 'transformed''' (Wink, 1989, p. 77), and 'a profound, durable process of change' (de Wit, 2015, p. 60). The small groups involved in this research also understood transformation in terms of a process of change:

Debs: 'Yes, I think you can have a massive change, can't you? Which, maybe that's the beginning of your journey, but then I think that continues, and as you say, it is a continual, it is a continuum.' (SGC – Focus Group)

Debs suggests that there may be an initial 'massive change', perhaps referring to a conversion experience, but this is then followed by a more gradual process of change that is 'continual' or a 'continuum'. That transformation may be such a gradual process of change is perhaps one of the reasons why it can be difficult to identify, which is raised both in the literature (Getu, 2002) and by members of the small groups:

Stephanie: 'It would have to be obvious, if it is transformation, then it's obvious, you don't miss it.'
Erin: 'Well, I suppose somebody might miss it, even if you felt transformed.'
(SGB – Focus Group)

That transformation is *an ongoing process of change* therefore appears to be a view that is held both by ordinary Christians and by the academy, and is also espoused in the Bible; it is present in both operant theology, formal theology and normative theology, and can also be seen in espoused theology, for example where churches refer to transformation as part of a mission statement, such as, 'We seek the transformation of individuals and communities'.

Interestingly, the groups tended to emphasize the individual rather than the corporate nature of transformation, whereas the Bible tends towards a more corporate understanding of transformation – as seen in the example considered above from Ezekiel 36. Generally, the groups majored on personal change and transformation, though Caleb did acknowledge that the Bible's vision for transformation is wider than personal transformation:

Caleb: 'I think as well as well as the characters that were all mentioned throughout and all the different angles we have on it I think the overall arc of the Bible is actually all about transformation...' (SGB – Focus Group)

This understanding of transformation is more akin to the approach of Contextual Bible Study, where the focus is on the context in which the readers are involved, and they read together in order to bring out 'community-based action' and 'particular projects of transformation' (West, 2007, p. 5). Similarly, Mezirow's (1978) research found that the women involved in re-entry programmes not only experienced personal changes, but also went on to be involved in and engaged with social action. Peterson, in discussing sanctification, also emphasizes the role of the church as the context for sanctification (1995). However, in our highly individualized culture, it is perhaps unsurprising that much of the emphasis during the small group discussions was on personal transformation, though this may be an occasion when the Bible may have a role of challenging currently held perspectives.

During the discussion of transformation, there was only one specific mention of coming to *more fully resemble Jesus Christ and glorify God*, though there was mention of the role and *the power of the Holy Spirit* in the process of transformation. The singular mention relating to coming to *more fully resemble Jesus Christ* was made by Philip:

Philip: '... and to becoming, because it is about becoming more Christ-like that is what sanctification is about and, you know, we can never plateau because there is, there is always more of Christ.' (SGC – Focus Group)

This very limited mention of transformation leading people to become more like Jesus or becoming more 'Christlike' is interesting, as it is a commonly held view. For example, Collicutt lists 'Christ is formed in you' as one of her seven characteristics of Christian formation (2015, p. 10), and later expands on this, saying, 'We are to be formed in accordance with the character of Christ' (Collicut, 2015, p. 41). However, there were several mentions of the role of the Holy Spirit in the process of transformation, for example, Adam's comment, 'It is the work of the Holy Spirit really' (SGA – Focus Group). While the role of the Holy Spirit in the process of transformation is attested to in some practical theology (Collicutt, 2015; Peterson, 1995), Root (2014) and Purves (2004) are right to acknowledge that this is not always the case, and that emphasis is often placed so entirely on the role of humans that the role of God is omitted. It is difficult to see how this omission would *glorify God*. There was no specific mention by the groups of transformation leading to the glorification of God, which might suggest that while they did recognize the role of the Holy Spirit in the process of transformation, they did not envisage the purpose of transformation as bringing glory to God.

Finally, while my original definition of transformation acknowledged the *anticipation of the future transformation of the whole of creation*, this was not mentioned by the groups, except on one occasion by Caleb, which we have previously considered:

Caleb: '... then it ends up in Revelation with, with the talk of the new, a newly recreated heaven and earth with a renewed heaven and earth which is about transformation as well so I think there is a whole arc of transformation I think going through the Bible.' (SGB – Focus Group)

Caleb makes reference to the book of Revelation and the new creation (Revelation 21) and acknowledges the wider scope of transformation found in the biblical texts. The wider lack of reference to any future or cosmic transformation perhaps again reflects the individual Western culture in which we live, though of course it could also reflect the fact that the groups may have assumed that I was only concerned with personal or individual transformation.

In summary, the data from the small groups was in accordance with certain aspects of my original definition, such as transformation being *an ongoing process of change* and resulting from the *power of the Holy Spirit*, but there was less accordance with other aspects, such as the community and future-focused elements and the aim of coming to *more fully resemble Jesus Christ and glorify God*. This first difference suggests that transformation was primarily conceived in individual terms by the groups. The second suggests that while groups have an understanding of the nature of transformation as a process involving the work of the Holy Spirit, they did not generally have as clear an understanding of the anticipated outcome of transformation, or this was not evidenced in the data. References were made to change, ageing, glowing, and references to changes in attitude, behaviour, thinking and feelings. Nevertheless, there was less clarity about what direction these changes were in, other than being changes. This suggests that while the word transformation is widely used in the church, and emphasis is placed on being transformed, there is less attention paid to what this transformation will look like. This might be why the groups struggled to offer examples of their own transformation, as their understanding of transformation was too broad to enable them to offer examples of specific instances.

Having revisited the concept of transformation, we will now move on to consider the three key themes identified in this research: expert, challenge and use of materials.

Note

1 As has already been noted, each small group participant has been allocated a randomly selected pseudonym. Where my words are recorded, I am identified by the initials 'AC'. Each extract is identified by Small Group (either SGA, SGB or SGC) and by when it occurred (extracts from the focus group discussions are identified as 'Focus Group', otherwise they are numbered as to which meeting the excerpt is taken from). Therefore, an excerpt taken from Small Group B that took place on the second occasion that I observed the group would be identified as (SGB – 2).

6

Theme 1 – Expert

One of the themes that emerged from the data was that of *expert*. First, it is important to identify what I mean by 'expert'. The term is commonly used to refer to someone who is especially knowledgeable about a particular field. In this context, I am using it to refer to those who are especially knowledgeable, or perceived to be especially knowledgeable, about the Bible. This expertise is in contrast to the level of knowledge displayed in so-called 'ordinary theology', which is defined by Jeff Astley as 'the theological beliefs and processes of believing that find expression in the God-talk of those believers *who have received no scholarly theological education*' (2002, p. 1, emphasis added). These 'ordinary' readers are distinguished from 'trained' readers (West, 1993, pp. 8–9) who *have* received scholarly theological education, or are perceived to have scholarly theological knowledge. I emphasize the role of perception, as in a small group, if one is perceived as an expert, then this will alter the group processes accordingly, regardless of whether one actually possesses scholarly theological knowledge. Indeed, as Raths notes in relation to the construction of power in small groups,

> For any individual the status which he [sic] has achieved for himself may not be the one that he desires; moreover *the status which he has earned may not be a sound reflection of his abilities*. Status is used in the sense that it is *that place or position in the hierarchy which members of the group bestow upon a participant*. (1954, p. 99, emphasis added)

In the case of this research, expertise or being seen as expert is a position awarded by the group to an individual, and not necessarily one which the individual has sought or claimed for themselves. The term 'expert' is an 'etic' term (Creswell, 2013, p. 291), meaning that it was not a term used by the groups, but one I consider to accurately reflect what was present in the data. The use of the term 'expert' in this way is not without basis in the literature (e.g. French and Raven, 1959) and in other work on small groups (e.g. West, 2011).

The data indicated that there were both internal and external experts that the groups considered authoritative; by 'internal' I am referring to members of the group who were considered expert, and by 'external' I am referring to individuals who were not in the group who were considered expert. This theme raises the question of what makes someone an expert. In some instances, it was due to group recognition or designation that someone became seen as an expert, in others – and the two are not mutually exclusive – it was because of someone's role, either within or beyond the group, that they were considered or took on the role of expert. Interestingly, there were also examples of members of the groups appearing not to wish to be seen as expert.

We will first look at each small group in turn before examining 1 Corinthians 3, then finally we draw the data and the biblical text together to consider how experts and expertise can best be used to facilitate rather than hinder transformative biblical engagement.

Small Group A

In Small Group A, the expert of the group was Adam, a retired minister and missionary, who had joined the group with his wife – Jessica – about 18 months ago. Adam also qualifies as an expert according to our definition, as he had not only received scholarly theological education, but had also been involved in the delivery of theological education. According to Grenz and Olson's spectrum of theology, Adam would be considered a 'professional theologian' as he had not only been trained in theology himself, but had also taught others (1996, p. 33). Cameron and her colleagues might also suggest that he offered a 'normative voice', as he was a member of the clergy and thus could be said to represent the 'theological authority' of the church (2010, p. 54).

I became aware that Adam was seen as an expert by the group due to the way that he was often deferred to in discussion. For example, during a discussion about what or who the group believed the devil to be, the following exchange took place:

Jane: 'He's within us, but sometimes we don't listen to him, and the devil is also there. You know, it, he's around, I don't know – Adam?'

Adam: 'Well the Bible depicts the devil as a real spiritual person. I mean what about the temptations? ...'

[Further discussion, then just as Louise says 'Anyway' to move the discussion on:]

Julia: 'Adam, do you think that the devil can get at you through dreams?'

Adam: 'In many ways, many ways, yes I do.'
Julia: 'Yes, I have felt that on occasion. Woken up praying that it wouldn't, won't, happen again.'
(SGA – 1)

While Adam was not leading the session, on two occasions during the discussion of the same topic, two different individuals deferred to Adam. Later during the same meeting, which Louise was leading, Louise deferred to Adam:

Louise: 'So, can I ask you Adam, what you think the connection is?'
Adam: 'I'm sorry, I've lost the question.'
[Laughter]
Adam: 'What's the question?'
Louise: 'See if I've got the same.' [laughs]
Adam: 'Is this verses 6 and 10?'
Louise: 'Yes, 6 and 10 verses.'
Adam: 'Well, I go along with Julia, and what she said, that when we recognize we don't know it all ...'
[Interrupting] Louise: 'But what's the connection though? That's what our question is.'
Adam: 'Humility, isn't it? You submit to God, you're humble when you say, "I don't know it all" so turn to God.'
[General agreement]
(SGA – 1)

So, while Louise was responsible for leading the session and had prepared to do so, she deferred to Adam, and implied that the reason for doing so was to check that she got the 'right' answer by conferring with Adam – 'See if I've got the same'. This could be considered an appeal to the 'normative theology' that Adam may have been seen to represent (Cameron et al., 2010). Interestingly, Adam began his response by agreeing with what another group member, Julia, had already said, which perhaps suggests that Adam either, felt confident in his own expertise and so deferred to someone else's response, or might have even been trying to avoid being seen as the singular expert and was therefore indicating the wider expertise of the group.

There were a number of occasions when there was evidence that it was due to Adam's prior roles, as both a church leader and a theological educator, that he was seen as expert. During a discussion about James 5.13–20 which Roger was leading, the following exchange took place:

Roger: 'It is about truth, isn't it? This last bit. Which you're qualified to comment on.' [Final comment is directed at Adam]
Adam: 'It's saying that the Christian faith is the truth about life.'
(SGA – 3)

The allusion to Adam being 'qualified to comment' suggests that at least part of the reason Adam was seen as expert was due to the fact that he was as an ordained minister, his teaching experience, and maybe his actual theological qualifications. Louise Lawrence refers to the clergy as being a 'professional class', 'educated and trained to teach and preach scriptures to others' (2009, p. 105). Small Group A certainly appeared to see Adam in this light. Indeed, the group seemed to rely upon him to clarify any questions they had, particularly around passages they found difficult to interpret:

Roger: 'Once again I didn't find it easy.'
Julia: 'No, I didn't. There were two questions I got, where I couldn't think of any answer at all.'
Adam: 'Well, maybe we share ignorance, maybe we share …'
[Interrupting] Julia: 'When I told Roger this, Adam, he said, "Oh, Adam will answer them."'
[all laughing and talking]
Julia: 'What a reputation!'
Adam: 'Can I live up to it? Anyway, I did have to look at commentaries for this one, so. Shall we start with a prayer? I asked Jessica [his wife] to pray. Let's pray.'
(SGA – 2)

The group, or at least certain more vocal, members of the group, appeared to have great confidence in Adam's expertise and presumed that even when they struggled with a passage, that he would be able to provide an interpretation that helped them understand it. However, on this occasion and on other occasions, Adam referred to the fact that he had deferred to commentaries in order to aid his understanding of the passage. This could be an example of Adam seeking to democratize the process of biblical engagement, as he was highlighting the fact that this knowledge was not somehow inherent, but gained through study. A further example is seen below, during a discussion about James 5.7–12:

Adam: 'Just a little bit on verse 7. Different versions here have early rain, late rain, you said spring rain and summer rain. Jessica, you had different ones?'

Jessica: 'Autumn and spring rains.'
[At the same time] Jane: 'Spring and summer rain, yes.'
Adam: 'Autumn and spring. Well I looked up the commentary on this, and the early rain is late October/early November, so that's autumn rain, isn't it? Late October/early November, they're in the Northern hemisphere, Israel. And the late rains are April/May, so really, autumn and spring is the best, best, um, description of these two types of rain. And obviously, he's aware of agriculture, James, isn't he?'
[Agreement]
(SGA – 2)

Adam encouraged the group to note the way that alternative translations have rendered the same passage differently, and that this led him to consider a commentary on the passage. Adam defers to the commentaries in a similar way to the group deferring to Adam. This an example of the interplay between internal and external experts; Adam, as the internal expert, defers to the authority of a commentator, an external expert.

In James Fowler's model of the stages of faith, one of the key aspects that differentiates one stage of faith from another is the shifting 'locus of authority', which is gradually transferred from external sources of authority to internal authority (1995, pp. 244–245). In order to move from Stage 3 faith to Stage 4,

> there must be an interruption of reliance on external sources of authority ... While others and their judgments will remain important ... their expectations, advice and counsel will be submitted to an internal panel of experts who reserve the right to choose and who are prepared to take responsibility for their choices. (1995, p. 179)

Fowler refers to this development as 'the emergence of an *executive ego*' (1995, p. 179). Therefore, it might be suggested that some members of Small Group A had not fully developed an executive ego and thus the locus of authority for them remained external, and was found in the expertise of individuals such as Adam. However, it might also be the case that while the group members outwardly accepted Adam's expertise, his comments were being 'submitted to an internal panel of experts'. Possible evidence of this can be seen in the following excerpt.

While Adam seemed to be generally accepted as expert by the group, this did not mean that other group members would not challenge him. During a discussion about healing, Adam referred to the fact that people do naturally age, but someone challenged this:

Adam:	'There is a natural ageing of the body. And one must expect the body to get weaker ...'
Roger:	'Yes, quite.'
	[Others making noises of agreement]
Adam:	'... through the normal processes. I was saying, someone coming forward who is full of arthritis and aged 80, can't expect to go away with the body of an 18-year-old.'
Roger:	'No.'
	[More murmurs of agreement]
Adam:	'You've got to be realistic.'
Roger:	'I think that's being realistic.'
Louise:	'Why, why not?'
Adam:	'Well, I think ...'
Louise:	'Why not?'
	[Laughter]
Adam:	'I think amazing things can happen, Louise, but the body does age ...'
Louise:	'Yes, I know, I can see that part of it, but I've seen people get release, when they're old, you know.'
Adam:	'Yes!'
Louise:	'From prayer.'
Adam:	'Yes, of course, of course. Release from pain is a great thing, isn't it?'
Louise:	'Yes, absolutely.'
	(SGA – 3)

Adam did not appear threatened by being challenged, and while Adam had been speaking more objectively before Louise's comment, his voice became more compassionate as he said, 'I think amazing things can happen, Louise, but the body does age'. Adam had perhaps sensed that this topic was potentially emotive in a group where the average was 75 years old. There was also an occasion when Adam challenged someone else in the group during a discussion about James 5.13–14 and Jewish worship:

Roger:	'Well, there are two things here. The early church, as I'm sure you well know, was a great one for singing, and every moment they would get up and sing the praises, and, er, and we have evidence of that in Corinthians and in Ephesians and in Colossians, but singing was most important, most vital ... Now, that's in comparison with the Jews, whose worship was virtually non-musical ...'
	[Adam indicates that he disagrees]

Roger: 'Is that not right?'
Adam: 'No, I don't know about that ...'
Roger: 'Sorry?'
Adam: 'They had the psalms, didn't they.'
[Others agree]
Roger: 'Yes, they had the psalms, but basically, their worship, at this time in particular, was non-musical.'
Adam: 'This must be synagogue worship then.'
Roger: 'Yes, oh sorry, sorry, the synagogue worship didn't have in contrast to the Christians who were always singing.'
(SGA – 3)

Adam appeared to feel somewhat responsible for intervening when he believed Roger was saying something that was incorrect, but the conflicting views were brought together when they agreed that synagogue worship at that time was unmusical. That they came together on their interpretation prevented, either, Adam undermining Roger's leadership of the session, or Roger undermining Adam's role as expert. While Adam's input was clearly highly valued, Roger, who organized the group, emphasized the need to hear from various people:

Roger: 'But I just said, I didn't I think, I have said this before, very essential that I don't lead every fortnight, it is not good, I mean I have always had to do it but, but other people, Keith has done it of course in the past.'
Jane: 'Louise has done it.'
Roger: 'And Louise came in and did it which is marvelous and Adam, I think it is very important because as I said before one voice, one opinion perhaps is not good...'
(SGA – Focus group)

Roger emphasized the need to have more than one voice, though this does not necessarily conflict with a desire to also have input from an expert voice.

Overall, Small Group A clearly saw Adam as their internal expert and would defer to him, both when something was challenging and also simply because they trusted and desired his input. Adam's position as expert appears to have developed due to his prior experience as a theological educator and his status as an ordained minister, which allowed him to become firmly established in the group, despite his membership of the group being significantly shorter than many other members.

Small Group B

Unlike in Small Group A, in Small Group B there was not a clearly designated internal expert, though there was still evidence of the role of experts in the group, especially external experts, as well as an apparent reticence by the group leader to be seen as expert.

On the first occasion I visited, John was leading the session, and as part of his preparation he had chosen one commentary for each of the passages being looked at.

John: 'Well, the first point, I totally agree with what Tessa said, I did think the chapter in there was particularly good [referring to Brian McLaren (2015), Chapter 40]. And often I don't find the book so helpful, so make that point. We can't get through though, the number of passages tonight, I mean, it's huge. We've got the John passage [John 3.1–21], which to be very succinct is, uh, "you must be born again" and "for God so loved the world" and for that I delved into the [indistinct] Greek, in order to read through that particular section [muttering "impressive"] and I've tried to, sort of like, look at commentaries for different reasons. Then we've got the passage from Acts [Acts 2.1–41] and again, uh, there's quite a lot of reading, um, the coming of the Holy Spirit, from Peter's sermon at Pentecost... And for that I've decided to use this one [indicating a commentary], which is more middle of the road, looking at two parts, the miracle of Pentecost and of course Peter's speech at Pentecost. And then we've got a third reading, which is from, er, Romans [Romans 6.1–14], and basically, the basis of that reading is about, um, the whole issue of dead to sin but alive to God, and for that I decided to use a very evangelical commentary, so I've kind of, like, had a dip into all three' ...
(SGB – 1)

Interestingly, John did not introduce the commentaries by referring to the author or title, but on at least two occasions, by the church tradition that he associated the commentary with. John begins by sharing that he found McClaren's input on the Biblical readings helpful, whereas this is not always the case, which makes clear he is happy to critique an 'expert'. However, despite finding McClaren's work helpful, John still opted to consider a number of commentaries, which is perhaps an example of the endorsement of one external expert over, and perhaps against, another. Interestingly, when John then went on to make use of one of the commentaries he had selected, the group members did not all seem convinced by the commentary:

John: 'Barrett [referring to C. K. Barrett "The Gospel According to St. John"] goes on, and these are his words, these are not my notes these are words I've taken from the commentary, that, by the way, he's very old fashioned, so he still talks about men ... but he says, 'Men', and I'll put in parentheses (women), 'must be prepared by a radical renewal of themselves, a new birth, effected by the Spirit who comes,' in parentheses '(as it were) as the advance guard of the new age'. What does he mean by that? What do the commentators mean by that? And, and what does that mean for us? Or what does that mean for you? I'll just read it again. 'Men', in parentheses (women), 'must be prepared by a radical renewal of themselves, a new birth, effected by the Spirit who comes (as it were) as the advance guard of the new age'. What does this mean for us?'
[Pause]
Alex: 'Could you read it one more time?'
John: 'Yeah, good question. OK. "Men", in parenthesis (women) ...'
Juliet: 'Just say men and women. It's easier.'
[Laughter]
John: 'Must be prepared by a radical renewal of themselves, a new birth, effected by the Spirit who comes (as it were) as the advance guard of the new age.'
Tabitha: 'I don't get the advance guard bit.'
Juliet: 'So the Holy Spirit is coming as the advanced guard.'
Tabitha: 'Yes, but I think the Holy Spirit stays.'
[Discussion continues as the group explore the quote.]
(SGB – 1)

The quote itself appeared to confuse some of the group, and the use of non-gender inclusive language and the subsequent alterations made by John did not necessarily help this. In both the USA and in the UK, there has been an acknowledgment of an 'anti-intellectualism' in society, one form of which has been identified as 'anti-elitism':

> In any society with democratic aspirations, we may expect a mistrust of claims to superior knowledge or wisdom on the part of an educated elite, especially when such claims are suspected to be instruments in the service of class privilege. (Rigney, 1991, p. 441)

This is not to say that the group were in any way opposed to intellectual enquiry, but they may have been suspicious of the use of overly intellectual or elitist language. They therefore sought to challenge the 'formal voice' (Cameron et al., 2010) of those such as McLaren or Barrett, and rather than appearing to show them any deference they appeared more inclined to critique them.

On another occasion, when looking at 1 Corinthians 13, which in McLaren's book is explored in Chapter 23 and is entitled 'Spirit of Love: Loving Neighbour' (2015, pp. 265–270), Tessa – who was leading – explicitly invited the group to consider whether or not they agreed with McLaren's use of the text:

Tessa: 'So, given that the love that he is speaking of is primarily the love that believers should have between them, and he has also got it right in the middle of the worship of the church, hasn't he, how you conduct your worship. Is it valid to widen this out to a more general blueprint for love? Brian McLaren using this to talk about love for your neighbour, so is it valid to use that in that way? [Pause] Or is it just for us believers?'
(SGB – 2)

Despite the way that Tessa framed the question, both Aaron and Caleb responded by supporting McLaren's use of the text, though on a later occasion, when Caleb was leading, he chose different passages to the ones identified by McLaren, as he did not agree with McLaren's choice:

Caleb: 'This chapter is on the "Spirit of Unity and Diversity", and it's actually primarily, well it's all, it is, it's about the Trinity really and he's actually explaining how the Trinity has come to be understood in his Brian McLaren way. Um, and he's got three passages, all of which I found were, a, slightly [pause] obscure, how it linked to the topic, and I thought actually, I would use his theme, which he's talking about the Trinity but actually pull out a few other verses instead ...'
(SGB – 3)

The pause before Caleb used the word 'obscure' indicates that he was being cautious about the justification he gave for opting to use alternative verses. The verses chosen by McLaren were: Proverbs 8, John 17.1–23, and Ephesians 4.1–16 (2015, p. 277), and the verses chosen by Caleb were: 2 Corinthians 13.14, Ephesians 3.14–17, John 14.15–17, and Ephesians 2.18. There is clearly some discernment taking place when it comes to McLaren's book, as Caleb was in support of his use of 1 Corinthians 13 to refer to love of neighbour during one meeting, but when he considered McLaren's choice of texts to discuss the Trinity, he opted to select different texts. Therefore Caleb, along with other members of the group, will not simply accept the opinion of external experts merely due to their status as such. This may be due to the relational nature of authority: as Raths notes, power is of an 'interpersonal nature ... to have power one must be empowered: power comes from others' (1954, p. 97). While McLaren may be seen as an expert, the extent to which his viewpoint is able to influence the group is limited by the fact that there is no relationship between him and the group.

Caleb, who co-hosts the group with his wife, Stephanie, and is also ordained, referred to a number of external experts during the period I observed the group, including Henri Nouwen, Rowan Williams, Jurgen Moltmann, and others, indicating his familiarity with their work. However, despite Caleb's potential to be seen as an expert, due to both his status as an ordained minister and due to his knowledge of external experts, he generally seemed reticent to be seen as such. For example, when discussing the Trinity, just after Ephesians 2.18 had been read ('Now all of us can come to the Father through the same Holy Spirit because of what Christ has done for us' (NLT version, which was the version used)), Caleb made the following comment:

Caleb: 'I don't think I need to say anything more on that ...'
       [Interrupting] Aaron: 'Snappy.'
Caleb: '... do you? It's just like, straight to the point. And describing the different roles of – I have to be – I'm not a doctrine specialist, alright? So, I have to be, you know. Doctrine specialists get all sorts of, get concerns about when you use the word "role" or "function" or whatever, and you've got to be careful, because you set up the wrong idea, because essentially its' a very complicated idea – it's simple but it's complex, the idea, and so, forgive me for my slightly agricultural language sometimes about it. Yeah, so [pause] how do you feel about the Spirit? What do you think– I thought it would be good to now just spend a bit of time opening up and saying, what do you think, how do you think believing in the Trinity impacts the way we might look at the world? Look at the world around us ...'
       (SGB – 3)

Caleb emphasized that he was not a 'doctrine specialist' and then went on to apologise for his 'slightly agricultural language' about the Trinity.

Caleb was aware that he was not an 'academic theologian' (Grenz and Olson, 1996, p. 33) and did not seek to offer a 'formal theology' (Cameron et al., 2010), and though he probably would not have referred to himself as a 'ministerial theologian' (Grenz and Olson, 1996, p. 33), by virtue of his training, according to Grenz and Olson's definition, this is what he is. However, due to his ministerial training, Caleb was aware of the huge amount of academic writing – 'formal theology' – on this area and that he could not hope to accurately present it in the limited time available, so he seeks to emphasize his limited knowledge. This may have also been due to his general reticence to be seen as the expert in the group.

Despite appearing concerned about dominating discussions, Caleb did on occasion offer contributions that highlighted his biblical knowledge, for example, the following comment on John 3.11–15:

Caleb: 'Well that's, the comparison is with the story of the Israelites when they had, was it a plague? Or a whatever? That came on them in, when they were journeying through the wilderness, and Moses brought a snake and put it up and whenever the people looked at the snake, the serpent on the stick, they were healed. So it's like saying, if we look to the son of God, risen, er, raised, then we will be healed. That's, that's what I take away from that.'
(SGB – 1)

Interestingly, Caleb offered this contribution after there was a significant pause after the passage was read, which may have been what encouraged him to contribute, as he may have felt that others were unable to do so.

Caleb's apparent reticence to fulfil the expert role that he may have naturally taken up may have been in part a response to the group's lack of a desire for an expert to guide their discussions, as is suggested by the following, which came out of a discussion about the divinity of Jesus:

Aaron: 'I would just very much like to hear other's people's views …'
[Interrupting] Caleb: 'Well maybe we could do for part of a session?'
Aaron: 'Yeah.'
Stephanie: 'I think it's gunna, that would fill up …'
[Interrupting] Aaron: 'Not somebody leading us to an answer.'
Caleb: 'Yeah.'
Aaron: 'But not so much right and wrong.'

Stephanie: 'But my personality will want to know the right answer at the end!'
[Laughter]
…
Caleb: 'Do you want me to have a go at, I'm not, I can't promise to prepare lots, but we just want a discussion, don't we? A good discuss …'
Stephanie: 'I would have thought that's, the balls in all our courts …'
Aaron: 'Yeah, that's what I'd most like, please.'
Stephanie: 'to come with thoughts of our own selves.'
(SGB – 3)

Aaron was very clear that he wanted everyone to contribute and did not want 'somebody leading us to an answer', but as the group co-ordinator, Caleb instinctively took responsibility for preparing for the session. This was then challenged by Stephanie, who noted that Aaron's primary interest was not in a right, or expert, answer, but in hearing about peoples' experiences. As has been acknowledged elsewhere, the postmodern turn has led many in the West to question and challenge received forms of authority (Middleton and Walsh, 1995), which would logically also include challenging experts. However, this has also led to the idea that everyone is, to an extent, an expert, as, from a social constructivist perspective, we all construct our own understanding of the world in which we live (Swinton and Mowat, 2016). Thus, everyone's perspective is considered to be equally valid, regardless of their level of 'scholarly theological education' (Astley, 2002, p. 1).

In summary, there appeared to be a desire to include external experts, not simply to follow their expertise, but in order to engage with it and at times challenge it. Caleb was the most obvious candidate to fulfil the internal expert role, and sometimes he seemed willing to do so, but at other times he seemed reticent to be painted in this light. Therefore, unlike in Small Group A, in Small Group B there was no one individual to whom the group deferred.

Small Group C

Small Group C was the group in which the theme of expert was least explicitly present. It was the only group that did not contain an ordained minister, which perhaps meant that there was no one specific individual who was especially likely to be identified as an expert. It may also be due to the fact that the group had only been running for about a year, so no one may have yet been identified by the group as being an expert. The hosts and leaders were a married couple, Philip and Gabi, and they were the two who *appeared* to sometimes seek to fulfill the expert role, though this may not have been their intention. An example of this is in the following discussion of Ezekiel 47, which Philip was leading:

Philip: 'So, what does the Ezekiel passage say to you? It's clearly a prophetic passage, that Ezekiel was led, um, I suppose, in a trance to see this. So, what does it say to you? [pause] About the river going ankle deep, knee deep, and up to the waist. What is the message?'

[Long pause]

Olivia: 'What, but, but going on from that in verse 6, he says, 'He asks me, 'Son of Man, do you see this? Then he led me back to the bank of the river". So, that's what I understand, almost that you could be, that you could face that river that you can't cross, but then he manages to take him back to a place where he showed it to him, that he could look onto it, you don't have to cross. He's not asking you to, no. The verse afterwards.'

Philip: 'But what's the …'

Olivia: 'Or are you talking about waiting for, on God, in time of difficult situation? What, what, what have I not understood here, everybody?'

[Number of people mutter about not being sure either]

Clive: 'I'm not very switched on to it either, I'm not sure what it means to me really. I can't think about things good from the temple and therefore it gets deeper and deeper the more you look into it, but that doesn't seem to be, you know.'

Philip: 'It's about the, the, water flowing from the temple, it's about …'

[Interrupting] Paul: 'Purifying.'

Philip: 'It could be an analogy for the Gospel, the truth, the love of God flowing out.'

Clive: 'Yes, yes, I can see that. But when you can't cross it, I mean, it gets too deep for you to understand? Or?'

Philip: 'Yeah, eventually.'

...

(SGC – 1)

At the start, Philip sought to frame the discussion by offering the comment that the passage is 'clearly a prophetic passage'. He then later sought to offer suggestions about how the passage should be interpreted; this input was met positively and seemed to be accepted, as it was not challenged.

THEME 1 – EXPERT

However, Philip's input may have simply been the way in which he chose to lead the discussion, and may not have been an indication of seeking to be seen as expert. Similarly, on an occasion when Gabi was leading, she also offered extra information:

Gabi: 'It says in the commentary, Stephen, that, um, the previous psalm, 90, under the title is says Moses wrote it …'
[At the same time as Gabi] Philip: '"A Prayer of Moses, the man of God".'
Gabi: 'And their thinking is that he wrote the next, and then, ten psalms, obviously one of which is 91. But it wasn't, um, David.'
Olivia: 'How interesting.'
(SGC – 3)

Like Philip, Gabi may have seen it as her responsibility to offer extra information about the passage as she was leading the meeting (on Psalm 91).

While there was not a clearly identifiable internal expert, there did appear to be a desire to hear from external experts. For example, on one occasion the group listened to a recording of 'Pastor Tom's' 'DriveTime Devotions', which focused on the passage that the group were looking at that week – Mark 5.21–34. 'Pastor Tom' is Tom Holladay, a teaching pastor at Saddleback Church in California; the DriveTime Devotions website (http://drivetimedevotions.com/) describes their purpose as helping people to 'know God's Word and put it into practice', with five recorded devotions uploaded each week. The recording lasted for just over ten minutes, and was then used by the group as the basis for a discussion. 'Pastor Tom' would either be considered a 'ministerial theologian' or a 'professional theologian', according to Grenz and Olson's model (1993).

On another occasion, there was a discussion about the current preaching series at church.

Joy: 'And I do think that, I think there is a place for study and learning, … You could have given the testimony and then we could have actually learnt who wrote this, you know we've got lots of people that don't know who wrote this psalm …'
[Interrupting] Gabi: 'Moses, they think Moses wrote it.'
[As Joy begins speaking again] Stephen: 'Really?'
Gabi: 'Yeah.'
Joy: 'Yeah, you know, all that sort of background. I think we come to, to understand that; what context, how it links into other passages, where that's used in the New Testament, [Gabi says

	"Yeah" a number of times as Joy is speaking] and actually, that, to me, that's what preaching is, but we seem to have moved away from that and it's all about how we feel, and there is a place for that ...'
Gabi:	'I know. You need both.'
Joy:	'... we need both.'
	(SGC – 3)

Joy appeared to want a deeper level of input from the preaching at the church, which may indicate a desire for those that preach to be experts, even if there is not a desire for there to be experts present at their small group meetings.

Small Group C neither contained an obvious internal expert nor sought one out; instead, there was some use made of external experts, such as 'Pastor Tom', and some desire expressed for input from external experts during sermons. There appeared little desire for anyone to provide expertise within the group.

Biblical case study: 1 Corinthians 3

We are now going to explore 1 Corinthians 3 in order to consider what bearing it may have in thinking about the role of experts in small groups. Paul is concerned that the Christians in Corinth are becoming divided because different factions are claiming to follow different leaders – Paul, Apollos and Cephas – so he challenges them on this. Paul uses a number of different images and metaphors – planting, watering, cultivating, building – to explain the role of himself, Apollos and Cephas. And he ends with a warning about being misled by worldly wisdom. What, then, might we learn from this passage about the role of experts?

Leon Morris (1958) has suggested that by using the term 'what' rather than 'who' when referring to Apollos and himself, Paul is focusing on the function rather than the individuals themselves. What is key is the function that Paul and Apollos have served, which is that of servant: their role was to serve the Christian community in a 'common purpose' (v.8). Paul begins with the imagery of planting and watering, with the emphasis being on God giving the growth (v.7). Then, in verses ten to fifteen, Paul swaps his metaphor from plants to buildings, and suggests that those who build will ultimately be judged by what they construct. As C. K. Barrett says, 'You are God's field, God's building; that is, the field which God, through his servants, is cultivating, the building which God, through his servants, is erecting' (1971, p. 86). The role of Paul, Apollos, Cephas or any other Christian leader is that of serving the community; the emphasis is on how leaders are building up the church (Prior, 1993), rather than on any importance that the leaders have in and of themselves. Again, Barrett expresses this well: 'The only significance of planter and waterer is that God accepts their labour and works through them (v.9); they have no independent importance.' (1971, p. 85). However, Paul does emphasize that he is 'like a skilled master builder' (v.10), so, while the emphasis is on being 'God's servants' (v.9), this does not mean that at the same time, Paul – and other leaders – are not skilled. Those who have been placed in positions of leadership, or have assumed positions of leadership or respect due to their perceived expertise, have a duty to use those skills that they possess to serve the communities of which they are a part.

Later in the passage, Paul refers to passages from Isaiah and Job to challenge 'the wisdom of the world' (v.19) and suggests that instead if the Corinthians wish to be wise, they should become fools. This is immediately followed by a warning: 'So let no one boast about human leaders' (v.21). This could be read both as a warning against placing Christians leaders on a pedestal due to their perceived wisdom, and a warning against any Christian considering themselves 'wise' according to worldly standards. Paul does not say that it is wrong that the community should be led, as he clearly sees the leader's role as an important part of enabling the community to grow, though he emphasizes that it is God who gives the growth. Paul's letter is aimed at the church community in Corinth, rather than to its leaders specifically, so there may also be a message here for members of small groups: 'So let no one boast about human leaders' (v.21) – or be wary of placing those you consider 'expert' on a pedestal. The chapter ends with the following proclamation: 'For all things are yours, whether Paul or Apollos or Cephas or the world or life or death or the present or the future – all belong to you, and you belong to Christ, and Christ belongs to God' (vs.21b–23). This expresses Paul's belief that all that we have is a gift from God in Christ, from church leaders to the earth to all that is to come (Prior, 1993), and that we belong to Christ and that Christ belongs to God. Thus, those who have particular expertise can be received by their communities as a gift from God, and those who possess expertise should also consider this expertise a gift, gifted in order that they might serve the community.

We are now going to draw together the data, 1 Corinthians 3 and other literature that is pertinent to the discussion, in order to consider how experts and expertise might best be utilised in order to facilitate transformative biblical engagement.

Experts and transformative biblical engagement

Given that this research was carried out among Church of England congregations, it is worthy of note that the two identifiable experts – Adam and Caleb – were both ordained ministers in the Church of England. Therefore, while it may be true that postmodernism has led many in the West to question and challenge received forms of authority (Middleton and Walsh, 1995), within the church at least, it appears that the clergy are still considered authoritative. Louise Lawrence refers to the clergy as being a 'professional class', 'educated and trained to teach and preach scriptures to others' (2009, p. 105). In a seminal article on the bases of power, French and Raven identified five different forms of power: reward, coercive, legitimate, referent and expert. They state that, 'the expert is seen as having superior knowledge or ability in very specific areas' (1959, p. 268). Indeed, those training for ordained ministry in the Church of England will study 'specific areas' of theology, including biblical studies, in order to fulfill their calling to 'unfold the Scriptures'. During the service for the Ordination of Priests (*Common Worship: Ordination Services*), as part of the Declarations, the congregation is reminded that those ordained priests must 'unfold the Scriptures', which is based in part on Luke 24.27, when Jesus appears on the road to Emmaus: 'Then beginning with Moses and all the prophets, he interpreted to them the things about himself in all the scriptures.' They offer a form of 'ministerial theology', a form of 'reflective faith as practiced by trained ministers and teachers in Christian churches' (Grenz and Olson, 1996, p. 31). Thus, it is not surprising that in the two small groups where members of clergy were present, they, to a greater or lesser extent, took on the role of expert, as this can rightly be considered to be a part of their calling. However, while still recognizing this, it is still possible to question whether there are ways of fulfilling this calling that are more or less likely to facilitate transformative biblical engagement.

Some models of biblical engagement have emphasized the importance of experts in enabling transformative biblical engagement, for example Contextual Bible Study (CBS), as pioneered by Gerald West. West noted that 'ordinary readers' (i.e. those who read the Bible without any scholarly theological education) read the Bible differently from biblical scholars, who do have scholarly theological education. Developing Meyer's (2002) idea, West suggested that ordinary readers are primarily 'trained' to read by their family and church community, whereas biblical scholars have been trained by the academy (West, 2007, p. 2). However, while the biblical scholars – the experts – are key to the process of CBS, the aim is empowering ordinary readers to interpret biblical texts for themselves (West, 2011). The intention is not that the expert will provide the interpretation and the ordinary readers will simply accept this. Indeed, Carlos Mesters, speaking of Roman Catholic communities in Brazil, has noted that it is an over-reliance on 'informational knowledge and the learned expert' that has prevented ordinary readers from interpreting biblical texts for themselves (1993, p. 9). John Riches, who has pioneered the use of CBS in Scotland, has suggested that 'the excitement of CBS lies in its ability to unlock "ordinary" readers' abilities and skills and to draw out their insights into the text' (Riches et al., 2010, p. xii). Hence, in order for transformative biblical engagement to take place, the expert must be working to empower ordinary readers to interpret texts for themselves, rather simply providing them with an 'expert' interpretation of the text. This connects with 1 Corinthians 3, where the role of an expert is to serve the community: as Paul says, 'For all things are yours, whether Paul or Apollos or Cephas or the world or life or death or the present or the future – all belong to you, and you belong to Christ, and Christ belongs to God' (verses 21b–23). The idea that leaders or experts 'belong' to the group emphasizes that they are there to use their expertise, their 'ministerial theology' (Grenz and Olson, 1996, p. 31), to serve and empower others. Louise Lawrence, speaking specifically of the role of clergy in the process of CBS, states, '[i]n such a process their [the clergy's] position would be transformed in the perceptions of the group from "clergy" (power role) to "person" (one voice among many in an egalitarian group)' (2009, p. 105). As Paul says, 'you belong to Christ, and Christ belongs to God' (verse 23) – we all have different roles in the body of Christ, but it is ultimately *his* body, not ours. In relation to French and Raven's suggestion that the expert role imbues the individual with certain power, which they define in terms of the ability to influence psychological change (1959, p. 260), it could be said that in relinquishing this power, others can be empowered.

So, to what extent did the experts in this research *appear* to hinder or facilitate transformative biblical engagement? It is important to note that any suggestions must be extremely tentative, hence the use of italics in the preceding sentence. However, I would suggest that the apparent over-reliance on Adam's expertise in Small Group A was more of a hindrance than an aid to transformative biblical engagement, because other group members indicated that they did not always continue wrestling with difficult biblical passages or study questions as they believed they could rely on Adam to answer any question. This also meant that when Adam was deferred to, it was often because there was a desire to know the 'right' answer, and so this did not facilitate other members coming to an answer or interpretation for themselves, or one forming out of a group discussion.

Adam did at times seek to encourage others to rely on their own knowledge and expertise, for example, when he simply said he agreed with the response of another member of the group. In Small Group B, Caleb's apparent reticence to contribute at times could be due to his concern at being seen as an expert and as the one with the 'right' answers. Caleb deliberately highlighted the fact that he was not a theologian: '... I'm not a doctrine specialist, alright?' (SGB – 3). Caleb was perhaps struggling to hold together Paul's instruction, to be both 'like a skilled master builder' (verse 10) and also 'God's servant' (verse 9), and appeared uncomfortable in the 'skilled master builder' role of the 'ministerial theologian' (Grenz and Olson, 1996). However, at other times, he appeared to feel a sense of responsibility for providing expertise, as when Aaron wanted to explore how people viewed Jesus (SGB – 3). Interestingly, on this occasion, this expertise did not appear to be desired by the group.

In Small Group C, the lack of expertise was something that the group appeared to miss, not only in the small group but as part of Sunday worship too. There was a desire to hear more from 'formal theology' (Cameron et al., 2010), and this led the group to seek to include expertise in their meetings, for example, recordings of 'Pastor Tom'. They were missing a 'skilled master builder' (verse 10), and some appeared to see this lack of expertise as detrimental to their growth in faith and, potentially, their transformation. This may have been related to the fact that the group predominantly identified as evangelicals, and as evangelicals are seen to possess an attitude of 'devotion to the Bible' (Bebbington, 1989, p. 12) and 'give scripture the primary place' (Wright, 1991, p. 8), they may have wished to have had deeper input on the biblical texts they were exploring, perhaps from someone who was perceived to be an expert. Thus, where an over-reliance on expertise potentially hindered transformative biblical engagement, a lack of expertise also potentially hindered transformative biblical engagement.

Within education, there has been a significant shift in how teachers and other educators are viewed; rather than being seen as experts who impart wisdom, the 'banking' model of education (Freire, 2005 [originally published 1968], p. 7), they are now often seen as facilitators who journey with their students. In the words of Paulo Freire, 'The teacher is no longer merely the-one-who-teaches, but one who is himself [sic] taught in dialogue with the students, who in turn while being taught also teach. They become jointly responsible for a process in which all grow' (2005, p. 80). Lawrence suggests this shift can also be seen in initial ministerial education, with those involved in training ordinands being encouraged to see themselves as facilitators not experts (2009). Interestingly, Small Group A had the highest average age (74.9) and was most reliant on an expert, whereas Small Group B and C had lower average ages (58.9 and 58.3, respectively) and were less reliant on experts, in some instances appearing to reject expertise – for example, when Aaron in Small Group B emphasized that he did not want 'somebody leading us to an answer' (SGB – 3). Hence, the shift in wider educational theory and practice can be seen to be at work within some of the small groups involved in this research.

In summary, it appears that experts are most likely to facilitate transformative biblical engagement if they embrace their role as 'skilled master builder' (verse 10), and use their expertise to serve the small group that they are part of. Most likely, as is the case in Contextual Bible Study, by using their expertise to enable other members of the group to engage with the biblical text at a deeper level, as was suggested by E. H. Robertson (1961), though this should not merely be at an intellectual level (e.g. Wink, 1989). Where experts function primarily by providing 'right answers', they are more likely to hinder transformative biblical engagement, as individuals may not seek to engage deeply with the biblical text, but may simply wait to hear what the expert has to say.

7

Theme 2 – Challenge

The second theme that emerged from the data was *challenge*. I use the term 'challenge', rather than perhaps 'disagreement' or 'conflict' for a number of reasons. First, it is a more neutral term than disagreement or conflict, which both carry more negative connotations: for example, 'I disagree with you' is more confrontational than, 'I would like to challenge that'. Secondly, it is broader; I can be challenged by something, or someone, I either agree *or* disagree with. Thirdly, it can be used comparably of interaction with texts and with people. Finally, it is a so-called 'emic' term (Creswell, 2013, p. 92), which was used by the participants and was thus a concept that was familiar to them. Despite being an emic term, the idea of challenge relating to transformation can also clearly be seen in the literature examined in Chapter 2.

Within the data, challenge emerged as a result of engagement with the text and as a result of engagement with others in the group, but it was also referred to more generally. We will begin with references to challenge, before looking at the other two forms of challenge that emerged: text-generated challenge and group-generated challenge, though as these two forms are not mutually exclusive they will be dealt with together. We will then explore Galatians 2.11–14 to assess what the biblical text might offer on this issue and end by considering whether challenge in small groups hinders or facilitates transformative biblical engagement.

Challenge as a desired practice

The questionnaire results offer a broad summary of how desirable challenge was seen to be. Question four of the questionnaire asked participants to identify how important a number of features of small groups were to them, using a scale of 'Very important', 'Fairly important', 'Not very important', 'Not at all important', or 'Not applicable'. The third feature was, 'Having your own views challenged', and Figure 1 shows how the three groups answered this question. While the numbers are not large enough to be significant, there is at least an indication that overall those in Small Group A showed slightly less inclination to be challenged than the other two groups.

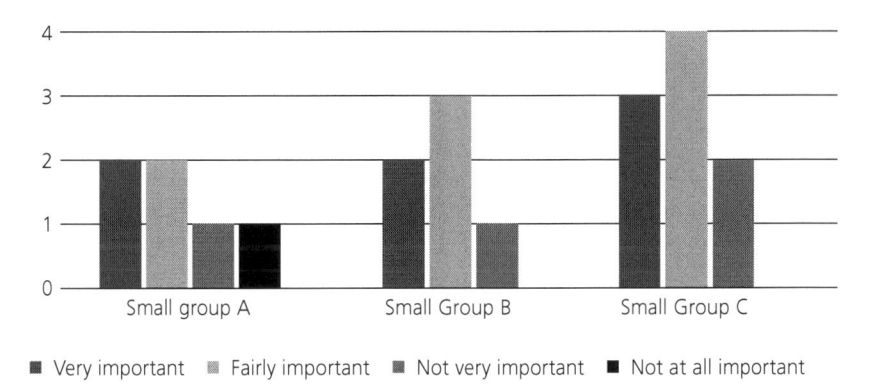

Figure 1: How important is it to you 'Having your own views challenged?'

However, in all the groups, the majority of the group considered it either very important or fairly important that their views were challenged in the small group. Nevertheless, the work of Anton Baumohl (1984) and John Hull (1985) has shown that change and learning can be painful experiences, therefore, while in hindsight we might recognize the value in being challenged, it may be that we do not especially enjoy being challenged at the time the challenge occurs. Thus these responses may partially reflect what the participants felt the 'right' answer was, as they may have felt that being open to being challenged was a virtuous characteristic – which leads us to consider the value that the groups placed on being challenged.

During the focus group discussions, there were a couple of instances when group members referred to the role of challenge in transformation. For example, the following exchange in Small Group C:

Philip: 'I think, I think, you know, the transformation that I, I suppose we look at in the Christian life is, is coming, coming to faith in the first instance and there can be big changes that we see when that happens but now there is this, you know, the theological word, it is the sanctification, which is the ongoing change and I think what we kind of touched on, the silly thing is that it's, it can be quite easy to get to a point where we are comfortable with the change that's happened in us and in the people around us and we are all kind of, we kind of plateau at a certain place but the challenge is to actually go on, to …'

Debs: 'Keep going.'

Philip: 'And to becoming, because it is about becoming more Christlike, because that is what sanctification is about and, you know, we can never plateau because there is, there is always more of Christ than we can find and I think that the danger, and I was quite challenged by the questions we had to fill in earlier [in the questionnaire] about, you know, have I been challenged to change my thinking, and I think, you know, I am quite comfortable with where I am now and I don't really want to get, get challenged to change again, and I think that is quite a dangerous place to be.'

Gabi: 'It evolves, it changes, evolves.'

Philip: 'But I think that, you know, we can get comfortable with where we are and not be prepared to be challenged to transform.'

Olivia: 'Not just for ourselves, but to other people so somebody else we are so comfortable with not changing that we are actually uncomfortable with other people changing so we try and say things to them meaning well, that actually can trans ... that actually is unloving.'

Clive: 'So that is the point of the preacher is to make you uncomfortable where you are to make you think yourself someone else because ...'

Philip: 'It makes the comfortable uncomfortable.'

Clive: 'Yes, exactly, because you see I don't like, I really don't like going to church and coming out comfortable, and I feel slightly and slightly challenged or something umm yes.'

Philip: 'Short changed.'

(SGC – Focus Group)

A group consensus emerged about the necessity of being challenged in order for ongoing transformation to take place, and concerns were raised about reaching a 'plateau' and being too comfortable. During the Small Group B Focus Group, there was another reference to being too comfortable:

Nathan: 'There's an element of being comfortable isn't there, being kind of too – word very carefully – too content with as you are, which isn't necessarily a bad thing, you know, depending on context but sometimes we can be too ... It is again like the same thing we don't expose ourselves to new things because we are happy with how we are and what we are and therefore you are less likely to change.'

(SGB – Focus Group)

There did appear to be a general perception that being too comfortable made one less likely to be challenged and thus less likely to be transformed. Indeed, Tim Shapiro, in referring to how challenge enables congregations to learn, states that, 'naming the challenge accurately will create discomfort' (2017, p. 46). Indicating that being too comfortable may well be closely associated with a lack of challenge or a lack of willingness to identify and confront a challenge. Returning to Small Group C, the apparent desire for challenge was so strong that if some of the individuals left church on a Sunday without being challenged, then they felt 'short-changed'.

The role of challenge was referred to on a number of other occasions, such as in the following discussion in Small Group B of 1 Corinthians 13, which was explored by looking at a number of real-life situations in order to consider what the most loving response was.

Martha: '… I think one of the hard things is, and I think it is hard in churches, because of the nice thing that is like a blanket over us all, you know, I like Tabitha's phrase, having the hard conversation, you know, confronting well if there is a conflict or a difference or a difficulty. I think that's one of the real challenges, to do that well and I just always think it's interesting, that it, does it say it in this passage? I thought I'd read it in one of the readings.'
Caleb: 'What, about love admonishing?'
Martha: 'Yes.'
Caleb: 'I don't think it was in todays.'
Tessa: 'But I think the whole tone of the letter is that.'
[Agreement]
Martha: 'Yes, but I do think that's, that's a real challenge, to do that in love. I suppose, because if you feel hurt by something, or overlooked, or hurt, and I'm thinking within a church community, then it's – or even in relationships, then it's, to do it in love and calmly is not what you feel like, if you're feeling hurt. Then that goes slightly hand in hand with the risk of being aggressive. It's going to translate so easily into attack.'
…
Martha: '… For my own life, I know that, I think I have learned most from when I'm challenged, you know. I don't like it if I'm criticized, or whatever, but I would say that, you know, there can be, they're much more learning points than someone just saying that was really good, or that was nice, or'

Tessa: 'Have you remained on good terms with people who have challenged you?'
Martha: 'Um, I'm trying to think, um. I mean, sometimes some of that's been professionally, so that's a kind of different situation, working with people, you know, a client has challenged so that's a bit different. I suppose it has, it has, yeah, it has happened with a couple of friends, one of them, something still rumbles on, but I'm still dealing with wanting to have a difficult conversation, and sort of it still rumbles on, well shall I, shan't I? Shall I raise this or just let it go …'
(SGB – 2)

This discussion highlights two key ideas, first, the difficulty of challenging others, and secondly, the role of challenge in learning. So first, the difficulty of challenging others: Martha identified the fact that many people find it difficult to have 'the hard conversation', because we may be feeling hurt or angry ourselves, or because we are concerned about hurting or angering someone else. Interestingly, some literature on group processes deliberately highlights the positive role that embracing challenge can have; for example, Jarlath Benson has this to say, 'Look for and bring into the open disagreement and difference of opinion. They are natural and to be expected. If properly used they are very helpful in widening the range of information and opinions, developing creativity and inventiveness' (1991, p. 120). Speaking specifically of the group context, Benson sees disagreement and difference, or challenge, as occurrences that should be normalized and embraced; there is also a sense in which they provide a learning opportunity, which we will consider in a moment. However, prior research on small groups has found that challenge and conflict are often avoided; Theresa Latini, summarizing research into small groups, states that, 'small groups homogenize ideas and censor expression … This chokes out potential constructive conflict' (2011, p. 42). On another occasion, she notes that small groups 'tolerate each other but avoid challenging each other' (Latini, 2011, p. 4). Indeed, social dynamics, including societal norms that influence behaviour, may mean that individuals are unlikely to challenge others, as they wish to avoid social friction or awkwardness. A key factor in enabling challenge to have a positive role in groups is the group leader or facilitator; in fact John Heron considers 'confronting' to be one of the dimensions of group facilitation, 'which is to do with how to raise consciousness about resistances to, and avoidances of, things that need to be faced and dealt with' (1999, p. 179). This links with Mezirow's work on transformative learning theory, and the role of constructive discourse in challenging our meaning perspectives and leading us to be become conscious of others' perspectives as we participate in 'perspective taking' (1978, p. 104). In order for challenge to become a normal and appreciated part of group life, the group members need to feel safe and secure with one another, which is why Daniel Schipani sees 'trust and mutual respect' as the key starting point for groups (2015, p. 105). So it may have been influential that two of the three groups involved in this study had been running less than two years (B and C).

Martha's assertion about the role of challenge in learning has been noted by a number of writers whose work we have already considered (Loder, 1989; Mezirow, 1978), and anecdotally it is an observation that is regularly expressed. Peter Jarvis, an educationalist, refers to the social context of adult learning (2011), which is in keeping with the examples shared by Martha, who referred to challenges that resulted from interactions with others in formal and informal settings. Jarvis refers to the occurrence of a 'disjuncture' that leads us to recognize a gap between our prior understandings and experiences of the world and a new experience; a disjuncture can be seen as a form of challenge. Thus a disjunctural experience forms the basis of the learning process and hence can lead to transformation (Jarvis, 2011). Speaking specifically of the role of disjuncture in social interactions, Jarvis notes, 'Social interaction involves exploring difference and adjusting our behaviour to enable the interaction to proceed smoothly. People are different and during interaction we learn to respond to those differences, to accommodate them and even to learn from them' (2011, p. 25). This assessment of the role of disjuncture in social interactions leading to learning appears to be in keeping with Martha's comment, 'For my own life, I know that, I think I have learned most from when I'm challenged, you know'. Sometimes when we come across a difference during a social interaction, we challenge it, and this leaves the other person with the option of adjusting their behaviour in order to maintain the relationship, or to respond with their own challenge. If there is no option but to continue with the relationship, then some form of accommodation will need to be made, and this is when learning and change may take place, perhaps on both sides. Jarvis' work is helpful in bringing together the role of challenging others, and being challenged by others, and the process of learning in a social context, such as a small group.

In summary, Small Groups B and C in particular appeared to value the role of challenge, both in their wider life, and in the church and small group context. Challenge was seen as stimulating growth and change, which were viewed positively. We will now move on to consider specific examples of challenge within the groups.

Text-generated and group-generated challenge

We will begin by considering three examples of when the text initially generated the challenge, before considering some examples of when the group initially generated the challenge.

Small Group A was discussing James 4.4–5 in response to a question by Wright – 'James doesn't call some of his readers 'adulterers' (vv.4–5) to accuse them of actual unfaithfulness in their marriages. What's he trying to communicate?' (2012, p. 44) – and the following exchange took place:

Louise: '… Verses 4 and 5, he's saying, 'You adulterous people, don't you know that friendship with the world means enmity against God? Anyone who chooses to be a friend of the world becomes an enemy of God'. So, what's he trying to say to us there?'
Roger: 'That's very harsh, isn't it?'
[Agreement]
Louise: 'Yes! It's all the way through really.'
Roger: 'Friendship with the world is enmity with God.'
[Pause]
Beth: 'Well that's very difficult, because God made the world. God created the world, so surely we've got to have friendship with some of it?'
Louise: 'Yes, he wants our friendship, he wants our relationship, yeah.'
Beth: 'I can't see that that's adulterous.'
Louise: 'No, it isn't, but we're unfaithful to him, that's adultery. So, if we're unfaithful to God, it's adultery, isn't it?'
Beth: 'But why is it unfaithful to God to not be at, uh, peace with everything that happens in the world?'
Adam: 'Because some of the standards the world are putting across, for instance not bothering to get married and just living together, are not Christian standards, [agreement from group] and you can go along with the world, and …'
Beth: 'Yeah, I see.'
Adam: 'That's only one example, but there are many others.'
Louise: 'And we're unfaithful when we're just loving ourselves and wanting our own way.'
(SGA – 1)

Beth appeared to be challenged by these verses from James, as they contradicted her view of God and creation, and potentially, other biblical passages she was familiar with – for example, 'God saw everything that he had made, and indeed, it was very good' (Genesis 1.31) – given her comment 'Well that's very difficult, because God made the world. God created the world, so surely we've got to have friendship with some of it?'. However, Louise and Adam sought to enable Beth to accept that both James' teaching and that of the Genesis account could be held together; one does not need to choose between either faithfulness to God or believing that God made the world. In *The Transforming Moment*, James Loder suggests that the process of transformation begins with 'conflict-in-context', and involves some form of challenge to our existing beliefs and behaviours, though we have a strong desire to resolve the conflict-in-context and to return to constancy (1989, pp. 3–4). Adam's and Louise's responses seem to reveal a desire for resolution; they did not want Beth to feel conflicted about this passage, and perhaps were wary of feeling conflicted themselves. It is difficult to know for sure if Beth felt that the discussion provided a resolution to the challenge that the passage elicited, but the fact that she cut Adam off during his example, suggests that she was able to see how she could hold together the fact that God made the world and the injunction, in certain circumstances, not to be 'friends' with the world.

On the third occasion I visited Small Group C, they were discussing Psalm 91. Gabi was leading and drew out a few aspects from that Sunday's talk on this psalm, especially from verses 1 and 2 ('Whoever dwells in the shelter of the Most High, will rest in the shadow of the Almighty. I will say of the Lord, "He is my refuge and my fortress, my God, in whom I trust."' (NIV)). In particular, she focused on the theme of dwelling, which was received very differently in the group:

Joy: 'I think for me, dwelling is like inhabit … I think it's that, being, dwelling for me, dwelling for me is being safe inside that dwelling, so it's a place that safe and secure, a bit like home, where you're safe, you're known, you're loved. You can be yourself and it's that, sort of, um …'
Gabi: 'Security?'
Joy: 'Security, yeah …'
Debs: 'Yes, it's a little bit like you're in like an igloo and the igloo is, is the Lord. Completely …'
Gabi: 'Dwelling in.'
Debs: 'Mmm, yeah.'
Olivia: 'I think for me, this is rather simplistic, this psalm. For me.'
Gabi: 'OK.'
Olivia: 'At the moment, I feel. Because dwelling and home and house, for me, at the moment, is a very unstable place, so the word to dwell in …'

Gabi:	'The physical? The physical is. But, yeah …'
Olivia:	'So, to dwell in, even when your physicals very shaky, it's very hard, this is making an assumption I feel, I've got to be in that place, where I'm feeling it is easy to dwell in the Lord, and I feel life is not easy, always, and so …'
Gabi:	'What … are you saying that this is suggesting it is easy to dwell in the Lord?'
Olivia:	'Yeah, yeah, that 'just come and dwell in the Lord and he will protect you'. But even just getting to the Lord and dwelling, in times of hardship or crisis, I think is more difficult for me, than easy, there's an assumption here. And I think you've got to journey before you can dwell in and feel OK. Maybe? You know? Just differently, at the moment, to me when I'm reading it …'
Gabi:	'Maybe this word …'
Olivia:	'And even in the past, when it's been given to me, I haven't connected as well with it, so I don't know, just a different take on it. I just found it …'
Gabi:	'So would the thing, Olivia, about, um, you know, when things are difficult and we say, maybe, 'It's not fair' or 'I don't like this' or 'I'm disappointed' and it's to you suggesting that we are able, the aim is to be able to say, 'Father, I trust you whatever'. How would that sort of phrase, sit with you? Rather than thinking about it as a dwelling? How easy is it …'
Olivia:	'No, that I like, because I do, I do say, I trust. I think, the word 'dwelling' for me …'
Gabi:	'Has other connotations.'
Olivia:	'… is a difficult word.'
Gabi:	'Yeah, that's fair enough. It's going to be different for each person.'
	(SGC – 3)

While both Joy and Debs found the concept of dwelling helpful and comforting, Olivia struggled with the concept, especially, as she said, she was in the process of considering moving house. Gabi noted this and interjected with 'The physical? The physical is. But, yeah …', however, Olivia then cut her off and elaborated further that her discomfort with the concept of dwelling went beyond her literal dwelling. This led Gabi to then offer a broader interpretation of the passage, suggesting that the psalm can be used to refer to trusting God in all circumstances; 'I will say of the Lord, "He is my refuge and my fortress, my God, in whom I trust"' (Psalm 91.2, NIV). This seemed to enable Olivia to see the verses were applicable to her, though she re-emphasized that the word 'dwelling' was difficult for her. Clearly, Joy, Debs and Olivia all experienced Psalm 91 differently, and Olivia used the phrase 'at the moment' on a number of occasions to indicate that at a different time she might experience the psalm differently again. Gabi summarized by saying, 'It's going to be different for each person', and this seemed to be accepted by the group. This reflects an approach in keeping with reader-response theory, with 'its promotion of the view that each reader can respond personally to a text rather than passively receiving an interpretation from someone else' (Pike, 2003, p. 38). Zoe Bennett and Christopher Rowland, in their jointly authored *In a Glass Darkly*, refer to the process of working together as producing a 'collaborative hermeneutic' (2016, p. 5), which led them to grapple with the variations in how they interpreted and lived with the Bible: 'The act of comparison has unearthed hidden features of similarity and dissimilarity: comparison offers fresh perspectives and fruitful contradictions, and so aids critical reflection' (2016, p. 5). As Olivia, in response to Gabi's prompts, reflected on why she found the word 'dwelling' difficult, she critically reflected on her own experiences, which had led her to find this phrase difficult. While Joy and Debs did not verbalize any critical reflection in response to Olivia's alternative perspective, they may have entered into an internal process of critical reflection too.

Gabi's comment, 'It's going to be different for each person', also raises the question of whether all interpretations are equally valid, and if biblical texts may lose their ability to challenge if we affirm all interpretations as valid, and may therefore interpret potentially challenging texts in ways that simply affirm our existing patterns of beliefs and behaviours. Andrew Todd researched three Bible-study groups in East Anglia (2009) and found that when the groups were faced with a biblical text that challenged their contemporary experience an 'alignment' took place, which privileged contemporary experiences over textual authority (2013). And this appears to be what occurs in the above example; Olivia's experiences make the psalm problematic for her, and rather than the text reshaping her experiences, her experiences reshape the text. Indeed, Anthony Thiselton has noted that texts can both transform readers and be transformed by readers, with him noting about the latter that, 'texts can suffer transformation at the hands of readers and reading communities' (1992, p. 31). However, Thiselton also warns against pursuing 'destructive iconoclastic critiques' (1992, p. 9) purely for the sake of being challenged, and Andrew Rogers (2009) has noted the affirmative role of texts. Indeed, both Joy and Debs could be said to have read the psalm affirmatively.

Returning to Small Group A, who were looking at James 4.7 ('Submit yourselves therefore to God. Resist the devil, and he will flee from you') and had been asked by Wright, 'What are practical ways you can resist the devil?' (2012, p.44), the following discussion took place:

Roger: 'You've got to define the devil, haven't you?'
Beth: 'Precisely.'
Roger: 'It's all very well, to like, resist him, and he will run, but what are we talking about?'
Beth: 'Our own conscience I think.'
Roger: 'Ah.'
Beth: '*I think.*'
Louise: 'Well I believe, I believe the devil is a person.'
Beth: 'I don't.'
Julia: 'He was a fallen angel, wasn't he?'
Louise: 'Yeah.'
Jane: 'Isn't he within us?'
Beth: 'That's what I believe, yeah.'
Jane: 'I've got a beautiful book that I bought at [shop], and it says that God is within us and the devil is within us, it's how we, if you hurt someone, if you go and rob somebody's house – it's a lovely book – and it says, if you go and rob someone, God is angry, and he's hurting, because you're not only hurting God, you're hurting the people around you. That's the devil working, so you've got to live, God's within each and everyone one of us, isn't he? He's within us, but sometimes we don't listen to him and the devil is also there, you know, it's, he's around. I don't know, Adam?'
Adam: 'The Bible depicts the devil as a real spiritual person. I mean what about the temptations Christ had and so on [agreement]. Their depicted as a real person ...'
Louise: 'I mean, where was he when Jesus died? You know, he was there, weren't he?'
Adam: 'Yes, yes. He can be invisible, can't he? [Agreement] You can't see angels and you can't see fallen angels, but the influence is there, as you say, in people's hearts.'
Louise: 'You see, we believe there's God, don't we?'
Beth: 'I believe in good and evil, I think that's what it is. God is good and the devil is evil.'
Louise: 'Well whoever he is and how he is, I know there is one ...'
Jane: 'Oh yes, oh yes.'
Beth: 'You've been tempted!'
[Laughter]
(SGA – 1)

THEME 2 – CHALLENGE

The different ideas that the group held about the devil may have been partially influenced by what Grenz and Olson term 'folk theology', which is strongly influenced by 'a tradition of some kind' (1996, p. 27). The idea of the angel on one shoulder and the devil on another could be considered a form of folk theology, which potentially appears to have influenced some of the beliefs expressed in the preceding excerpt. Andrew Village has suggested that a diversity of interpretations might reflect the 'God-given necessity' of the 'innate diversity of creation' (2007, p. 165), where a diversity of interpretations is seen as a positive occurrence rather than as problematic. The passage enabled the group to have a discussion about different views on the devil, though there did appear to be a desire to resolve the diversity of views, as seen in the previous example from Small Group A. The invitation made by Jane for Adam to contribute was perhaps made in the hope that Adam would offer a definitive answer that the group could agree upon. Interestingly, the disagreement was ultimately diffused with humour, with Beth joking that Louise knows the devil exists because she has experienced temptation. Indeed, Heron proposes the use of laughter in groups helps to avoid people becoming defensive (1999, p. 66). On this occasion, laughter certainly helped to diffuse the tension that had been slowly building as a result of the disagreement. We will now move on to consider some instances when the group context initiated the challenge.

During a discussion in Small Group B about the work of the Holy Spirit, based on John 3.1–12, Caleb refers to Mother Teresa's work:

Caleb: 'You remind me of Mother Teresa's autobiography, I don't know if any of you have read it? I didn't read it, but one of my good friends read it and, um, it was quite, it was commentated about it at the time, that actually, this amazing woman who did so many incredible things, she felt very distant from God for much of her, much of the time she was doing it, she actually felt quite a dryness, which is …'

Stephanie: 'Or …'

Caleb: 'I'm actually agreeing with what you're saying. Go on my love [directed at Stephanie, his wife].'

Stephanie: 'Or that was the times she wrote in her journal.'

Robert: 'Do you think she only wrote when she felt bad?'

Stephanie: 'Well I only write when- If you read my journal you would think I'm about to jump off a bridge, most days, but I only write in it when I'm really upset. I'm not trying to diminish that …'

Caleb: 'No, it's true, I hadn't thought about that.'

Stephanie: 'It was, she didn't write every day, but that doesn't diminish the point that someone like Mother Teresa had many days where she felt unloved and not sure what she was doing in the world, which is kind of hard to see from the outside. That point is very valid.'
(SGB – 1)

The challenge here emerged as Stephanie challenged how Caleb has interpreted Mother Teresa's autobiography; speaking from personal experience, Stephanie noted that it cannot be assumed that a journal will necessarily reflect the totality of someone's inner life or emotional state. However, Stephanie highlighted where she agreed with Caleb and emphasized this by saying, 'That point is very valid.' This raises an interesting aspect relating to group processes, which is the impact of particular relationships in groups, in this instance marriage. Inevitably, the presence of married couples within a group affects the processes of a group, as those who are married have a distinctive relationship that exists beyond the group. There seems to be very limited literature on relationships between group members, aside from references to it within literature on group therapy, where it is referred to pejoratively as 'clique formation and pairing' (Aveline and Dryden, 1988, p. 178). This is an area in which greater research would be of real value, as based purely on this sample, small groups often include married couples among their members.

As well as the way that relationships in groups may lead to challenge, two other features were identified by Small Group B as part of their discussions: sex or gender, and culture.

Aaron: '... I think Paul and Peter both told it like it was ...'
Tessa: 'Oh, they were very straight talkers, weren't they?'
Aaron: 'And Jesus had a bit of a way with words, on occasions. He was quite insulting to people, wasn't he? If he thought they deserved it. So ...'
Tessa: 'I think there is a male-female dynamic though, I'm doing sweeping statements there, but I think sometimes the female way is very much round the houses when it comes to dealing with situations like this. And of course, I work in a predominantly female profession.'
...
Caleb: 'I would slightly challenge the male-female thing actually ...'
Tessa: 'Would you? I'm glad somebody would.'
Caleb: 'From my experience, I can just think of the last place I worked at [ ]. There was just a hopeless manager at my level

	'... And our director wasn't doing anything about that, and we managed to beat around the bush brilliantly for the three, four years I was there.'
Aaron:	'This was all blokes?'
Caleb:	'Yes, all blokes ... Very male environment, that was a blokey context. In fact, it was the women in the team, [name], who was probably the toughest and the best at- So my experience would challenge that ...'
	...
Stephanie:	'Sometimes going round the houses is a – it depends what you mean by going round the houses – but that's a really loving thing, way. Just speaking up for going round the houses.'
Tessa:	'Procrastination.'
	[Laughter]
Stephanie:	'It depends what it means by going round the houses, we've been talking a lot about cross cultural communication in our last week at our conference, and watching people, some going round the houses is cultural; you have to tell a story to get somewhere, which isn't quite what you're- I don't know how that works in conflict, I haven't seen it, I'd be interested to know, if I tell a story, do you tell a story? Does that, if you tell a story that's opposite to mine, I don't know how that looks, but then maybe it doesn't apply to your situation.'
	(SGB – 2)

Tessa suggested that women may take a less direct route to challenging others, and therefore implied men may be more direct. Caleb challenged this, which is perhaps ironic given that he is a man; Tessa welcomed this challenge, and Caleb went on to share an example from a previous workplace, which indicated that men may also seek to avoid directly challenging others. Some suggest that the higher levels of testosterone present in men's bodies makes them naturally slightly more aggressive than women (Rhoads, 2004), which would therefore potentially make them more likely to challenge others. However, others have noted the role that stereotypes play (Baker, 2014), and because men are often seen as more aggressive, this trait may be noted as normal in men but extraordinary in women – as perhaps in Caleb's example, where he noted that it was actually his female colleague who was most likely to challenge others. During group meetings, there did not appear to be a pattern of either men or women being more likely to challenge others, except perhaps within marriage relationships, when it appeared that wives were more likely to challenge their husbands than be challenged by them.

Stephanie then raised the question of culture and whether within certain cultures it is more or less acceptable to directly challenge someone, and if one might instead share one's story in order to offer an opposing view. N. T. Wright makes this point well:

> Stories are, actually, peculiarly good at modifying or subverting other stories and their worldviews. Where head-on attack would certainly fail, the parable hides the wisdom of the serpent behind the innocence of the dove, gaining entrance and favour which can then be used to change assumptions which the hearer would otherwise keep hidden away for safety. (2013, p. 40)

Here is a clear acknowledgment of the power of stories to challenge, while avoiding a more confrontational approach, which may lead some individuals to withdraw. Inevitably, different cultures will handle challenge and conflict in different ways, and the whole process of biblical engagement will be approached differently by different cultures. However, based on the data, it is not possible to draw any firm conclusions about the role of culture in influencing challenge, despite the fact that across the groups a number of different cultures and ethnicities were represented. Interestingly, Alma Lanser-van der Velde, who was involved in the intercultural Bible-reading project 'Through the Eyes of Another', has suggested that group dynamics have a greater influence upon the 'hermeneutic process' than culture (2004, p. 288). Further research would need to be carried out to establish the truth, or otherwise, of this claim.

During two focus groups, there was some discussion of the role of others in either providing challenge or enabling individuals to cope with textual challenges. First, the role of others in providing challenge:

AC: 'And then linking back to the whole small group idea, do you think engaging with the Bible in a small group has the potential to be transformative?'
Sally: 'Yes.'
[Laughter]
AC: 'And if so, kind of how and why?'
Sally: 'I think having people's different perspectives can make one think differently, see something totally differently to the way one had before, or give, perhaps give you a sort of more depth of view.'
...
Aaron: 'Yes, so, so what, what I was thinking about is you, you see the caterpillar living it's life and then it sort of goes and sits

somewhere and turns into a you know whatever it is called and, and then you don't see the stuff changing, you don't see the transformation, until at a particular point then quite rapidly it emerges, doesn't it as a butterfly? So, I suppose what I am trying to think from that, is that on Sunday we heard an example of somebody who'd been challenged by her stepfather and it, it made a change but actually there might have been all sorts of other change that was going on. So, it is a very long and clumsy metaphor, but transformation can be happening underneath the surface slowly, gradually and, you know, the big dramatic thing possibly isn't the most important part of it or it is just a stage, and groups can do that.'

...

John: 'Sometimes in the group, I think, a small group, it is not so much the Bible, if we can move away from the Bible as such, I mean, I think sometimes it's things that people say that really make you think, and that really kind of like, you go away thinking even more, um, rather than it necessarily being the Bible, I, I don't know, that's what I think sometimes.'
(SGB – Focus Group)

The overall sense from the members of Small Group B was that other people had a role in providing challenge which then led to transformation. Indeed, as is clear from the final comment, it was primarily seen to be other group members, rather than the Bible, that provided the stimulus for change and transformation. This is supported by the questionnaire data: while two out of seven people said it was 'Very important' to have their own views challenged (as seen above), when asked how important 'Hearing the views of others' was, six people said it was 'Very important'. There was a desire to hear the view of others, which, as a result, meant there was an openness to being challenged, but this was not a driving factor. This emphasis on relationships is in keeping with the findings of other studies which have found that fellowship is a key feature of small groups (Todd, 2009, 2013; Walton, 2011, 2014). However, valuing fellowship need not come at the expense of all the other potential positive characteristics of small groups, such as the opportunity to be challenged. Indeed, Timothy Gorringe (1986) has suggested that God works in and through others in order to bring about our growth in Christ-likeness.

Small Group A noted the way that other members of the group enabled them to cope with texts or Bible study questions they found challenging.

AC: 'So then the final question. Do you find engaging with the Bible reading the Bible in this group to be transformative or to challenge you to change or anything like that?'
Julia: 'Oh I think it is quite challenging isn't it. I think this Tom Wright one has been very challenging.'
Jane: 'Yes, it is very.'
Roger: 'Some of the things I didn't feel I could answer until we discussed.'
Jane: 'Very interesting.'
(SGA – Focus Group)

The emphasis here seems to be on the challenging nature of some of the questions set by Wright (2012), which during or after the group discussion the members felt more able to answer. The challenge was not necessarily coming from the text or from the group, but from the materials the group were using, and the group was able to address the challenge posed by the materials. We will be considering the use of materials in Chapter 8.

In summary, there is a complicated relationship between the role of the text and the role of the group in providing challenge. For example, Olivia may not have been challenged by Psalm 91 if Gabi had not focused on the word 'dwelling' as part of leading the group discussion, and this challenge may have been exacerbated for Olivia when other members of group shared how helpful and comforting they found the psalm. This highlights the complex nature of the interaction between the group members and the text, and trying to discern where the challenge originates from.

We will now move on to consider a biblical case study before we discuss the broader question of the role of challenge in transformative biblical engagement.

Biblical case study: Galatians 2.11–14

Galatians 2.11–14 is commonly referred to as the incident at Antioch (Moo, 2013) or the conflict at Antioch (Bruce, 1982), and is Paul's account of a dispute between himself and Peter (referred to here by his Aramaic name, Cephas). An account of this incident is also found in Acts 15. This incident directly follows a meeting in Jerusalem between Paul and the leaders there, where the 'right hand of fellowship' is extended to Paul and Barnabas (verse 9) and they encourage them in their mission to the Gentiles. While it has been suggested that this episode (vs.11–14) may have been 'chronologically displaced' (Moo, 2013, p. 141), others have defended the ordering as being chronologically accurate. For example, Moo (2013) contends that the strength of Paul's rebuke suggests that this event took place after it had already been agreed at Jerusalem that Gentiles were not required to be circumcised in order to become part of the worshipping community (v.3). Similarly, Fee (2007) proposes that Paul intended the Galatians to read this incident in the light of the earlier account. So, what is the nature of the incident? Paul is challenging Peter due to the fact that he has withdrawn from eating with the Gentiles, having been previously doing so, in response to people who came from James and out of 'fear of the circumcision faction' (v.11). Paul publicly challenges Peter on this, asking him, 'If you, though a Jew, live like a Gentile and not like a Jew, how can you compel the Gentiles to live like Jews?' (v.14) – which Wright rephrases as,

> 'Peter, you've been living like a Gentile, making no distinction between Jews and non-Jews. How can you now insist, as your behaviour is insisting, on Gentiles becoming Jews in order to become part of the inner circle of God's people?' (2002, p. 23)

What, then, might we learn about the role of challenge from this passage in Galatians?

First, it shows that it is acceptable to challenge. Some Early Church fathers were so concerned about the idea of a conflict between Paul and Peter that they suggested it was 'staged' to demonstrate the matters at stake (Hansen, 1994, p. 61). However, the evidence suggests that the conflict did indeed take place. So if Paul considered it not only acceptable to publicly challenge Peter but to record the fact that he had done so, this suggests that, on occasion, it is appropriate for one believer to challenge a fellow believer. This leads on to a second point: the reason Paul challenges Peter suggests the kind of issues about which it might be appropriate to challenge a fellow believer. Various commentators emphasize the fact that Paul's concern was with defending the truth of the gospel (Longenecker, 1990; de Boer, 2011); for example, Hansen states that, 'Paul was willing to endure the pain of conflict with Peter in order to defend the truth of the gospel' (1994, p. 62). This suggests that it is not only acceptable but expected that one believer might challenge a fellow believer if they felt that the truth of the gospel was in jeopardy. In this instance, by Peter refusing to continue eating with Gentiles, Paul felt that Peter was undermining the gospel and that the unity of the church and the mission to the Gentiles was under threat (Longenecker, 1990). So the implication is that we should not be seeking to challenge others for the sake of it, but only when we are concerned that they are holding to a belief that undermines the truth of the gospel, or perhaps any belief that is central to the Christian faith.

Thirdly, what can we learn from the way that Paul goes about challenging Peter? Interestingly, Longenecker asks, 'Though in the right, did Paul have to be so quarrelsome, even vitriolic [in his challenge of Peter]?' (1990, p. 79). Longenecker goes on to note that Paul seems to ignore his own advice written to the Galatians: 'if anyone is detected in a transgression, you who have received the Spirit should restore such a one in a spirit of gentleness' (6.1). Or as Bruce (1982) notes, Paul did not appear to follow the instruction of Matthew 18.15: 'If another member of the church sins against you, go and point out the fault when the two of you are alone'. Does Paul's approach to challenging Peter offer a model for our own behaviour? It might be suggested that due to the seriousness with which Paul viewed Peter's behaviour, and his concern that others, such as Barnabas (v.13), were following his behaviour, Paul felt he had no choice but to publicly challenge Peter. It was also a matter that was applicable to the whole Christian community, and not just to Peter and Paul; it could therefore be considered logical that Paul should raise the issue in public (Bruce, 1982). This suggests that it might be appropriate for some matters to be challenged publicly, for example, in a small group. However, it was still dealt with within the Christian community (de Boer, 2011), rather than even more publicly, which is in keeping with Paul's teaching in 1 Corinthians 6. Interestingly, we do not know how this matter was resolved (Bruce, 1982), but it is clearly important in a small group setting to ensure that positive relationships are maintained even when people challenge one another.

We will now draw together the data relating to challenge, and the teachings drawn from Galatians 2, as well as other relevant literature, in order to consider whether challenge hinders or facilitates transformative biblical engagement.

Challenge and transformative biblical engagement

As was already mentioned, there exists a range of sources, from various academic disciplines, that suggest that challenge (referred to by various terms: 'disorientating dilemma' (Mezirow, 1978), 'conflict-in-context' (Loder, 1989), 'trigger event' (Brookfield, 1987, p. 26), 'crisis' (Browning, 1996, p. 281), to name a few) leads to change, or indeed, transformation. So does the data from this research support this? Certainly, there was a belief amongst members of the small groups that challenge was a key factor in leading to transformation and small group members were able to identify times that being challenged had led them to change, but what evidence was there that challenge, or a lack of challenge, hindered or facilitated transformative *biblical engagement*?

We've already seen that the role of the group was seen as highly important, for example, John in Small Group B referred to the 'things that people say that really make you think' (SGB – Focus Group). John's emphasis on the role of others, I would suggest, reflects the overall trend of the data; members of the group provided the key form of challenge, in that even when the text initially generated the challenge, it was the discussion following which either concentrated or diffused the challenge. This reinforces Mezirow's findings, who saw that it was in the context of small groups that women had the opportunity to critically reflect, particularly on cultural expectations about women, and were able to challenge these expectations (1978). A key feature of the process of transformation was the reflective or constructive discourse with others (Mezirow, 2000). Thus, it is in the context of small group discussions that challenges, perhaps generated from the biblical text, can be explored. In the same way, Bennett and Rowland found that a 'collaborative hermeneutic' facilitated comparison, which enabled 'critical reflection' (2016, p. 5).

Summarizing recent research amongst small groups, Theresa Latini states, 'Small groups homogenize ideas and censor expression … This chokes out potential constructive conflict' (2011, p. 42). In Loder's (1989) terminology, an over-emphasis on resolution during the 'conflict-in-context' – the challenge – may inhibit the challenge being fully realized and embraced, thus also hindering transformative biblical engagement. Indeed, in the same way that some of the Early Church fathers were so concerned about the apparent conflict between Paul and Peter that they sought to interpret the incident as 'staged' (Hansen, 1994, p. 61), small group members might be concerned about challenging one another out of fear of causing offence. Martha, in Small Group B, expressed the difficulty of this, however, Martha was also able to note that on a number of occasions she had experienced a great deal of learning as a result of being challenged. So I would support Benson's reflection: 'If properly used [challenges] are very helpful in widening the range of information and opinions, developing creativity and inventiveness' (1991, p. 120). This research has certainly indicated that challenge can lead to change, and that small groups can provide this challenge, however, what has not been clearly seen is how the challenge provided by small groups leads to transformative biblical engagement.

We have considered the four voices of theology model offered by Cameron and her colleagues, and they note the importance of operant and espoused theologies challenging normative and formal theologies. They state, 'What becomes essential in this task [the task of Theological Action Research] is a practical and attitudinal commitment to a complex theology disclosed through a conversational method' (Cameron et al.,

2010, p. 56). We might say that Paul challenged Peter because his operant theology appeared to be at odds with his espoused theology; his practice of separating from the Gentiles disclosed an operant theology that was at odds with the espoused theology of the church in Jerusalem, who had agreed that Gentiles were fully part of the Christian community. Being willing to hear the different theological voices, and allowing those voices to challenge one another where necessary, might enable small group members to challenge those theologies –both operant, espoused, normative and formal – that seem to be at odds with the truth of gospel as seen in the Bible. For challenge to enable transformative biblical engagement, the Bible must be enabled, when necessary, to challenge.

To conclude, it appeared that for challenge to lead to transformative *biblical* engagement, greater openness to not simply being challenged but being challenged by the biblical text was needed, but that small groups *can* provide a facilitative context for this challenge to take place.

8

Theme 3 – Use of Materials

Here we consider the *use of materials*. The focus will be on two questions: *What* materials were used? and *How* were the materials used?, with the emphasis being primarily on *how* the materials were used. We will also consider a biblical case study in order to enhance our understanding of this area. We will end by considering whether the choice and use of materials hindered or facilitated transformative biblical engagement.

First, we need to consider the significance of materials in general. I use the term 'materials' to refer to any resources used by the groups in order to aid their engagement with and understanding of biblical material. Andrew Rogers (2009) makes use of the concept of 'mediators' and 'mediation' in his work on congregational hermeneutics, defining mediation as 'the process of transmitting hermeneutical characteristics through a variety of mediators' (p. 35). Rogers then specifically identified 'print mediators' to refer to those mediators in printed from, for example, commentaries or Study Bibles (2009, p. 35). Rogers sees these mediators, both print and other, as key in establishing and maintaining hermeneutical approaches. In this chapter we will mostly focus on print mediators, as this was the form that was primarily used by the groups – though one group did make use of an audio-recording on one occasion. It is important to note that none of the materials used by the groups were 'neutral', as they all mediated certain theological convictions through their hermeneutical approaches. As well as this, how the groups chose to use their materials also carried theological and hermeneutical significance.

One of our previous themes – expert – has a close relationship to the use of materials. However, while the focus of our consideration of experts was primarily on internal experts who were individuals present in the room, our focus here is primarily on inanimate resources – 'print mediators' – and how these are used. What was also significant when considering experts was the relationships between the internal experts and the group. As Raths notes, power is of an 'interpersonal nature … to have power one must be empowered: power comes from others' (1954, p. 97). However, when it comes to materials or 'print mediators', while the author may be considered an expert and may be a well-known author, they do not possess any 'interpersonal' power. Thus, while closely related, experts and the use of materials are not the same and have distinctively different effects on the groups.

As each small group used different materials, we will consider each group individually before drawing together the findings to address whether or not transformative biblical engagement was hindered or facilitated. We now turn to the materials.

Small Group A

What materials were used?

Small Group A were using a Bible study guide from the *For Everyone* series on the book of James, authored by Tom Wright with Phyllis J. Peau (2012).

The book of James is broken down into nine studies, prefaced with advice on how to use the guide both individually and in groups, and with some guidelines for leaders at the end. Each study follows a set pattern. First, each begins with an introductory section, which is generally a story or reflection that leads to an 'Open' question that draws out a theme from the story or reflection. For example, at the start of the study on James 2.1–13, which is entitled 'No Favorites [sic]', Wright begins with a story about someone showing favouritism to him, and then asks 'Describe a time when you were on the receiving end of favoritism [sic] or showed favoritism [sic] to someone else' (2012, p. 28). The next stage in the study, 'Study', is reading the passage, and Wright recommends that users re-read the passage (p. 9) before moving on to look at the questions, which fall into three categories: observation questions 'which ask about the basic facts in the passage', interpretation questions 'which delve into the meaning of the passage', and application questions 'which help you discover the implications of the text for growing in Christ' (p. 9). Throughout the study are sections from the *For Everyone* Bible commentary series, which is also authored by Wright. The final part of the study is a 'Pray' section, which includes suggestions for a time of prayer following the study, either immediately or at a later stage.

When groups make a selection about what materials to use to aid their engagement with the Bible, they are, intentionally or unintentionally, making a choice about what theological and hermeneutical perspectives they will allow to influence their engagement. While the Bible study guide chosen by the group was jointly authored, the group always referred to Tom Wright as the author; for example, Adam on one occasion said,

'… Tom Wright gives us a number of questions …' (SGA – 2). As it is only Tom Wright's name that appears on the cover of the book we will focus here on him, and what the choice to use material associated with Tom Wright tells us about the group; this is not intended to diminish the work of Phyllis Peau, but simply to reflect who the group credited with the authorship of the guide.

Tom Wright (or N. T. Wright) is a New Testament scholar who is also a Bishop in the Church of England; he is usually associated with the evangelical tradition of the church (Wright, 1991). As Small Group A was part of a Church of England church and attended by members of that church, the fact that Tom Wright had held a position of authority in their denomination may have been significant. In relation to evangelicalism, Wright does not shy away from at times critiquing the evangelical tradition, though he does self-identify as evangelical (Wright, 1991). Bebbington famously characterized evangelicalism as being defined by conversionism, activism, biblicism and crucicentrism (1989, p. 3). Of particular relevance for this study, Bebbington understood biblicism as an attitude of 'devotion to the Bible' and a belief that it is inspired by God, though what it means for the Bible to be inspired by God is interpreted differently (1989, p. 12). Indeed, Wright in explaining the evangelical position on the Bible, states that evangelicals 'take it for granted that we are to give scripture the primary place and that everything else has to be lined up in relation to scripture' (1991, p. 8). In his guide, Wright does appear to give the Bible the 'primary place', and the questions are very much 'lined up' to follow the biblical text very closely. For example, in the chapter on James 5.13–20, the questions lead users to follow the text closely: 'What instructions does James give to his readers in verses 13–14?' and then, 'What are the results of following these instructions (v. 15)?' (Wright, 2012, p. 56). However, as well as closely following the biblical text, Wright also seeks to encourage users to reflect on their own contexts: in the same chapter, two further questions are, 'In what ways would you like to grow as a person who prays powerfully?' and 'How could your Christian community engage more in prayer?' (2012, p. 59). This could be considered an example of what Stevens (1999) sees as the theological task of not only interpreting the Bible but also interpreting life, and doing these two things simultaneously. Wright might also be seeking to encourage the 'faithful improvization' that he argues for in his other work, where he suggests that God is like a divine playwright who has authored the Bible, and now wishes us to join him in authoring the final act (Wright, N. T., 2013, p. 143). Having engaged deeply with the Bible, we are then able to live in a way that is faithful to the biblical texts – 'faithful improvisation'.

Having considered the materials that were selected and used by Small Group A, we will now move on to explore how these materials were actually used by the group.

How were the materials used?

As suggested at the beginning of the book, in a section entitled 'Getting the Most Out of James' (2012, p. 7), members read the passage and went through the questions before coming to the meeting. During the period of time that I was observing the group, the final three studies were completed, which were: 'Humility and Faith' (James 4.1–17), 'The Rich and the Suffering' (James 5.1–12), and 'Praying in Faith' (James 5.13–20). I will provide examples below of how each of the individuals leading made use of the materials.

At the start of the session focused on Chapter 7, 'Humility and Faith', which is based on James 4.1–17, Louise – who was leading – prayed aloud and then introduced the session as follows:

Louise: 'Now we know that James is the brother of Jesus and he didn't believe who Jesus was until the … after the resurrection, and then he became a leader in the church at Jerusalem. And he wrote this letter to the Christians everywhere, so, it is for us today, isn't it? And we're looking at Tom Wright's commentary of it, and he starts saying about relationships, and he mentions start off with children's relationships, you know that a young child can have a friend, their very best friend and then that friend falls out and goes and has another friend. That's the kind of fellowship, er, friendship that, um, children can have, but then he mentions the exclusive relationship in a marriage, and often, um, in the Bible, marriage is an example of the relationship with God. So, there's a question to start with, for you married couples [laughter]: 'What are some of the benefits of the exclusive relationship in marriage?' I hope you've thought about it and got some answers. [More laughter] What do you think are the benefits of an exclusive relationship?'
(SGA – 1)

After Louise's introductory statements about who James was and his role in the Early Church, which is in keeping with Wright's comments about James in the introduction of the study guide (2012, p. 7), she then went on to paraphrase Wright and quoted directly his 'Open' question

THEME 3 – USE OF MATERIALS

('What are some of the benefits of the exclusive relationship in marriage?' (p. 43)). Louise followed the study guide questions closely throughout the meeting, and also guided the group back to the question or next question when discussions veered away from the focus of the question.

Louise had also reflected on the questions and brought some notes with her in order to guide the discussion, as she acknowledged towards the end of the meeting:

Louise: '... to be honest I found it fairly difficult to study it out and bring it up to date, um, talking about our relationship, uh, with God, our daily journey of faith with him, and, because that's what it's been all about: relationship, that we should have, you know. But 'the chapter ends with a warning' [Wright, 2012, 47], I'll read that last, section 12, and if we look at the last verse of the chapter ...'
(SGA – 1)

So while Louise followed Wright's questions throughout the study, she also felt a sense of responsibility to have made sense of the passage, by studying it and bringing it 'up to date', in order to lead the discussion: although she was reliant on Wright's questions to guide the discussion, she ensured that she felt confident in leading it. Louise ended the discussion by reading some lyrics from a song, so she also included her own material, as well as the material of Wright.

The next meeting was led by Adam, and was focused on Chapter 8, 'The Rich and the Suffering' (James 5.1–12). Like Louise, Adam began the meeting by inviting someone to pray aloud, and then read the anecdote and reflection from Wright at the start of Chapter 8 (Wright, 2012, pp. 49–50) before asking the 'Open' question: 'What have you had difficulty being patient for recently?' (Wright, 2012, p. 50). After sharing some of the things that the group had struggled to be patient about, Adam then asked Roger to read part of the Bible passage (James 5.1–6), and asked the following:

Adam: 'Any have any comments on it before we look at the questions? What's your reaction to this passage? And to the writer of it?'
(SGA – 2)

As Adam indicated, this was not one of Wright's questions but his own. This approach, starting with a very open question, is used by a number of researchers involved in the Contextual Bible Study method – for example, 'What are your first reactions to this story?' (Lawrence, 2009, p. 34), or 'What jumps off the page at you?' (Riches et al., 2010, p. 62). This can also be seen in the research carried out by Ruth Perrin, who began by asking, 'What are your thoughts, observations or questions about that passage?' (2016, p. 35). This allowed the group to share their initial reactions to the passage, then after a few comments some further discussion occurred that was not focused explicitly on the material, so Adam then moved the discussion on.

Adam: '... Well let's not say anything more until we've looked at the questions here, because Tom Wright gives us a number of questions ...'
(SGA – 2)

Adam then went on to read out question two from Wright (2012, p. 50), and the discussion followed Wright's questions for the rest of the discussion of James 5.1–6. They then moved on to consider James 5.7–12, at which point Adam said that he had looked up some commentaries in order to understand what the reference to the early and late rains were. Adam therefore drew on materials other than Wright in order to expand his understanding of the passage, so as to guide the group's discussion appropriately. After the discussion went slightly off topic, Adam brought the group back to verse 9 and asked them what is happening in the delay, while the early Christians are waiting for Jesus' return. There was a discussion about the gossip and bickering that was going on, and then as Wright (2012, p. 53) also notes, the passage moves on to talk about Job, at which point Adam introduced some material from a commentary by William Barclay.

Adam: 'I want to read to you from William Barclay on Job, because he writes rather well about him: "We generally speak of the patience of Job ..." It's a good one, isn't it?'
Roger: 'Yes, that's splendid.'
(SGA – 2)

While there was no discussion of the quotation from Barclay, this was another example of Adam introducing further material to the group. There was then a discussion of verse 12 and the concept of taking oaths, and Adam quoted from the Thirty-Nine Articles of Religion, one of which deals specifically with taking oaths. Perhaps as Adam introduced extra material, he didn't appear to feel it necessary to include all of Wright's material:

THEME 3 – USE OF MATERIALS

Adam: 'I think we've really taken the heart out of this.'
Roger: 'Yes.'
Adam: 'And we don't really need to go through question by question now ...'
Roger: 'We could read the note on page 54, which is interesting.'
Adam: 'Well, would you be kind enough to read it?'
(SGA – 2)

Roger then went on to read the note from Wright at the end of the chapter. It is interesting that while Adam was happy to set aside the second half of the questions from Wright, Roger did want to at least read the note at the end of the chapter. Unlike Louise, Adam did not follow or use each of Wright's questions: in fact, none of the questions on James 5.7–12 were used, but Adam did introduce a significant amount material from other sources instead as well as introducing his own questions.

Roger led the final meeting that I observed, which was also the final meeting using Wright, and was focused on 'Praying in Faith' (James 5.13–20). Roger, like Louise and Adam, began by asking someone to pray and then asked Julia to read the introduction of Chapter 9 (p. 55) and the 'Open' question: 'How does prayer both make sense and at the same time seem incomprehensible?' (Wright, 2012, p. 56). No-one offered a response, so Roger suggested that they read the passage and then go back to the question. However, once they have read the passage, Roger then suggested that they look at the first section from the 'Study' section, which he asked Jessica to read. Roger then asked the first question of the 'Study' section:

Roger: '... Why is it quite appropriate for James to finish this letter with a call to prayer?' [p. 56] [Pause] It's fairly obvious, no?'
[Long pause]
Louise: 'Well he's already said about praying in all different circumstances, hasn't he? When we're sad, when we're happy, when we're ill. So that means praying is vital, and er, anyone without a prayer life, well, I've written here, is spiritually dead.'
Roger: 'Yes. I put down just most important. Anyhow, I think we shall come back on that one. Can we look at verses 13 and 14, 'What instructions does James give to his readers in verses 13 and 14? ...'
(SGA – 3)

Roger then went on to read the verses. Like Louise, Roger stuck to Wright's questions and worked through all of the questions in the 'Study' section, and asked Jane to read the 'Pray' section at the very end. However, Roger did include some additional material; during a discussion of section 8, which ends with the question, 'Why do you think prayer is so terribly neglected in our culture?' (p. 58), Roger offered the following input:

Roger: 'Can I read you, because I can't remember it, but many of you will, Tennyson, Victorian, 'More things are wrought by prayer than this world dreams of. Wherefore, let thy voice, rise like a fountain for me night and day. For what are men better than sheep or goats, that nourish a blind life within the brain, if, knowing God, they lift not hands of prayer, both for themselves and those who call them friend? For so the whole round earth is every way, bound by gold chains about the feet of God.' Marvellous!'
Julia: 'Visionary.'
Roger: 'Yeah, visionary. [Pause] I suppose that has some relevance for what we're talking about? I hope so.'
Adam: 'Yes ...'
(SGA – 3)

The poem did not lead to a discussion but it did allow for a moment of reflection. Of all of the leaders, Roger kept most closely to Wright's material and did not seek to paraphrase it, though he did offer his own reflections and contributions. Louise also kept closely to Wright's material, but Adam only used select aspects of Wright's material.

In summary, Small Group A generally followed the questions set by Wright, and while extra material was at times introduced, this was generally used to complement the set material.

Small Group B

What materials were used?

Small Group B were using Brian D. McLaren's *We Make the Road by Walking: A Year-Long Quest for Spiritual Formation, Reorientation and Activation* (2015).

McLaren helpfully summarizes the book in the following comments, which are taken from the preface to the book,

> You are not finished yet. You are 'in the making'. You have the capacity to learn, mature, think, change and grow. You also have the freedom

to stagnate, regress, constrict and lose your way. Which road will you take? ... I've written *We Make the Road by Walking* to help individuals and groups seize this moment and walk wisely and joyfully into the future together ... It is a work of *constructive* theology – offering a positive, practical, open, faithful, improvable and fresh articulation of Christian faith suitable for people in dynamic times. It is also a work of *public* and *practical* theology – theology that is worked out by 'normal' people in daily life. (2015, pp. ix–x)

The emphasis is on individuals and groups taking ownership of their life and faith and taking a lead in determining how it will evolve; they make their own road. Thus McLaren emphasizes that the interpretation he offers of biblical passages 'is one of many possible responses to each text ... and you should feel free to prefer another interpretation' (p. xi). This can also be seen is the wide variety of ways that McLaren suggests the book may be used: individually, in small groups, and in public worship.

There are 52 chapters, as one of the ideas underlying the book is that it can be used weekly over the course of the year. The chapters are split into four sections: 'Alive in the Story of Creation', 'Alive in the Adventure of Jesus', 'Alive in a Global Uprising', and 'Alive in the Spirit of God'. Each chapter begins with three suggested Bible readings and a quote from one of the readings. For example, for Chapter 1, 'Awe and Wonder', the suggested Bible readings are Genesis 1.1–2.3, Psalm 19 and Matthew 6.25–24, and the quote comes from Psalm 19: 'The heavens are telling the glory of God' (p. 3). McLaren suggests in the preface that the users' 'enjoyment of the chapter will be enriched' if they read the designated Bible passages (p. xi), but this is clearly not presumed or deemed to be essential. There then follows a reflection on the passage which ends with an application for today. Finally, there is a section entitled 'Engage', which includes six questions that are identical or follow a similar format for each session:

1 'What one thought or idea from today's lesson especially intrigued, provoked, disturbed, challenged, encouraged, warmed, warned, helped or surprised you?'
2 'Share a story ... [relevant to the focus of the session]?'
3 'How do you respond to ... [something related to the focus of the session]?'
4 'For children: [varies every session]?'
5 'Activate: [some form of practical response to the session]'
6 'Meditate: [some form of prayerful response to the session]'.

In the preface, McLaren invites readers to 'skip, ponder for a few minutes on your own, or perhaps respond to in a private journal or public blog' (p. xi). The impression given is that readers should feel free to use the material in whatever way they find most helpful.

Brian McLaren has authored a large number of books, including *The Great Spiritual Migration* (2016), *Naked Spirituality* (2011) and *A Generous Orthodoxy* (2004). His website (https://brianmclaren.net/about-brian/) describes him as an 'author, speaker, activist and public theologian', who 'is a passionate advocate for "a new kind of Christianity" – just, generous, and working with people of all faiths for the common good'. McLaren's emphasis on spirituality as opposed to religion is a widespread trend in both the USA (McLaren's home country) and Europe (Hardy, 2001). Daniel Hardy notes that at times this can lead to conflict and division in the Church, 'between those trying to appeal to the "spirituality" of generations being lost to the churches and others intent on recalling them to "Christian truth" and fixed Christian moral standards' (2001, p. 96). McLaren's work is seeking to not only take spirituality seriously, but also to develop 'a new kind of Christianity'. As we have already noted, when asked to identify their church tradition, members of Small Group B identified as Broad Church, Central, Liberal and Open; additionally, three opted to offer their own description: one put, 'Christian (Try and avoid labels!)' and the other two commented 'Generously orthodox (but I don't like labels!)' and 'An individual searching for understanding'. These responses indicate that Small Group B were open to McLaren's perspective and approach; indeed, one described themselves as 'generously orthodox', which given that McLaren authored a book entitled *A Generous Orthodoxy* (2004) suggests a level of cohesion between the viewpoint of the group and the viewpoint of McLaren – though as we have already noted and will continue to find, this did not mean that Small Group B used McLaren's material unquestioningly. We will now move on to look at how Small Group B used McLaren's material.

How were the materials used?

Small Group B made much looser use of their material than Small Group A. While McLaren provides questions at the end of each chapter for discussion, these were not used in any of the meetings that I observed. Instead, each leader did something different.

John, who led on Chapter 40, 'The Spirit Is Moving! (Pentecost Sunday)', with three set readings (John 3.1–21, Acts 2.1–41 and Romans

6.1–14), did not appear to use McLaren's material, but instead selected some commentaries to use:

John: 'Well, the first point, I totally agree with what Tessa said, I did think the chapter in there was particularly good [referring to Brian McLaren (2015), Chapter 40]. And often I don't find the book so helpful, so make that point. We can't get through though, the number of passages tonight, I mean, it's huge. We've got the John passage [John 3.1–21], which to be very succinct is, uh, "you must be born again" and "for God so loved the world", and for that I delved into the [indistinct] Greek, in order to read through that particular section [muttering "impressive"] and I've tried to, sort of like, look at commentaries for different reasons. Then we've got the passage from Acts [Acts 2.1–41] and again, uh, there's quite a lot of reading, um, the coming of the Holy Spirit, from Peter's sermon at Pentecost. It might be quite a good idea just to stop and not say anything tonight and just talk about the sermon we had on, er, Sunday and the worship we had then, which was brilliant. And for that I've decided to use this one [indicating a commentary], which is more middle of the road, looking at two parts, the miracle of Pentecost and of course Peter's speech at Pentecost. And then we've got a third reading, which is from, er, Romans [Romans 6.1–14], and basically, the basis of that reading is about, um, the whole issue of dead to sin but alive to God, and for that I decided to use a very evangelical commentary, so I've kind of, like, had a dip into all three …'
(SGB – 1)

As the group chose to focus on the reading from John, John then made use of the Barrett commentary on a number of occasions during the session, but did not use the questions or any other material from McLaren.

The next meeting was led by Tessa and was based on Chapter 43, 'The Spirit of Love: Loving Neighbour'; the two Bible readings were Acts 10 and 1 Corinthians 13. Tessa opted to focus on 1 Corinthians 13, and began by summarizing what McLaren said in the previous chapter, as they had not looked at this. She then asked Aaron to read 1 Corinthians 13, before offering an initial focus for discussion.

Tessa: 'So, I thought we could start positively, thinking about that passage and about what Brian McLaren said about where the Spirit is moving, love for God always overflows in love for neighbour [2015, p. 265]. Have we seen examples of that in our churches? The churches perhaps we belong to now or we've been part of in the past. Where the Spirit is moving and that love pours out. If anybody could think of anything, where they've witnessed, been part of that, been on the receiving end of that?'

(SGB – 2)

In combination with the reading from 1 Corinthians 13, Tessa drew out a statement from McLaren – 'Where the Spirit is moving, love for God always, always, always overflows in love for neighbour' (2015, p. 265) – in order to frame her first question. While the question Tessa asked was not one of McLaren's 'Engage' questions, it was based on McLaren's material.

A bit later, Tessa referred to the context of the Corinthian church and framed a question by challenging something that McLaren said in his chapter:

Tessa: 'So, given that the love that he's [Paul] speaking of is primarily the love the believers should have between them and he's also got it right in the middle of the worship of the church, hasn't he? How you conduct your worship. Is it valid to widen this out to a more general blueprint for love? Brian McLaren's using this to talk about love for your neighbour, so, is it valid to use that in that way? [Pause] Or is it just for us believers?'

(SGB – 2)

Tessa used the material as a basis for discussion by suggesting that it may be right to critique McLaren's interpretation of the passage, rather than by assuming McLaren was correct in his interpretation. This is a different approach to that taken by Small Group A, who were inclined to follow Wright's reflections and leading. This may reflect the fact that the two groups had different attitudes towards authority. The average age of those in Small Group A was 75 in contrast to Small Group B where it was 59, so the educational experiences of these two groups may have been somewhat different: those in Small Group A are more likely to have been influenced by an approach to teaching and education that saw the teacher as the one with knowledge to be shared, rather than as one to accompany students in learning (Freire, 2005). Baumohl (1984) has noted this over-reliance on experts and those in authority in the Church, and the expectation that they will have the answers. Small Group B's confidence in critiquing the materials they are using shows a move away from an over-reliance on experts and authorities.

During the final meeting I observed, Caleb was leading on Chapter 45, 'Spirit of Unity and Diversity', for which the suggested readings were Proverbs 8, John 17.1–23 and Ephesians 4.1–16. However, Caleb decided to use alternative readings to those suggested by McLaren.

Caleb: 'This chapter is on the "Spirit of Unity and Diversity", and it's actually primarily, well it's all, it is, it's about the Trinity really and he's actually explaining how the Trinity has come to be understood in his Brian McLaren way. Um, and he's got three passages, all of which I found were, a, slightly [pause] obscure, how it linked to the topic, and I thought actually, I would use his theme, which he's talking about the Trinity but actually pull out a few other verses instead …'
(SGB – 3)

Caleb instead opted to use 2 Corinthians 13.14, Ephesians 3.14–17, John 14.15–17, and Ephesians 2.18, which were much shorter, and provided an introduction or framework for the discussion. Caleb then went on to use a quote from Rowan Williams and referred to some other authors in his discussion of the Trinity, but did not make further use of McLaren.

Small Group B tended to use McLaren's material as a starting point for their discussions, but significant preparation was then done by the person leading each meeting, and there was also a variety of approaches to how additional material was incorporated. On the whole, where used, the additional material took precedence over McLaren's material.

Small Group C

What materials were used?

Small Group C were using small group material produced by their church as part of a series on 'Bearing fruit in every season', which was also the focus of the main Sunday worship.

There were some general questions for the whole series, which were:

- What season of life are you in?
- In what areas of life is God getting your attention – and how?
- How is God calling and enabling you to bear fruit in the season you're in?

There were also specific questions for each of the small group sessions. The notes for the sessions always included the full text of the main Bible passage for that session, and sometimes also included other possible biblical texts. The main message from Sunday's talk was then summarized directly after the passage, followed by a series of questions for discussion. There was not a set style or pattern for the questions, and they varied in number from three to five. Given the range in style of question, it appears that the speaker for each Sunday set the questions for the following small group discussions, hence the varied style and number of questions.

The three sets of questions were based on the particular biblical passages which had been selected to accompany the previous Sunday's sermons, and also drew on the sermons themselves – which, during the period of time that the group was observed, took the form of testimonies. This meant that on some occasions the questions were focused more on the biblical passage and on other occasions they were focused more on what was said during the testimony. The latter approach at times was slightly problematic if not all the small groups members had been present for the Sunday service and had therefore not heard the testimony. Of the different types of question that Riches and his colleagues developed as part of their Contextual Bible Study approach, the type that was primarily used sought 'resonance between the text and the contemporary context' (2010, p. 62). This type of question can be seen in material that Small Group B were using, for example, the first (two-part) question based on Mark 5.21–34 asked, 'As you read through the passage, are there any words or phrases that stand out for you? Are you able to identify with the woman in any way?'. The second part of this question is clearly encouraging the small group members to consider how this text resonates with them. In Ruth Perrin's research, she found that seeking the relevance of biblical texts for everyday life was a common trait amongst the young evangelicals (2016). We have already seen that there was a belief amongst members of Small Group C that the biblical text could speak directly to them in their specific contexts, as with Joy's comment, 'Well it is the Holy and living word, so it can always, I find it speaks to me' (SGC – Focus Group). So the way that the questions sought to encourage group members to make connections between the text and their everyday lives was in keeping with their expectations about what happens when they read the Bible. However, as we will see in our next section on the use of the materials, some members of Small Group C were not satisfied that the materials were entirely suitable.

THEME 3 – USE OF MATERIALS

How were the materials used?

Philip was leading the first week that I visited Small Group C, and the focus was on Ezekiel 47. As the small group material and Sunday material were linked, Philip began by asking if those that had been at church on Sunday had any particular reflections on what was said. Then, after hearing the Bible passage read aloud, Philip asked:

Philip: 'So, what does the Ezekiel passage say to you? It's clearly a prophetic passage, that Ezekiel was led, um, I suppose, in a trance to see this. So, what does it say to you? [pause] About the river going ankle deep, knee deep, and up to the waist. What is the message?'
(SGC – 1)

This initial question was not included in the material provided by the church, but did allow members of the small group to share their initial reactions to the passage. However, for the rest of the meeting, Philip followed the material provided and did not include any other material, other than offering his own suggestions and contributions.

On the second occasion that I visited the group, Clive and Debs jointly led the discussion. This meeting was focused on Mark 5.21–34, and Clive began by summarizing what had been said on the Sunday for those who were not there. Debs then read the passage, in *The Passion Translation*, which was provided as part of the notes for the session. They then listened to a recording of 'Pastor Tom' speaking about this passage, as part of his 'DriveTime Devotions', which was not part of the set material; this lasted about ten minutes. After the recording, Clive asked,

Clive: 'So [pause] anything in particular that resonated with anybody?'
(SGC – 2)

This is similar to the first question provided in the small group material, which asks, 'As you read through the passage, are there any words or phrases that stand out for you? Are you able to identify with the woman in any way?'. While Clive did not specifically mention the woman, he did provide an opportunity for the group to share those things that resonated with them, which may have been words or phrases that stood out or they may have felt some resonance with the woman. However, as the group had just listened to the 'Pastor Tom' recording, their discussion became far more shaped by this material than by the material provided by the church. Nevertheless, at one stage in the discussion, Olivia returned to the questions and directed one at Stephen:

Olivia: 'As a bloke then, you know the second question, sorry, over to you Clive, just looking at the questions ...'
Clive: 'Yes.'
Olivia: 'I just wondered how ...'
Gabi: 'How you persevere?'
Olivia: 'How Stephen answers that one? You know the second question?'
(SGC – 2)

The second question was 'Romans 12.15: Calls us to "rejoice with those who rejoice and weep with those who weep". How do we persevere with this challenge when we don't see immediate answers to our prayers for others, and their pain and suffering endures for months or even years?'. However, the conversation then moved on, but Olivia bought up the question a second time:

Olivia: 'What I wondered was, sorry to ask, but it's been bothering me, this second question, 'How do we persevere with this challenge when we don't see immediate answers to our prayers for others, and their pain and suffering endures for months or even years?'. Does that mean we have to change the nature of our prayers? When that doesn't happen.'
Gabi: 'Well maybe that's a challenge, or maybe that's a question we ask ourselves.'

...

(SGC – 2)

While the majority of the group simply allowed the discussion to develop, Olivia wanted to explore the challenge posed by question two. The group then addressed this question more fully. However, they did not go on to discuss the other three questions set for the session, but instead ended with a time of open prayer. The emphasis on prayer in small groups has been noted in other research, such as that of Bielo, who found that one of the groups he studied placed such a high priority on 'cultivating intimacy' (with each other, leading to greater intimacy with God) that they regularly shortened their period of Bible study in order to spend more time praying (2009, p. 89). In this instance from Small Group C, high value was placed on both biblical engagement and on developing relationships, and thus a balance was struck between time for Bible study and time for prayer requests to be shared and time for prayer.

At the third visit, Gabi led and the focus was Psalm 91; she brought together material from the Sunday's talk, the small group material and further material, in order to guide the discussion.

THEME 3 – USE OF MATERIALS

Gabi: 'We're going to do a bit of this and a bit of that. How many people heard [Sunday's speakers]?'
...
Gabi: 'Anyway, we're going ... I don't think it particularly matters if you heard them or not actually as some of the questions kind of stand-alone, but what I've done, just first of all, just had a quick look, or listen, to Joyce Meyer on this psalm, and actually, she's got some really good things, which come under some of the titles that [Sunday's speakers] talked about. So would somebody like to pray? Stephen, would you like to pray for us?'
(SGC – 3)

Joyce Meyer is an American minister who is also president of Joyce Meyer Ministries; she is an author and broadcaster. Following this introduction and a time of open prayer, Gabi asked the group to take it in turns to read a few verses of the psalm and then drew out some key points from the Sunday talk in order to frame the discussion. This sparked a conversation which led to further discussions that were not explicitly focused on the small group questions or on the Joyce Meyer material. However, later on, Gabi did refer back to one of the questions, asking the group to consider 'What is on your heart at the moment to pray for?', which Gabi extended to include 'What our dreams are?'. And then, as Gabi asked for final reflections on the psalm, Olivia asked for a question to guide their responses, and Gabi shared the final question of the small group material, 'How are you creating an environment for growth and for God to move in your life?', which had been a guiding question throughout the series.

Interestingly, during the meeting led by Gabi, Olivia made the following comment:

Olivia: '... We're happy to go along with the series, we're happy to go along with the series of home group [referring to the small group material], which might not be meaty enough for it. Why are we doing it? Because it's correct and supportive to the church, and its being done, and we're dutifully following it.'
Stephen: 'Gor, Olivia, that was an outpouring, wasn't it?'
[Laughter]
Gabi: 'Yeah, well ...'
Olivia: 'It's challenging to us, isn't it? We ourselves. I mean, I'm guilty, I'm not necessarily learning anything from it, but I'm drifting with it. I'm going, I'm attending. Do you know what I mean?'
(SGC – 3)

This is particularly interesting, as on a number of occasions, it was Olivia who encouraged the group to return to the questions provided. However, she clearly does not see the material as fulfilling her expectations about what small group material should be.

Small Group C exhibited a variety of approaches to the use of material, with Philip following the set material closely, but both Clive and Debs, and Gabi, all putting greater emphasis on the additional material that they introduced or had utilized in preparation. There was also at least one member of the group who appeared not to find the set material overly valuable.

We will now move to consider a biblical passage – Romans 4 – in order to consider what this might suggest to us about the use of materials in small groups.

Biblical case study: Romans 4

In the NRSV translation, Romans 4 is entitled, 'The Example of Abraham', and in this chapter Paul makes use of Old Testament material in developing his main point: that justification is through faith (Ziesler, 1989). Paul relies most heavily on Genesis 15.6 in his argument, which says, 'And he [Abraham] believed the Lord; and the Lord reckoned it to him as righteousness'. Walter Brueggemann has noted that Genesis 15 'is pivotal for the Abraham tradition' (1982, p. 140), so it is highly significant that Paul chose to use this particular story in his argument. Paul quotes Genesis 15.6 directly on three separate occasions in Romans 4 (v.3, 9, 22), and also uses it implicitly throughout the passage. Paul also refers to Genesis 17 in verses 10, when he refers to the fact that Abraham had already been reckoned by God as righteous before he had been circumcised, as this does not occur until Genesis 17 – which, in terms of the narrative of Abraham's life, is over sixteen years after the events described in Genesis 15 (McKeown, 2008). Genesis 17 is referred to again in verse 17, when Paul quotes the promise made to Abraham that, 'I have made you the father of many nations' (Rom. 4.17 and Gen. 17.5). However, Paul not only quotes and refers to Genesis, but also to Psalm 32:

> So also David speaks of the blessedness of those to whom God reckons righteousness apart from works:
> 'Blessed are those whose iniquities are forgiven,
>   and whose sins are covered;
> blessed is the one against whom the Lord will not reckon sin.'
> (Rom. 4.6–8)

Verses seven and eight are a direct quotation of Psalm 32.1-2, which reveal that justification is attained 'on the basis of divine grace ... The psalm is thus central to the gospel and points out the path of true happiness to sinners aware of their need for forgiveness' (Craigie, 2004, p. 268). Tanner (2014) notes that the passive voice used in the psalm indicates that it is God's action that justifies, not human action. Finally, Paul also appears to challenge some Old Testament passages: in verse 5 he says, 'But to one who without works trusts him who justifies the ungodly, such faith is reckoned as righteousness'. This may be seen to contradict passages such as Exodus 23.7 ('Keep far from a false charge, and do not kill the innocent and those in the right, for I will not acquit the guilty'), or Isaiah 5.23 (which condemns those 'who acquit the guilty for a bribe, and deprive the innocent of their rights!'), or Proverbs 17.15 ('One who justifies the wicked and one who condemns the righteous are both alike an abomination to the Lord') (Ziesler, 1989). However, as Achtemeier notes, 'in its best moments, Israel knew that it had been chosen not because of its worth but because of God's grace' (1985, p. 79), and he appeals to texts such as Deuteronomy 7.7-8 to support this:

> It was not because you were more numerous than any other people that the Lord set his heart on you and chose you—for you were the fewest of all peoples. It was because the Lord loved you and kept the oath that he swore to your ancestors, that the Lord has brought you out with a mighty hand, and redeemed you from the house of slavery, from the hand of Pharaoh king of Egypt.

Nevertheless, Paul does offer an interpretation that challenges some Old Testament passages, or at least requires them to be radically reinterpreted. He also uses an episode that was foundational in Israel's history and identity in order to develop a perspective that challenged existing interpretations of this episode. What then can we learn from Paul's use of Old Testament material for our current discussion?

It is important to note that we cannot draw a direct correlation between Paul's use of the Old Testament, and the use of resource materials by small groups; the former is an example of the use of biblical materials within the Bible, and the latter is the use of non-biblical materials to aid the understanding and interpretation of the Bible. Paul's writings are part of the canon of Scripture, whereas small group materials are not. Despite this, I believe there are still insights to be gleaned from this passage for our current discussion. First, Paul chose passages of the Bible that were relevant to his hearers: the story of Abraham would have been familiar to the Jewish Christians that Paul was addressing. This suggests that in selecting what materials to use as the basis for small group discussion, leaders need to take into account the context of their group; age, gender, education, life stage, and various other factors which will all have an impact on what kind of materials will or will not be appropriate. Secondly, Paul was not afraid to offer a new, and potentially challenging, interpretation of the passages that he made use of. We saw that Small Group B routinely adapted the materials they were using in order to make it appropriate for their context and in order to engage with the Bible passages more fully. Even if the materials are already appropriate for a particular small group, it will almost always be beneficial to adapt them slightly in order to enable them to be as relevant as possible to the group. However, this does mean that small groups should remove or avoid difficult texts or challenging questions: as we have seen from the previous chapter, challenge needs to be embraced. Thirdly, and related to the second point, Paul appears to have deeply engaged with the Old Testament passages he relies on and to have wrestled with the challenge they posed to his beliefs about justification. Good small group materials should enable group members to engage deeply and meaningfully with the Bible in ways that open them up to transformation. They should seek to avoid superficial readings of the text by asking closed questions with 'right' answers; instead, they should lead small group members to enter into meaningful dialogue with the text and with one another.

We will now draw together the data we have considered on the use of materials, and the insights gained from Romans 4, and other relevant literature, to consider to what extent the use of materials by small groups hinders or facilitates transformative biblical engagement.

The use of materials and transformative biblical engagement

As Fleischer has noted, 'it is the quality of the discourse generated ... that creates transformative moments for each person' (2006, p. 153), thus, alongside group processes, the choice and use of material is highly significant. The data points towards the conclusion that the deeper discussions emerged from material that had been altered or specially chosen by the group leader. This was perhaps because they knew the other members well, and so selected material that they thought was especially relevant (as Paul selected Gen. 15.6), or because by moving away from set questions the discussion was able to evolve and develop more freely, without a sense of searching for a right answer. Many of the leaders had clearly prepared very carefully for the session, either by producing their own questions, as in Small Group B, or by incorporating additional material, as in Small

THEME 3 – USE OF MATERIALS

Groups A and C. While there is the possibility that the leaders had done more preparation as they knew they were being observed (Cameron and Duce, 2013), there was no indication from anyone's behaviour that it was unusual for the leaders to have prepared in the way they did, therefore, I can only assume that the level of preparation reflected the groups' normal practices. This process of preparation is significant, as it has been suggested that the careful preparation of questions is key to transformational engagement (Wink, 1989). The additional material used included commentaries, poetry, song lyrics, recordings, and quotations from authors and theologians. This meant multiple voices (Cameron et al., 2010) were able to be heard together. At times the additional materials were used to supplement the primary material, in a complementary way, and at others the additional material became the focus of the discussion, and the primary material was relegated or dispensed with altogether. We saw in Chapter 3 that Walter Wink suggested an approach that sought to bring together the workings of the right and left sides of the brain, in order that 'critical study' (associated with the left-side of the brain) and 'personal encounter' (associated with the right-side of the brain) can be unified within the process of biblical engagement (1981, p. 14). Wink believed that we overuse of the more logical, analytical left-side of our brains and underuse the more creative, emotional right-side of our brains. He therefore suggested the use of more creative approaches, such as mime or drawing, as part of the process of biblical engagement. In considering the materials used by the three small groups in this research, none of them explicitly encouraged these more creative approaches. Thus, when groups did incorporate further materials, it is interesting that some included poems and song lyrics, which perhaps express the more creative and emotional aspects of the right-side of the brain. It might be suggested that the fact the materials did not seek to engage the right-side of the brain could have been a hindrance to transformative biblical engagement.

Considering the choice of materials raises questions about authority and leadership, and who has the authority to select the material to be used and how it will be used. Each group seemed to take a democratic approach to the choice of material, with a collective decision being made about what materials to use. This was evidenced by discussions in Small Group A and B about what material they should use next, as both groups were coming to the end of their current material. In Romans 4 we see Paul use a text (Gen. 15.6) that would have been highly significant to his original hearers – it could be considered to be an example of their normative theology – and he offers a new interpretation of this text, which challenged their espoused theology. If groups only select material that reinforces their espoused theologies, meaning 'the theology embedded within a group's articulation of its beliefs' (Cameron et al., 2010, p. 54), then this theology will only ever be reinforced and other voices will not be heard. In selecting material, groups should ideally seek material that enables all four voices to be heard, so that they can be brought into conversation. In the words of Timothy Gorringe, 'The God of whom Jesus speaks is engaged in an "alternative education", the goal of which is the realization of human creative potential, and thus that education proceeds through dialogue' (1986, p. 18). The materials that small groups use to facilitate their biblical engagement must enable the Bible (a normative voice) to be brought into dialogue with the espoused and operant theologies of the group, and where appropriate, draw upon formal theologies in order to broaden this dialogue. Thus, even when experts are not present, the materials that small groups use can offer expertise, which can enable the fullest discussion possible 'that creates transformative moments for each person' (Fleischer, 2006, p. 153).

In conclusion, there is not enough evidence to show that any specific material used either directly hindered or facilitated transformative biblical engagement. Nevertheless, the data does suggest that incorporating a range of material, either in one session or across a number of sessions, provides a wider range of material to engage with, so may be more likely to generate a great diversity of insights into the biblical text, and thus potentially lead to transformative engagement. It was also seen that deeper biblical engagement occurred when materials were adapted for an individual small group, which suggests that this may also be influential in facilitating transformative biblical engagement.

9

Transformation, biblical engagement and small groups: Some practical and theological implications

This chapter will draw together the data and reflections from the preceding four chapters, along with material from throughout this study, in order to consider how small groups might better facilitate transformative biblical engagement. However, those who lead small groups will be best placed to consider how the findings and tentative suggestions of this research might best be incorporated into their own practice in order to facilitate transformative biblical engagement. The overall aim is to 'increase our knowledge and understanding of God and to enable us to live more loving and faith-filled lives' (Swinton and Mowat, 2016, p. xiii), or in other words, in order that we might continue to be transformed to more fully resemble Jesus Christ and glorify God.

The subheading of this chapter – 'some practical and theological implications' – should not be read as implying that some of the implications of this research are practical and some are theological; instead, as a piece of practical theological research, the implications are both practical *and* theological. This research has sought to be 'theological all the way through' (Cameron et al., 2010, p. 51).

I wish to offer two key suggestions about what the practical theological implications of this research might be. The first implication relates to the purpose of small groups and the second relates to the leadership of small groups.

Some practical and theological implications

The purpose of small groups

When looking at transformation, participants noted that it was important that people *wanted* to be transformed or changed:

Debs: 'It is choice, isn't it, it is a choice, I suppose.'
Gabi: 'Yes.'
Debs: 'So if we don't choose, to open ourselves and to look then we won't change.'
(SGC – Focus Group)

Debs is clear that choice is key. This means that people need to not only be open to transformation, but see transformation as a key aim or purpose of their small group. What then did the participants in this research see as the key purpose of their small groups? When considering the questionnaire responses to question 2 ('What do you believe to be the primary purpose of a church-related small group?' – see Appendix B for full questionnaire), it became clear that relationships were highly valued by the groups. Across all the groups, seven out of twenty-two participants used the word 'fellowship', eight used the word 'support' or 'supporting', and four used the word 'share' or 'sharing'. However, even responses that did not use these terms referred to others; indeed, *every response included relating to others in some way*. The responses either regarded the development of relationships as the primary purpose of small groups, for example, one participant said, 'Increasing fellowship, sharing and support between church members' (SGB), or the responses regarded relationships as enabling other purposes to be achieved, for example, 'To build and encourage Christians in the faith – to run the race together in Christ in the world' (SGC).

Apart from the emphasis on relationships and relationality, 'grow', 'growth' and 'growing' were also referred to by four participants as the primary purpose of a small group, for example, 'Fellowship and spiritual growth' (SGA). As well as this, 'build' was used by three, as seen in the previous quote and also in the following quote: 'Build each other's faith to live better as Christians in the world and live God's mission' (SGB). There was also one reference to 'discipleship': 'Discipleship, fellowship, friendship' (SGC).

The overriding impression was that building and maintaining of relationships was a key purpose of small groups, and that these relationships enabled growth and built faith. The emphasis on relationships, fellowship and support has also been apparent in other research on small groups (Todd, 2009; Walton, 2014).

In some instances, it was also seen that transformation was not necessarily something that small group members aspired to or sought from the group:

Gabi: 'I think yes, I think my response to the question ['Do you find being in this small group transformative? Why?'] is I don't find that word particularly helpful in terms of valuing the group. I value the group, I value the relationships and value the honesty and I, and I value that it has got many dimensions to it, so it has spiritual, it has got the emotional, it has got the physical, feeling, you know, so it is just, yes, it is fellowship in the broader sense for me which I think is, is really good, really good. And I like the different personalities and what each person has to bring, yes, that feeds me.'
(SGC – Focus Group)

Gabi clearly values the relational aspects of the group, and refers to relationships and fellowship, but, as she says, she does not find the word 'transformation' helpful in explaining why and what she values about the group. For Gabi, the main purpose of being in the small group appears to be relational rather than transformational. However, it is important to note that an emphasis on relationships need not be in any way detrimental to or prohibitive of transformation. For example, Small Group B produced a document that identified their small group values, which stated that they hoped to provide: 'A safe and supportive setting', 'A place for growth' and 'A place for discerning God's mission'. Small Group B clearly saw it as important to create a safe and supportive setting in order to enable growth and the discernment of God's mission. Indeed, Daniel Schipani has noted that groups must begin with 'trust and mutual respect' in order for transformative biblical engagement to take place (2015, p. 105). However, Schipani also recognized that 'receptive expectation' (2015, p. 105) was essential in order for transformation to take place, meaning that there must be some desire for and openness to transformation among small group members in order to enable transformation to occur. As we noted earlier, Timothy Gorringe sees relationships as key to God's work in making us more Christ-like: 'God "dwells" in, and his education is conducted in and through relationships of friendship, kindness, mutual acceptance and forgiveness, and beyond that in those aspects of human work upon the world which are life-enhancing and life-fulfilling' (1986, p. 18). However, these relationships do not exist in and of themselves, but as a means to 'the realization of human fullness' (Gorringe, 1986, p. 8). Therefore, valuing and building relationships in small groups is not necessarily mutually exclusive from seeking transformation, in fact, these relationships can themselves be a means for transformation to take place.

Walter Wink, who wrote *Transforming Bible Study* in order to suggest an approach that facilitated transformative engagement, has the following to say on the purpose or goal of small groups:

> If in this approach, we make our conscious goal the transformation of persons toward the divine possibilities inherent in them, then we cannot be content with simply 'having a good group', or helping people to 'understand the Bible better', or 'giving them more information', or even 'trying to build fellowship'. These are temptations to do the good, not the better. If nothing less than human transformation is our goal, then everything we do must be aimed at enabling people to become more precisely and fully the selves that they need to be in order to be available to God as effective agents of the kingdom. (1981, p. 82)

For Wink, any purpose or goal that is less than 'human transformation' is a diminishment of what small groups should be aspiring to. Similarly, Dakin states, 'Transformation is therefore the Task of the house group' (1989, p. 18). However, as we have seen from the data, the groups highly valued 'trying to build fellowship' and one participant even stated that the value she placed on the group was not related to its capacity to lead to transformation. How then should small groups and small group leaders in particular engage with the question of purpose?

From this research, the data points towards a number of possible suggestions. First and foremost, it is important for small groups to have an explicit and clearly defined purpose. As we have already noted (see section 3.2), Whitaker suggests that groups can be used to help participants move from a 'current state' to a 'preferred state', but that this is only possible if one has a clear idea of what this 'preferred state' is (1987, p. 8). This may have been developed by small group members themselves or have been developed by the church and small groups are requested to adopt this purpose as their own. The former is more likely to be effective in situations where the group has developed organically – for example, where a group of people who are already friends have decided to start meeting together more formally. The latter is more likely to be effective in situations where a new group is being established by the church, and having a predetermined purpose may enable potential members to consider if this is a purpose they wish to subscribe to. In the case of Small Group B, the values of the group ('A safe and supportive setting', 'A place for growth' and 'A place for discerning God's mission'), which are akin to a purpose statement, were developed prior to the commencement of the group and any new members – including myself as researcher – were asked to read through the values and agree to support them. It may therefore be helpful for all small groups to start by considering what they would like the purpose of their small group to be and to develop some form of purpose statement which they regularly review and, if necessary, revise. As well as sharing their own hopes for the group, small groups might also wish to consider a biblical passage in order to aid their consideration of the purpose of small groups. For example, Acts 2.42–47:

> They devoted themselves to the apostles' teaching and fellowship, to the breaking of bread and the prayers. Awe came upon everyone, because many wonders and signs were being done by the apostles. All who believed were together and had all things in common; they would sell their possessions and goods and distribute the proceeds to all, as any had need. Day by day, as they spent much time together in the temple, they broke bread at home and ate their food with glad and generous hearts, praising God and having the goodwill of all the people. And day by day the Lord added to their number those who were being saved.

Having a clearly defined purpose will also enable groups to consider the means by which they can achieve this purpose. What will facilitate or hinder the attainment of this purpose? This leads us back to the themes we have been exploring in the preceding chapters.

In summary, small groups regularly operate without having a predetermined purpose that has been explicitly discussed and agreed by the group; instead, each member may have their own implicit conception of what the purpose of the group is, though this may not have been consciously acknowledged. The data from this research highlighted the fact that for many of the participants, relationships and relationality was, from their perspective, the primary purpose of their small group. In order to give small groups, especially small group leaders, a clearer sense of identity and focus, having an agreed purpose would be advisable. While Wink would suggest that this purpose should be 'the transformation of persons toward the divine possibilities inherent in them' (1981, p. 82), if this were to be seen as the purpose of a given small group, then this would need to be unpacked; for instance, what is understood by 'transformation' and what is meant by 'divine possibilities'? Once the purpose has been agreed, a group can move on to consider how they will achieve this purpose.

The leadership of small groups

We will now consider how the findings of this research might enable those who lead small groups to more effectively facilitate transformative biblical engagement, especially in relation to how they utilize expertise, challenge and materials.

In *Let's Do Theology*, Laurie Green identifies the role of the 'People's Theologian' as those who build bridges between academic theologians and 'those doing theology in the field' (2009, p. 134). Green's conception of the role of the People's Theologian has much to offer in developing a conception of the role of the small group leader. Green identifies four key characteristics of the People's Theologian; first, they must be a member of the group and act as the 'animator' in order to 'provide appropriate learning exercises and opportunities for the group' to help them develop their own theological positions (2009, p. 134). Secondly, People's Theologians have the responsibility to be knowledgeable about Christian tradition and theology, though '[t]hey will have responsibility to be servants of the Christian faith tradition and not controllers of it' (2009, p. 135). Thirdly, People's Theologians 'must have integrity among the poor to be acceptable to them' (2009, p. 135) or, in other words, they must be seen as one of the people or one of the group. And fourthly, 'the People's Theologians must affirm the theological responsibilities and abilities of the group and never allow a group or its members to give the theological task away to others' (2009, p. 135).

It should be noted that a focus on transformation can also be seen in Green's work, for example, when speaking of his approach to theology, he states:

> So we will not be espousing a more participatory and practical way of doing theology just because it is educationally more sound (although it is), nor simply because it will help people to grow personally in the faith (although it will), but because it will address today's issues and allow the Kingdom of God to beckon us forward, so that we might participate in the transformation of society (2009, p. 6).

Thus, to make use of his work here is not to impose a transformation agenda onto his approach, as an emphasis on transformation can already be seen in his work.

So how does Green's conception of the People's Theologian inform our understanding of the role of the small group leader, especially in relation to our themes of expert, challenge and use of materials? And how does this relate to the transformative potential of biblical engagement in small groups? First, a number of the characteristics offered by Green relate closely to the theme of expertise, and how this might function most conducively in a small group. For example, in relation to Green's second characteristic, while small group leaders may be expected to have some expertise, they are expected to act as 'servants' (2009, p. 135), which is in keeping with Paul's teachings in 1 Corinthians 3 and the emphasis on leaders serving the Christian community. As well as this, all four characteristics have much in common with the approach of Contextual Bible Study (CBS), where the expert's role is to empower others in their engagement with and interpretation of the text. For example, Riches states that, 'the excitement of CBS lies in its ability to unlock "ordinary" readers' abilities and skills and to draw out their insights into the text' (Riches et al., 2010, p. xii). The emphasis in CBS is on empowering the group to take on the 'theological task' (Green, 2009, p. 135) of interpretation for themselves. This means that alternating who leads the discussion, as the groups involved in this research did, may be one strategy for empowering others – though it is important that the small group leader still regularly leads in order to model best practice.

Second, what about challenge? Green's suggestion that the People's Theologian should act as 'animator' (2009, p. 134), providing a context for learning, suggests that the small group leader should take responsibility for ensuring there is enough challenge in the group in order to facilitate transformative biblical engagement. As we have seen, Jarlath Benson suggests that leaders, 'Look for and bring into the open disagreement and difference of opinion. They are natural and to be expected. If properly used they are very helpful in widening the range of information and opinions, developing creativity and inventiveness' (1991, p. 120). Rather than seeking to smooth over differences of opinion, small group leaders may instead seek to highlight these differences, in order to enable these to challenge members of the group. When explaining the 'reflection' stage of his Let's Do Theology Spiral, Green entitles one section 'Challenge from the Christian tradition' (2009, p. 77). This is perhaps where expertise and challenge come together: the small group leader may use their expertise about a particular biblical passage or theological position in order to 'provide appropriate learning exercises' (Green, 2009, p. 134) that provide challenge to group members. Again, combining the themes of expert and challenge, and in contrast to Green's position, I would suggest that at times, and in the accordance with the context in which Paul challenges Peter, it may be appropriate for small group leaders to challenge members when it is a matter of 'the truth of the gospel' (Hansen, 1994, p. 62). While I agree with Green that the People's Theologians or small groups leader should not be seen as the 'controllers'

(2009, p. 135) of theological tradition, there may be times where their expertise enables them to see that a particular belief or trajectory is at odds with the truth of the gospel, and on these occasions, I believe there should be the opportunity for this to be challenged.

Finally, does Green's model help us to think through the use of materials? Green suggests that the People's Theologian 'will need to be soaked in the tradition' in order to draw from it (2009, p. 135). In Romans 4 we saw that Paul was so 'soaked' in the Jewish tradition that he was able to select a text that was 'pivotal for the Abraham tradition' (Brueggemann, 1982, p. 140) – Genesis 15 – in order to develop his argument for justification by faith. Not only will small group leaders need to develop and use biblical expertise, but they will also need to develop expertise when it comes to discerning what materials might be most effective in assisting their small group with engaging with the Bible. This also relates to Green's emphasis on the need for People's Theologians to be seen as 'of the people' and to 'learn the language' (2009, p. 135) of the group; small group leaders will need to know their small group members in order to discern what materials may or may not be appropriate for their small group context.

It will have become apparent that the role of the small group leader is not insignificant! In fact, a high level of responsibility is laid on the shoulders of small group leaders. This means that churches need to carefully consider the selection and training of small group leaders and also ensure that they receive enough ongoing support and direction. It may be helpful to hold a regular meeting for all those involved in leading a small group so that expertise, encouragement and challenges can be shared.

In conclusion, we have seen how expertise, challenge and the use of materials can be influential on whether or not transformative biblical engagement is hindered or facilitated. It is has become clear that careful consideration needs to be taken as to how they are incorporated into small groups to prevent them becoming hindrances to transformative biblical engagement. We have seen that, for a small group to create an environment for transformative biblical engagement, both the purpose and the leadership of the small group need to be thoughtfully considered. We explored the importance of having a clear purpose for a small group so that there was an understanding of what the group was for, in order to guide the group's priorities and activities. Laurie Green's model of the People's Theologian has enabled a consideration of how small group leaders might most effectively incorporate expertise, challenge and materials in ways that facilitate, and do not hinder, transformative biblical engagement. And it has become clear that the role of the small group leader is one of significant responsibility and importance.

10

Conclusion

In this book, I have explored the way that small groups' practices hinder or facilitate transformative biblical engagement, based on research carried out with three specific small groups. Here I identify the contribution that this research makes to wider work in this area as well as the implications of this research, before considering its limitations, and outlining some areas for potential further research.

Contribution of this research

This research has provided a unique insight into the way that ordinary readers conceive of the concept of transformation. It has raised awareness of the potential for small group practices to facilitate transformative biblical engagement; it has also been shown that these same factors – experts, challenge, and use of materials – may act as hindrances to transformative biblical engagement. Unlike much prior research into small groups (Bielo, 2009; Perrin, 2016), this research was not focused solely on evangelical Christians, but sought to include those from a range of different traditions in the Church of England. Only one other researcher has focused their research on small groups affiliated with Church of England churches (Todd, 2009).

This book has highlighted the complex and multi-faceted nature of the concept of transformation. It has sought to bring together the work of an educationalist (Mezirow), a biblical scholar (Brueggemann) and a number of theologians (Loder, Schipani and Green), in order to develop a fuller understanding of the process of transformation. The data has shown that while ordinary readers have a clear grasp of the fact that transformation is a process, they are less clear about the intended outcomes of this process. This perhaps highlights the fact that the concept is used so widely in Christian communities and in such varying ways, that it is difficult to discern exactly what form of transformation is being referred to in a given context. This in keeping with Makonen Getu's assertion that not all aspects of transformation can be 'quantified' (2002, p. 97), and Walter

Wink may also be partly correct when he asserts that 'transformation, when it occurs, is a profound mystery' (1981, p. 81). This is partly due to the fact that only some factors relating to the process of transformation are measurable by the researcher.

At the start of this book, transformation was defined as *an ongoing process of change whereby individuals and communities come to more fully resemble Jesus Christ and glorify God by the power of the Holy Spirit, in anticipation of the future transformation of the whole of creation.* This could be said to reflect a more formal, or even normative, understanding of transformation. However, this research has enabled this initial definition of transformation to be brought into dialogue with the understanding of transformation held by three groups of so-called 'ordinary' Christians (Astley, 2002) and their operant theologies of transformation. In response to this dialogue, it seems appropriate to reshape my original definition, which is in keeping with the work of Cameron and her colleagues (2010) who suggest that the four voices of theology should enter into dialogue and where necessary seek to challenge one another. Therefore, a definition that seeks to bring together the four voices of theology found in this work *might* define transformation as *an ongoing and complex process of change whereby individuals, with the help of and alongside their communities, come to more fully resemble Jesus Christ, in both their being and doing, by the power of the Holy Spirit, and in anticipation of the future transformation of the whole of creation.* This revised definition seeks to draw together biblical (normative), academic (formal) and 'ordinary' (operant) understandings of transformation, perhaps in the hope of enabling espoused understandings of transformation to be clearer. Espoused theology is 'the theology embedded within a group's articulation of its beliefs' (Cameron et al., 2010, p. 54), therefore, if churches offer a clearer articulation of their understanding of transformation, then this will enable greater clarity as to what this might look like in practice – ultimately, leading us 'to live more loving and faith-filled lives' (Swinton and Mowat, 2016, p. xiii).

The themes that emerged from the research (experts, challenge and use of materials) can offer something to the wider conversation about what makes small groups – especially Bible study groups – effective. Indeed, as de Wit notes, 'a lot has been written about transforming reading but very little about the conditions that reading (the Bible) must meet if change is intended' (2004a, p. 30). It is hoped that in identifying these three key themes, a little more light has been shed on the conditions that may best facilitate Bible-reading that might enable transformation and change. The theme of expert in particular relates to a wider discussion, especially in relation to Contextual Bible Study, about the role of expertise in a postmodern society that has largely rejected received forms of authority.

Finally, the specific combination of research methods used are also unique to this piece of research with small groups. Walton (2014) notes that questionnaires, interviews and case studies have become the norm in researching small groups, thus the decision to use questionnaires, focus groups and observation was unique, and also offered an alternative approach to small group research. The decision to use focus groups as opposed to interviews also allowed for group processes to be observed under different conditions.

Implications of this research

There are two key implications that arise from this research; one relates to transformation and one relates to small group leadership.

The first implication of this research relates to the concept of transformation. While there is a wealth of academic literature on transformation (such as Green, 2009; Kim, 2011; Loder, 1989; Mezirow, 1978; Rogers, 2015; Schipani, 2015), and while the term 'transformation' is used widely in the Church, there is not much dialogue between the two. Thus, ordinary readers – those who have received no formal training in biblical studies – are not aware of the literature relating to transformation, and academic theologians are not aware of the views of ordinary readers on transformation. It would be of great benefit if there could be greater dialogue between the four voices of theology, so that operant and formal theology in particular could be mutually enriched in their understanding of transformation. Greater sharing of knowledge between the two groups would be mutually informative and has the potential 'to enable us to live more loving and faith-filled lives' (Swinton and Mowat, 2016, p. xiii). It is hoped that this book might help to foster a conversation between ordinary theology and academic theology on the nature of transformation. The second implication of this research relates to the leadership of small groups. It became clear that the three themes or factors that emerged as the focus of this research all related not only to the hindrance or facilitation of transformative biblical engagement, but also to the leadership of small groups. While it has already been widely acknowledged that group leaders have a key role to play in the effectiveness of any group (Aveline and Dryden, 1988; Heron, 1999), this has not necessarily led churches to invest proportionally in their small group leaders. If small group leaders are recognized to be highly influential in either hindering or facilitating transformative biblical engagement, then this implies that great care should be taken in selecting, training and supporting small group leaders in order to enable them to facilitate transformative biblical engagement.

Limitations and further research

All research is limited, and this research was limited in a number of specific ways. First, this research was time-limited: as the period of time available for data collection was limited to a period of months this meant that it was not possible to observe the small groups for a long period, which would have been beneficial in enabling the observation of the potentially *ongoing* process of transformation.

Another limitation of this research was the fact that I had to allow gatekeepers – such as church leaders or small group coordinators – to select which small group to put me in contact with. Thus, groups may have been selected because a gatekeeper thought they were representative in some sense, or because they thought a group was especially 'effective', or because they thought a group was 'interesting', and so on – there are many reasons why gatekeepers may have chosen to put me in contact with certain groups and not others. Therefore, while no qualitative research seeks to be representative in the sense that quantitative research does, it is still important to acknowledge this as a potential limitation.

Finally, only three small groups were included in this research, and while this in keeping with previous research carried out on small groups (Perrin, 2016; Todd, 2009), it would have been interesting to have had a wider sample in order to see whether the themes identified in this research would also have been present in other small groups. And as the average age of all three groups was over 50, it would have been interesting to see if the findings would have been different if the research had been conducted with groups with a younger average age. This leads us on to consider areas for further research.

One area in which further work would be of benefit is the area of intra-group relationships, especially marriage. There seems to very limited literature on relationships between group members, aside from references to it within literature on group therapy, where it is referred to pejoratively as 'clique formation and pairing' (Aveline and Dryden, 1988, p. 178). This is an area in which greater research would be of real value, as based purely on this data, small groups often include married couples among their members. To what extent does the presence and behaviour of married couples in small groups hinder or facilitate transformative biblical engagement?

While this research initially considered taking a more interventionist approach and providing the groups with Bible study materials that had

CONCLUSION

been produced specifically for the research, it was decided that observing 'normal' small group practices was more likely to yield data that addressed the research question. However, an interventionist approach, perhaps one that took into account the findings of this research and sought to incorporate expertise and challenge into specially written materials, could shed further light on how these factors effect transformative biblical engagement. A final area for further research, which could not have been envisaged at the beginning of this study, would be to explore the impact of the global coronavirus pandemic on small group practices. At the time of writing, we are still very much in the midst of the pandemic, and some small groups are not meeting at all, whereas others have altered their practices to enable meetings through the use of technology, such as online video conferencing systems. It would be very interesting to explore the extent to which small groups meeting in an online context might hinder or facilitate transformative biblical engagement.

This research sought to address the question: *What factors in small groups might hinder or facilitate transformative biblical engagement?* The data produced three key themes – expert, challenge and use of materials – which were all seen to affect the likelihood of biblical engagement in small groups leading to transformation. These factors were understood in terms of either hindering or facilitating transformative biblical engagement. It was seen that each of them could potentially hinder or facilitate transformative biblical engagement, and that the role of small group leader could be key in enabling these factors to facilitate rather than hinder transformative biblical engagement. Thus, greater attention needs to be paid to the role of small group leaders in order to best facilitate transformative biblical engagement.

Appendix A

Exerts of 'Appendix B: The Small Group Survey' from Robert Wuthnow's (1994) *Sharing the Journey: Support Groups and America's New Quest for Community*. New York: The Free Press.

'Q53.   Was each of the following a reason why you became involved [in this small group], or not?

  A. Feeling like you didn't know anyone in your community
  B. Having problems in your personal life
  C. Being invited by someone you knew
  D. Hearing about it through your church or synagogue
  E. Needing emotional support
  F. Being in another group like it previously
  G. Wanting to become more disciplined in your spiritual life
  H. Experiencing a crisis in your life
  I. The desire to grown as a person' (p. 410).

'Q61.   As a result of being in this group, which of these, if any, have you experienced ...?

  A. Answers to prayer
  B. Healing of relationships
  C. A new depth of love toward other people
  D. Feeling closer to God
  E. Less interested in people outside your group
  F. Conflict with people in your group
  G. More understanding of people with different religious perspectives
  H. More open and honest with other people
  I. More open and honest with yourself
  J. Feeling better about yourself
  K. The Bible has become more meaningful to you
  L. Better able to forgive others
  M. Better able to forgive yourself

APPENDIX A

      N. Has helped me share my faith with others outside the group'
      O. Has helped me to serve people outside the group' (Wuthnow, 1994, pp. 413–414).

'Q62. In getting help from the group, how has each of the following been to you? Very important (VI), fairly important (FI), not very important (NVI), or not at all important (NAAI)?

      A. Studying particular passages from the Bible
      B. Hearing other members share their views
      C. Seeing how to apply ideas to your life
      D. Having a leader who could answer your questions
      E. People in the group giving you encouragement
      F. Having one person in the group you could discuss things with
      G. Someone in the group that you could admire and try to be like
      H. Hearing people tell stories about what worked and what didn't work for them
      I. Seeing love and caring acted out in the group' (Wuthnow, 1994, p. 414).

'Q68. As a result of being in this group, have you done any of the following?

      A. Become involved in volunteer work in your community
      B. Taken a more active part in your church or synagogue
      C. Worked with the group to help other people in need outside the group
      D. Worked with the group to help someone inside the group who was in need
      E. Become more interested in social or political issues
      F. Changed your own attitudes on some social or political issue
      G. Become more interested in peace or social justice
      H. Participated in a political rally or worked for a political campaign
      I. Donated money to a charitable organization, other than your church or synagogue
      J. Increased the amount of money you give to your church or synagogue (Wuthnow, 1994, pp. 416–417).

Appendix B

Questionnaire

> Gender:
>
> Age:
>
> Occupation:
>
> (If retired, feel free to describe your main occupation during your working life)
>
> Church tradition (please circle any of the following that you would use to describe yourself):
>
> Anglo-Catholic   Broad Church   Central
> Conservative   Charismatic   Evangelical
> Liberal   Open   Traditional
>
> Other – please offer any terms you would prefer to describe your church tradition as:
>
> Length of time you have been attending this small group (in weeks, months or years):

1. Of the reasons listed below, please circle **all** of those that influenced you to join *this* small group:

    A. To become more part of the church community
    B. Being invited by someone you knew
    C. Hearing about it through your church
    D. Mutual support
    E. Being in another group like it previously
    F. Wanting to become more disciplined in your spiritual life
    G. Feeling you ought to join
    H. Experiencing a crisis in your life
    I. Habit
    J. The desire to grow as a person
    K. In order to pray with others

APPENDIX B

    L. Wanting to develop a better understanding of the Bible
    M. Because you wanted to learn more about the Christian faith.
    N. Other, please specify:

2. What do you believe to be the primary purpose of a church-related small group?

3. Please indicate below to what extent you feel your current small group fulfils this purpose. Feel free to explain your answer below the table.

Completely fulfils this purpose	Partially fulfils this purpose	Sometimes fulfils this purpose	Does not fulfil this purpose

4. How important have the following features been to you, please select one option by ticking in the relevant box.

	Very important	Fairly important	Not very important	Not at all important	Not applicable
Studying and discussing the meaning of biblical passages					
Having a leader who could answer your questions					
Having your own views challenged					
Developing deep relationships with people in the group					
Praying with others					

	Very important	Fairly important	Not very important	Not at all important	Not applicable
Being encouraged by other group members					
Seeing how to apply ideas to your own life					
Hearing the views of others					

5. As a result of being in this group, have you been influenced to do any of the following? (Please circle all that apply)

   A. Shared your faith with someone
   B. Become involved in leading or teaching, either at church, in your small group or in another Christian context
   C. Become involved in volunteer work in your community
   D. Changed your attitude on a social or political issue
   E. Made changes to your lifestyle choices in order to limit your impact on the environment
   F. Been involved in an evangelistic event or programme
   G. Taken a more active part in your church
   H. Either independently, or with other members of the group, helped someone who was in need
   I. Signed a petition, joined a demonstration or carried out some other form of activity to challenge injustice
   J. Considered participating in, or participated in, an activity to renew the environment of your local community, e.g. litter picking
   K. Other. Please explain:

6. Do you think you have changed as a result of being in this small group? If so, what do you think caused this change?

Any other comments:

Thank you for taking the time to complete this questionnaire.

Appendix C

Focus Group Questions

1. What is 'transformation'?

2. What does transformation look like?

3. How does transformation happen?

4. What prevents transformation happening?

5. What, if anything, does the Bible say about transformation?

6. What, if anything, does the Bible have to do with transformation?

7. Do you find being in this small group transformative? Why?

8. Do you find engaging with the Bible in this group to be transformative? Why?

Bibliography

All biblical quotations are taken from the New Revised Standard Version (NRSV) unless otherwise stated.

Achtemeier, P. J., 1985, *Romans: Interpretation: A Bible Commentary for Teaching and Preaching*, Louisville: John Knox.
Archer, M. S., Collier, A. and Porpora, D. V., 2004, *Transcendence: Critical Realism and God*, London: Routledge.
Astley, J., 2002, *Ordinary Theology: Looking, Listening and Learning in Theology*, Farnham: Ashgate.
Aveline, M. and Dryden, W. (eds.), 1988, *Group Therapy in Britain*, Milton Keynes: Open University Press.
Baker, J., 2014, *Enjoying gender equality in all areas of life*, London: SPCK.
Ballard, P., 2014, 'The Use of Scripture', in Bonnie J. Miller-McLemore (ed.), *The Wiley Blackwell Companion to Practical Theology*, Chichester: Wiley Blackwell, pp. 163–172.
Ballard, P. and Holmes, S. R. (eds.), 2005, *The Bible in Pastoral Practice: Readings in the Place and Function of Scripture in the Church*, London: Darton, Longman and Todd.
Ballard, P. and Pritchard, J., 2006, *Practical Theology in Action: Christian Thinking in the Service of Church and Society*, 2nd edn, London: SPCK.
Barclay, W., 1975, *The Letter to the Corinthians*, revised edn, Edinburgh: The Saint Andrew Press.
Barret, C. K., 1971, *A Commentary on the First Epistle to the Corinthians*, 2nd edn, London: A and C Black.
Barrett, C. K., 1991, *The Epistle to the Romans*, 2nd edn, London: AandC Black.
Barth, K., 2010 [originally published 1932], *Church Dogmatics: Vol. I.1 The Doctrine of the Word of God*, translated by G. W. Bromiley, G. T. Thomes and H. Knight, London: T and T Clark.
Bauckham, R., 2003, 'Reading Scripture as a Coherent Story', in R. Hays and E. Davis (eds.), *The Art of Reading Scripture*, Grand Rapids: Eerdmans, pp. 38–53.
Baumohl, A., 1984, *Making Adult Disciples: learning and teaching in the local church*, London: Scripture Union.
Bebbington, D. W., 1989, *Evangelicalism in Modern Britain: A history from the 1730s to the 1980s*, London: Unwin Hyman.
Bennett, Z. and Rowland, C., 2016, *In a Glass Darkly: The Bible, Reflection and Everyday Life*, London: SCM Press.
Benson, J. F., 1991, *Working More Creatively with Groups*, London: Routledge.
Bhaskar, R., 2008, *A Realist Theory of Science*, London: Verso.
Bielo, J. S., 'Recontextualizing the Bible in Small Group Discourse', *SALSA, XIV: 2006, Texas Linguistic Forum*, 50 (2007), pp. 1–9.

BIBLIOGRAPHY

Bielo, J. S., 2009, *Words upon the Word: An Ethnography of Evangelical Group Bible Study*, New York: New York University Press.

Boff, L. and Boff, C.,1987, *Introducing Liberation Theology*, translated by Paul Burns, Tunbridge Wells: Burns and Oates.

Bowald, M. A., 2015, *Rendering the Word in Theological Hermeneutics: Mapping Divine and Human Agency*, Bellingham: Lexham Press.

Bradshaw, J., 1994, 'The conceptualization and measurement of need: A social policy perspective', in J. Popay and G. Williams (eds.), *Researching the People's Health*, London: Routledge, pp. 45–58.

Brewer, J. D., 2000, *Ethnography*, Buckingham: Open University Press.

Briggs, R. S., 'The Role of the Bible in Formation and Transformation: A Hermeneutical and Theological Analysis', *Anvil*, 24:3 (2007), pp. 167–182.

Briggs, R., 2011, *Reading the Bible Wisely: An Introduction to Taking Scripture Seriously*, revised edn, Eugene: Cascade Books.

Brookfield, S. D., 1986, *Understanding and Facilitating Adult Learning: A Comprehensive Analysis of Principles and Effective Practices*, Milton Keynes: Open University Press.

Brookfield, S. D., 1987, *Developing Critical Thinkers: Challenging Adults to Explore Alternative Ways of Thinking and Acting*, Milton Keynes: Open University Press.

Browning, D. S., 1996, *A Fundamental Practical Theology: Descriptive and Strategic Proposals*, Minneapolis: Augsburg Fortress.

Bruce, F. F., 1982, *The Epistle of Paul to the Galatians: A Commentary on the Greek Text*, Exeter: Paternoster Press.

Brueggemann, W., 1982, *Genesis. Interpretation: A Bible Commentary for Teaching and Preaching*, Louisville: Westminster John Knox Press.

Brueggemann, W., 2007, *Praying the Psalms: Engaging Scripture and the Life of the Spirit*, 2nd edn, Eugene: Wipf and Stock.

Cameron, H., Bhatti, D., Duce, C., Sweeney, J. and Watkins, C., 2010, *Talking about God in Practice: Theological Action Research and Practical Theology*, London: SCM Press.

Cameron, H. and Duce, C., 2013, *Researching Practice in Ministry and Mission: A Companion*, London: SCM Press.

Capps, D., 2014, *Still Growing: The Creative Self in Older Adulthood*, Eugene: Cascade Books.

Cartledge, M. J., 2015, *The Mediation of the Spirit: Interventions in Practical Theology*, Grand Rapids: William B. Eerdmans.

Chapman, M., 2006, *Anglicanism: A very short introduction*, Oxford: Oxford University Press.

Cohen, L., Manion, L., and Morrison, K., 2011, *Research Methods in Education*, 7th edn, Abingdon: Routledge.

Collicutt, J., 2015, *The Psychology of Christian Character Formation*, London: SCM Press

Collins, H. M., 2016, 'Weaving Worship and Womb: A Feminist Practical Theology of Charismatic Worship from the Perspective of Early Motherhood', PhD Thesis. Bristol University and Trinity College, Bristol.

Craigie, P. C. with Tate, M. E., 2004, *Psalms 1–50: World Biblical Commentary. Volume 19*, 2nd edn, Mexico City: Thomas Nelson.

Cranton, P., 2016, *Understanding and Promoting Transformative Learning: A guide to theory and practice*, 3rd edn, Sterling: Stylus.

Creedon, A. C., 2019, 'An analysis of the small group processes that hinder or facilitate transformative biblical engagement', PhD Thesis. University of Aberdeen with Trinity College, Bristol.

Creswell, J. W., 2013, *Qualitative Inquiry and Research Design: Choosing Among Five Approaches*, 3rd edn, London: SAGE.

Croft, S., 2002, *Transforming Communities: Re-imagining the Church for the 21st Century*, London: Darton, Longman and Todd.

Crossan, J. D., 1988, *The Dark Interval: Towards a Theology of Story*, Sonoma: Polebridge Press.

Dakin, T. J., (1989) *House Groups: What are they for? – a pastoral theology of house groups*, Oxford: Communication, Education and Development.

Davies, O., Janze, P. D. and Sedmak, C., 2007, *Transformation Theology: Church in the World*, London: TandT Clark.

de Boer, M. C., 2011, *Galatians: A Commentary*, Louisville: Westminster John Knox Press.

de Wit, H., Jonker, L., Kool, M. and Schipani, D. (eds.), 2004, *Through the Eyes of Another: Intercultural Reading of the Bible*, Amsterdam: Institute of Mennonite Studies.

de Wit, H., 2004a, 'Through the eyes of another: Objectives and backgrounds', in Hans de Wit, Louis Jonker, Marleen Kool and Daniel Schipani (eds.), *Through the Eyes of Another: Intercultural Reading of the Bible*, Amsterdam: Institute of Mennonite Studies, pp. 3–53.

de Wit, H., 2012, *Empirical Hermeneutics, Interculturality, and Holy Scripture*, Amsterdam: Institute of Mennonite Studies.

de Wit, H. and Dyk, J. (eds.), 2015, *Bible and Transformation: The Promise of Intercultural Bible Reading*, Atlanta: SBL Press.

de Wit, H., 2015, 'Bible and Transformation: The Many Faces of Transformation', in de Hans de Wit and Janet Dyk (eds.), *Bible and Transformation: The Promise of Intercultural Bible Reading*, Atlanta: SBL Press, pp. 53–74.

Donahue, B. with the Willow Creek Small Groups Team, 2002, *Leading Life-Changing Small Groups*, Grand Rapids: Zondervan.

Douglas, T., 1983, *Groups: Understanding people gathered together*, London: Tavistock Publications.

Dugud, I. M., 1999, *Ezekiel: The NIV Application Commentary*, Grand Rapids: Zondervan.

Dulles, A., 1983, *Models of Revelation*, Maryknoll: Orbis Books.

Eagleton, T., 1983, *Literary Theory: An Introduction*, Oxford: Basil Blackwell.

Eddo-Lodge, R., 2018, *Why I'm No Longer Talking to White People about Race*, London: Bloomsbury.

Ehrensperger, K., 2008, 'Feminist criticism', in Gooder, P. (ed.), *Searching for Meaning: An Introduction to Interpreting the New Testament*, London: SPCK, pp. 135–137.

Engelke, M., 2013, *God's Agents: Biblical Publicity in Contemporary England*, London: University of California Press.

Fee, G. D., 2007, *Galatians: Pentecostal Commentary*, Blandford Forum: Deo Publishing.

BIBLIOGRAPHY

Fiddes, P. S., 2012, 'Ecclesiology and Ethnography: Two Disciplines, Two Worlds?', in Pete Ward (ed.), *Perspectives on Ecclesiology and Ethnography*, Cambridge: William B. Eerdmans, pp. 13–35.

Fink, L. D., 2004, 'Beyond Small Groups: Harnessing the Extraordinary Power or Learning Teams', in Michaelsen, L. K., Knight, A. B. and L. Dee Fink (eds.), *Team-Based Learning: A Transformative Use of Small Groups in College Teaching*, Sterling: Stylus, pp. 3–26.

Fiorenza, E. S., 1994, *In Memory of Her: A Feminist Theological Reconstruction of Christian Origins*, 2nd edn, London: SCM Press.

Firth, D. G. and Grant, J. A. (eds.), 2008, *Words and the Word: Explorations in Biblical Interpretation and Literary Theory*, Downers Grove: IVP Academic.

Fish, S., 1980, *Is There a Text in This Class?: The Authority of Interpretive Communities*, Cambridge: Harvard University Press.

Fleischer, B. J., 'Mezirow's Theory of Transformative Learning and Lonergan's Method in Theology: Resources for Adult Theological Education', *Journal of Adult Theological Education*, 3:2 (2006), pp. 147–162.

Ford, D. G., 2015, 'Reading the Bible outside the church: A case study', PhD Thesis. University of Chester.

Ford, D. G., 'The transformative potential of Bible engagement for ordinary Catholics', *Practical Theology*, 2019, pp. 1–13.

Fowler, J. W., 1995, *Stages of Faith: The Psychology of Human Development and the Quest for Meaning*, London: Bravo Ltd.

Fowler, R. M., 2008, 'Reader-response criticism', in Paula Gooder (ed.), *Searching for Meaning: An introduction to interpreting the New Testament*, London: SPCK, pp. 127–134.

Freire, P., 1972, *Cultural Action for Freedom*, Middlesex: Penguin Books.

Freire, P., 2005 [originally published 1968], *Pedagogy of the Oppressed. 30th Anniversary Edition*, London: Continuum.

French Jr., J. R. P. and Raven, B., 1959, 'The Bases of Social Power', in Dorwin Cartwright (ed.), *Studies in Social Power*, University of Michigan: Institute for Social Research, pp. 259–269.

Gadamer, H-G., 2013 [originally published 1960], *Truth and Method*, translation revised by Joel Weinsheimer and Donald G. Marshall, London: Bloomsbury.

Geertz, C., 1973, *The Interpretation of Cultures*, New York: Basics Books.

Getu, M., 'Measuring Transformation: Conceptual framework and indicators', *Transformation*, 19:2 (2002), pp. 92–97.

Goheen, M. W., 'The Urgency of Reading the Bible as One Story', *Theology Today*, 64 (2008), pp. 169–183.

Gorringe, T., 1986, *Redeeming Time. Atonement through Education*, London: Darton, Longman and Todd.

Graham, E., 1996, *Transforming Practice: Pastoral Theology in an Age of Uncertainty*, London: Mowbray

Green, L., 1990, *Let's Do Theology: a pastoral cycle resource book*, London: Mowbray.

Green, L., 2009, *Let's do theology: Resources for Contextual Theology*, London: Bloomsbury.

Grenz, S. J. and Olson, R. E., 1996, *Who Needs Theology?: An Invitation to the Study of God*, Downers Grove: IVP Academic.

Grey, M., 2007, 'Feminist theology: a critical theology of liberation', in Rowland, C. (ed.), *The Cambridge Companion to Liberation Theology*, 2nd ed, Cambridge: Cambridge University Press, pp. 105–122.

Grimell, J., 'Revisiting the courage to be to understand the transition from military to civilian life', *Practical Theology*, 11:5 (2018), pp. 387–400.

Hansen, G. W., 1994, *Galatians. The IVP New Testament Commentary Series*, Downers Grove: IVP Academic.

Hardy, D., 2001, *Finding the Church: The Dynamic Truth of Anglicanism*, London: SCM Press.

Hare, A. P., 1995, 'Introduction', in A. Paul Hare, Herbert H. Blumberg, Martin F. Davies and M. Valerie Kent (eds.), *Small Group Research: A Handbook*, Norwood: Ablex Publishing Corporation.

Harris, T. A., 1995, *I'm OK – you're OK*, London: Arrow Books.

Haughton, R., 1967, *The Transformation of Man: A Study of Conversion and Community*, London: Geoffrey Chapman.

Heron, A. I. C., 1983, *The Holy Spirit: The Holy Spirit in the Bible, the History of Christian Thought, and recent Theology*, Philadelphia: The Westminster Press.

Heron, J., 1999, *The Complete Facilitator's Handbook*, London: Kogan Page.

Heywood, D., 2017, *Kingdom Learning: Experiential and Reflective Approaches to Christian Formation*, London: SCM Press.

Hitchcock, G and Hughes, D., 1995, *Research and the Teacher: A Qualitative Introduction to School-based Research*, 2nd edn, London: Routledge.

Hopewell, J. F., 1988, *Congregation: Stories and Structures*, London: SCM Press.

Hull, J., 1985, *What Prevents Christians Adults from Learning?*, London: SCM Press.

Jaques, D., 1991, *Learning in Groups*, 2nd edn, London: Kogan Page.

Jarvis, P., 2011, 'Learning from everyday life', in Peter Jarvis (ed.), *The Routledge International Handbook of Lifelong Learning*, Abingdon: Routledge, pp. 19–30.

Johnson, D. W. and Johnson, F. P., 1982, *Joining Together: Group Theory and Group Skills*, 2nd edn, Englewood Cliffs: Prentice-Hall.

Johnson, R. B. and Onwuegbuzie, A J., 'Mixed Methods Research: A Research Paradigm Whose Time Has Come', *Educational Researcher*, 33:7 (2004), pp. 14–26.

Johnson-Miller, B. C., 'The Complexity of Religious Transformation', *Journal of Adult Theological Education*, 2:1 (2005), pp. 31–49.

Kahl, W., 2007, 'Growing Together: Challenge and Chances in the Encounters of Critical and Intuitive Interpreters of the Bible', in Gerald O. West (ed.), *Reading Other-wise: Socially Engaged Biblical Scholars Reading with Their Local Communities*, Atlanta: Society of Biblical Literature, pp. 147–158.

Keener, C. S., 2005, *1–2 Corinthians*, Cambridge: Cambridge University Press.

Kerr, N. R., 2009, *Christ, History and Apocalyptic: The Politics of Christian Mission*, Eugen: Cascade Books.

Kessler, R., 2004, 'From bipolar to multipolar understanding: Hermeneutical consequences of intercultural Bible reading', in Hans de Wit, Louis Jonker, Marleen Kool and Daniel Schipani (eds.), *Through the Eyes of Another: Intercultural Reading of the Bible*, Amsterdam: Institute of Mennonite Studies, pp. 452–459.

Kim, Y. S., 'Rational and Proposal for the Journal of Bible and Human Transformation', *Journal of Bible and Human Transformation*, 1:1 (2011), pp. 1–15.

Kim, Y. S., 2013, *A Transformative Reading of the Bible: Explorations of Holistic Human Transformation*, Eugene: Cascade Books.

BIBLIOGRAPHY

Kitzinger, J., 'The Methodology of Focus Groups: the importance of interaction between research participants', *Sociology of Health and Illness*, 16:1 *(1994)*, pp. 103–121.

Kleisser, T. A., LeBert, M. A. and McGuinness, M. C., 1991, *Small Christian Communities: A Vision of Hope*, New York: Paulist Press.

Knowles, M. S., 1980, *The Modern Practice of Adult Education: From Pedagogy to Andragogy*, revised and updated edn, Englewood Cliffs: Cambridge.

Kolb, D. A., 1984, *Experiential Learning: Experience as the Source of Learning and Development*, Englewood Cliffs: Prentice Hall.

Lanser-van der Velde, A., 2004, 'Makings things in common: The group dynamics dimension of the hermeneutic process', in Hans de Wit, Louis Jonker, Marleen Kool and Daniel Schipani (eds.), *Through the Eyes of Another: Intercultural Readings of the Bible*, Amsterdam: Institute of Mennonite Studies, pp. 288–303.

Latini, T. F., 2011, *The Church and the Crisis of Community: A Practical Theology of Small-Group Ministry*, Grand Rapids: William B. Eerdmans.

Lawrence, L. J., 2009, *The Word in Place: Reading the New Testament in Contemporary Contexts*, London: SPCK.

Le Grys, A., 2010, *Shaped by God's Story: making sense of the Bible*, London: Lulu Publishing.

Lees, J., 2007, 'Remembering the Bible as a Critical "Pedagogy of the Oppressed"', in Gerald O. West (ed.) *Reading Other-wise: Socially Engaged Biblical Scholars Reading with Their Local Communities*, Atlanta: Society of Biblical Literature, pp. 73–86.

Liefeld, W. L., 1978, 'Transfigure, transfiguration, transform', in Colin Brown (ed.), *The New International Dictionary of the New Testament. Volume 3*, Exeter: Paternoster Press, pp. 861–864.

Loder, J. E., 1989, *The Transforming Moment*, 2nd edn, Colorado Springs: Helmers and Howard.

Lonergan, B. J. F., 1971, *Method in Theology*, Toronto: University of Toronto Press.

Longenecker, R. N., 1990, *Galatians: World Biblical Commentary. Volume 41*, Nashville: Thomas Nelson.

Loughlin, G., 1999, *Telling God's Story: Bible, Church and narrative theology*, Cambridge: Cambridge University Press.

Lyotard, J-F., 1992, *The Postmodern Condition: A Report on Knowledge*, translated by G. Bennington and B. Massumi, Manchester: Manchester University Press.

Maslow, A. H., 1970, *Motivation and Personality*, 2nd edn, London: Harper and Row.

Mason, J., 'Mixing methods in a qualitatively driven way', *Qualitative Research*, 6:9 (2004), pp. 9–25.

Merriam, S. B. and Brockett, R. G., 2007, *The Profession and Practice of Adult Education: An Introduction*, San Francisco: Jossey-Bass.

Mesters, C., 1993, 'The Use of the Bible in Christian Communities of the Common People', in N. K. Gottwald and R. A. Horsley (eds.), *The Bible and Liberation: Political and Social Hermeneutics*, revised edn, Maryknoll: Orbis Books, pp. 3–16.

Mezirow, J., 'Perspective Transformation', *Adult Education*, 28:2 *(1978)*, pp. 100–110.

Mezirow, J., 1991 *Transformative Dimension to Adult Learning*, San Francisco: Jossey-Bass.
Mezirow, J., 'Understanding Transformation Theory', *Adult Education,* 44:4 *(1994)*, pp. 222-232.
Mezirow, J., 2000, 'Learning to Think Like an Adult: Core Concepts of Transformation Theory', in Jack Mezrow (ed.), *Learning as Transformation: Critical Perspectives on a Theory in Progress*, San Francisco: Jossey-Bass, pp. 3-33.
McGrath, A., 2002, *A Scientific Theology: Volume 2: Reality*, London: TandT Clark.
McKeown, J., 2008, *Genesis*, Grand Rapids: William B. Eerdmans.
McLaren, B. D., 2015, *We Make the Road by Walking: A Year-Long Quest for Spiritual Formation, Reorientation and Activation*, London: Hodder.
Middleton, J. R. and Walsh, B. J., 1995, *Truth Is Stranger Than It Used to Be: Biblical Faith in a Postmodern Age*, Downers Grove: InterVaristy Press.
Miller-McLemore, B. J., 2014, 'Introduction: The Contributions of Practical Theology', in Bonnie J. Miller-McLemore (ed.), *The Wiley Blackwell Companion to Practical Theology*, Chichester: Wiley Blackwell, pp. 1-20.
Miranda-Feliciano, E., 2004, 'Shaping our lives, transforming our communities, reaching out to the world: The power of reading together', in Hans de Wit, Louis Jonker, Marleen Kool and Daniel Schipani (eds.), *Through the Eyes of Another: Intercultural Readings of the Bible*, Amsterdam: Institute of Mennonite Studies, pp. 261-272.
Moo, D. J., 2013, *Galatians: Baker Exegetical Commentary on the New Testament*, Grand Rapids: Baker Academic.
Morris, L., 1958, *The First Epistle of Paul to the Corinthians: An Introduction and Commentary*, London: The Tyndale Press.
Myers, J. R., 2003, *The Search to Belong: Rethinking Intimacy, Community, and Small Groups*, Grand Rapids: Zondervan.
Ogden, G., 2003, *Transforming Discipleship: Making Disciples a Few at a Time*, Downers Grove: InterVaristy Press.
Osmer, R. R., 2008, *Practical Theology: An Introduction*, Grand Rapids: William B. Eerdmans.
Owens, J., 2011, 'An Introduction to Critical Realism as a Meta-Theoretical Research Perspective', *Centre for Public Policy Research*, King's College, London.
Perrin, R. H., 2016, *The Bible Reading of Young Evangelicals: An Exploration of the Ordinary Hermeneutics and Faith and Generation Y*, Oregon: Pickworth Publications.
Peterson, D., 1995, *Possessed by God: A New Testament theology of sanctification and holiness*, Leicester: Apollos.
Phillips, E., 2012, 'Charting the "Ethnographic Turn": Theologians and the Study of Christian Congregations', in Pete Ward (ed.), *Perspectives on Ecclesiology and Ethnography*, Cambridge: William B. Eerdmans, pp. 95-106.
Phillips, P. M., 2017, *Engaging the Word: Biblical Literacy and Christian Discipleship*, Abingdon: The Bible Reading Fellowship.
Pike, M. A., 'The Bible and the Reader's Response', *Journal of Education and Christian Belief*, 7:1 (2003), pp. 37-51.
Prior, D., 1993, *The Message of 1 Corinthians: Life in the local church*, Nottingham: Inter-Varsity Press.

BIBLIOGRAPHY

Prior, J. M., 2015, 'The Ethics of Transformative Reading: The Text, the Other, and Oneself', in Hans de Wit and Janet Dyk (eds.), *Bible and Transformation: The Promise of Intercultural Bible Reading*, Atlanta: SBL Press, pp. 75–97.

Purves, A., 2004, *Reconstructing Pastoral Theology: A Christological Foundation*, Louisville: Westminster John Knox Press.

Raths, L., 'Power in Small Groups', *The Journal of Educational Sociology*, 28:3 (1954), pp. 97–103.

Rhoads, S. E., 2004, *Taking Sex Differences Seriously*, New York: Encounter Books.

Riches, J., Ball, H., Henderson, R., Lancaster, C., Milton, L. and Russell, M., 2010, *What is Contextual Bible Study? A practical guide with group studies for Advent and Lent*, London: SPCK.

Ricoeur, P., 1976, *Interpretation Theory: Discourse and the Surplus of Meaning*, Fort Worth: Texas Christian University Press.

Ricoeur, P., 1981, *Hermeneutics and the human sciences: Essays on language, action and interpretation,* edited, translated and introduced by John B. Thompson, Cambridge: Cambridge University Press.

Rigney, D., 'Three Kinds of Anti-Intellectualism: Rethinking Hofstadter', *Sociological Inquiry*, 61:4 (1991), pp. 434–451.

Robertson, E. H., 1961, *Take and Read: A Guide to Group Bible Study*, London: SCM Press.

Rogers, A., 2009, 'Ordinary Biblical Hermeneutics and the Transformation of Congregational Horizons within English Evangelicalism: A Theological Ethnographic Study', PhD Thesis. King's College, London.

Rogers, A. P., 2015, *Congregational Hermeneutics: How Do We Read?*, Farnham: Ashgate.

Root, A., 2014, *Christopraxis: A Practical Theology of the Cross*, Minneapolis: Fortress Press.

Root, A., 'Regulating the Empirical in Practical Theology: On Critical Realism, Divine Action, and the Place of the Ministerial', *Journal of Youth and Theology*, 15 (2016), pp. 44–64.

Scharen, C. B. (ed.), 2012, *Explorations in Ecclesiology and Ethnography*, Cambridge: William B. Eerdmans.

Scharen, C. B. and Vigen, A. M. (eds.), 2011, *Ethnography as Christian Theology and Ethics*, London: Continuum.

Schipani, D. S., 2015, 'Transformation in Intercultural Bible Reading: A View from Practical Theology', in Hans de Wit and Janet Dyk (eds.) *Bible and Transformation: The Promise of Intercultural Bible Reading*, Atlanta: Society of Biblical Literature, pp. 99–116.

Schipani, D. and Schertx, M., 2004, 'Through the eyes of practical theology and theological evaluation', in Hans de Wit, Louis Jonker, Marleen Kool and Daniel Schipani (eds.) *Through the Eyes of Another: Intercultural Readings of the Bible*, Amsterdam: Institute of Mennonite Studies, pp. 437–451.

Schneiders, S. M., 1991, *The Revelatory Text: Interpreting the New Testament as Sacred Scripture*, San Francisco: Harper.

Scott, D. and Morrison, M., 2006, *Keys Ideas in Educational Research*, London: Continuum.

Shapiro, T., 2017, *How Your Congregation Learns: The Learning Journey from Challenge to Achievement*, Lanham: Rowman and Littlefield.

Silverman, D., 2014, *Interpreting Qualitative Data*, 5th edn, London: SAGE.
Stackhouse Jr., J. G., 2015, *Partners in Christ: A Conservative Case for Egalitarianism*, Downers Grove: IVP Academic.
Steiner, G., 1975, *After Babel: Aspects of Language and Translation*, Oxford: OUP.
Stevens, R. P., 1999, *The Abolition of the Laity: Vocation, Work and Ministry in a Biblical Perspective*, Carlisle: Paternoster Press.
Stott, J., 1989, *The Message of Ephesians: God's New Society*, Nottingham: Inter-Varsity Press.
Swinton, J. and Mowat, H., 2006, *Practical Theology and Qualitative Research*, London: SCM Press.
Swinton, J. and Mowat, H., 2016. *Practical Theology and Qualitative Research*, 2nd edn, London: SCM Press.
Tanner, B. L., 2014, 'Psalm 32', in Nancy deClaissé-Walford, Rolf A. Jacobson and Beth LaNeel Tanner (eds.), *The Book of Psalms*, Grand Rapids: William B. Eerdmans, pp. 306–309.
Taylor, J. B., 1969, *Ezekiel: An Introduction and Commentary*, Leicester: Inter-Varsity Press.
Thielman, F., 1995, *Philippians: The NIV Application Commentary*, Grand Rapids: Michigan.
Thiselton, A. C., 1992, *New Horizons in Hermeneutics: The Theory and Practice of Transforming Biblical Readings*, London: HarperCollins.
Thiselton, A. C., 2013, *The Holy Spirit – In Biblical Teaching, through the Centuries, and Today*, Cambridge: William B. Eerdmans.
Thompson, S. and Kahn, J. H., 1976, *The Group Process as a Helping Technique*, Oxford: Pergamon Press.
Tindale, R. S. and Anderson, E. M., 1998, 'Small Group Research and Applied Social Psychology: An Introduction', in R. Scott Tindale et al. (eds.), *Theory and Research on Small Groups*, New York: Springer Science+Business Media, pp. 1–8.
Todd, A., 'Repertories or nodes? Constructing meanings in Bible-study groups', *Journal of Applied Linguistics*, 2:2 (2005), pp. 219–238.
Todd, A., 2009, 'The talk, dynamics and theological practice of Bible-study groups: A qualitative empirical investigation', PhD Thesis. Cardiff University.
Todd, A., 'The Interaction of Talk and Text', *Practical Theology*, 6:1 (2013), pp. 69–85.
Tompkins, J. P., 1988, 'An Introduction to Reader-Response Criticism', in Jane P. Tompkins (ed.), *Reader-Response Criticism: From Formalism to Poststructuralism*, Baltimore: The John Hopkins University Press, pp. ix–xxvi.
Tuckman, B. W. and Jensen, M. A. C., 'Stages of Small-Group Development Revisited', *Group and Organization Studies*, 2:4 (1977), pp. 419–427.
van Daalen, D. H., 1986, *A Guide to the Revelation*, London: SPCK.
Van Maanen, J., 2011, *Tales of the Field: On writing ethnography*, 2nd edn, London: The University of Chicago Press.
Vanhoozer, K. J., 1998, *Is there a meaning in this text?: The Bible, the reader and the morality of literary knowledge*, Leicester: Apollos.
Vanier, J., 2010, *Community and Growth. Revised edition*, London: Darton, Longman and Todd.
Veling, T. A., 2005, *Practical Theology: 'On Earth as It Is in Heaven'*, New York: Orbis Books.

BIBLIOGRAPHY

Village, A., 2007, *The Bible and Lay People: An Empirical Approach to Ordinary Hermeneutics*, Farnham: Ashgate.

Village, A., 2013a, 'Biblical Interpretative Horizons and Anglican Readers: An Empirical Enquiry', in Clare Amos (ed.), *The Bible in the Life of the Church*, Norwich: Canterbury Press, pp. 143–167.

Village, A., 2013b, 'The Bible and Ordinary Readers', in Jeff Astley and Leslie J. Francis (eds.), *Exploring Ordinary Theology: Everyday Christian Believing in the Church*, Farnham: Ashgate, pp. 127–136.

Village, A., Francis, L. J. and Craig, C., 'Church Tradition and Psychological Type Preferences among Anglicans in England', *Journal of Anglican Studies*, 7:1 (2009), pp. 93–109.

Walton, R. L., 'Disciples Together: The Small Group as a Vehicle for Discipleship Formation', *Journal of Adult Theological Education*, 8:2 (2011), pp. 99–114.

Walton, R. L., 2014, *Disciples Together: Discipleship, Formation and Small Groups*, London: SCM Press.

Ward, P. (ed.), 2012, *Perspectives on Ecclesiology and Ethnography*, Cambridge: William B. Eerdmans.

Ward, P., 2017, *Introducing Practical Theology: Mission, Ministry, and the Life of the Church*, Grand Rapids: Baker Academic.

Ward, P. and Dunlop, S., 'Practical Theology and the Ordinary', *Practical Theology*, 4:3 (2011), pp. 295–313.

West, G. O., 1993, *Contextual Bible Study*, Pietermaritzburg: Cluster Publications.

West, G. O., 1999, *The Academy of the Poor: Towards a Dialogical Reading of the Bible*, Sheffield: Sheffield Academic Press.

West, G. O. (ed.), 2007, *Reading Other-Wise: Socially Engaged Biblical Scholars Reading with Their Local Communities*, Atlanta: Society of Biblical Literature.

West, G. O., 'Do Two Walk Together? Walking with the Other through Contextual Bible Study', *The Anglican Theological Review*, 93:3 (2011), pp. 431–449.

Whitaker, D. S., 1987) *Using Small Groups to Help People*, London: Routledge.

Whitmore, T. (2011, 'Whiteness Made Visible: A Theo-Critical Ethnography in Acoliland', in Christian B. Scharen and Aana Marie Vigen (eds.), *Ethnography as Christian Theology and Ethics*, London: Continuum, pp. 184–206.

Wilkinson, S., 2004, 'Focus group research', in David Silverman (ed.), *Qualitative Research: Theory, Method and Practice*, 2nd edn, London: SAGE, pp. 177–199.

Wink, W., 1981, *Transforming Bible Study. Second edition*, London: SCM Press.

Woolf, M. A., 2011, 'Middle age', in Peter Jarvis (ed.), *The Routledge International Handbook of Lifelong Learning*, Abingdon: Routledge, pp. 45–55.

Wright, A., 2013, *Christianity and Critical Realism: Ambiguity, truth and theological literacy*, Abingdon: Routledge.

Wright, C. J. H., 2006, *The Mission of God: Unlocking the Bible's grand narrative*, Nottingham: Inter-Varsity Press.

Wright, N. T., 'How Can the Bible be Authoritative? (The Laing Lecture for 1989)' in *Vox Evangelica*, 21 (1991), pp. 7–32.

Wright, N. T., 2013 [originally published 1992], *The New Testament and the People of God*, London: SPCK.

Wright, T., 2002, *Paul for Everyone: Galatians and Thessalonians*, London: SPCK.

Wright, T. with Le Peau, P. J., 2012, *James: 9 studies for individuals or groups*, London: SPCK.

Wuthnow, R., 1994, *Sharing the Journey: Support Groups and America's New Quest for Community*, New York: The Free Press.

Yong, A., 2002, *Spirit-Word-Community: Theological Hermeneutics in Trinitarian Perspective*, Aldershot: Ashgate.

Younghusband, E., 1976, 'Introduction', in Sheila Thompson and J. H. Kahn, *The Group Process as a Helping Technique*, Oxford: Pergamon Press, pp. xiii–xvii.

Ziesler, J., 1989, *Paul's Letter to the Romans*, London: SCM Press.

Index of Names and Subjects

accountability, in small groups 2, 43
Achtemeier, Paul J. 155
affirmation, and transformation 34
ageing, and transformation 73, 77, 93
agency:
  divine 34, 79–81, 84
  human 21, 78–81, 92
anti-elitism 103–4
Archer, Margaret 52
Astley, Jeff 5, 7, 95
Augustine of Hippo 19, 85
author, and text 21, 138
authority:
  and experience 125
  postmodern challenge to 107, 112, 169
  in small groups 95–9, 105, 112, 137–8, 148, 157–8

Ballard, Paul 2
Barclay, William 142
Barrett, C. K. 103–4, 110–11, 147
Barth, Karl 20, 85
Baumohl, Anton 26, 78, 80, 117, 148
Bebbington, David 139
being, three modes 24
Bennett, Z. and Rowland, C. 13, 125, 135

Benson, Jarlath F. 38, 39–40, 120, 135, 165
Bhaskar, Roy 52, 53–4
Bible:
  as divine revelation 20, 89
  formative role 18
  intercultural reading 30–1, 45, 78, 130
  as meta-narrative 81–4
  normative role 18
  and practical theology 50
  study guides 138–88
  transformation in 12–18, 81–5, 91
  as transformative 1–2, 18, 19–25, 84–5, 88–90, 134–6
  see also challenge, text-generated; engagement with the Bible; interpretation; Old Testament
Bible study groups 1–2, 5, 36–7, 46–7, 60–71
  and evangelical churches 66–7, 70, 114, 139, 167
  see also small groups
Bielo, James 46–7, 55, 59, 152
Boff, Leonardo and Boff, Clodovis 22
Bowald, Mark 3, 4, 21
Brewer, J. D. 58
Briggs, Richard 8, 18, 20, 48
Brookfield, Stephen 30, 134
Browning, D. S. 30, 34, 134
Bruce, F. F. 134

189

Brueggemann, Walter 28–9, 31–2, 33, 154, 167

Cameron, Helen 51
Cameron, Helen and Duce, Catherine 62
Cameron, Helen et al. 7–8, 96, 135, 157–8, 159, 168
Capps, Donald 73
Cartledge, M. J. 80
case studies 56, 110–11, 132–4, 154–6, 169
catalyst, in transformation 78–9, 81, 84, 88–9
challenge:
  challenging others 120, 132–4
  and culture 129–30
  as desired practice 116–21
  of experts 99–100, 106–7, 148
  and Galatians 2.11–14 132–4
  group-generated 127–32, 135, 155
  and I Corinthians 13 119, 148
  as key theme in research 65, 116–36, 171
  and learning 119–21, 135
  as painful 117
  text-generated 88–90, 122–7, 135–6, 152
  in transformation 21–3, 27, 33–4, 48, 134–6, 165–6
change:
  corporate 27, 45–6, 91
  and human agency 21, 78–81
  individual 17, 23, 27, 91–2
  in small groups 38–9, 41
  social 22–4, 46
  and transformation 9, 13–18, 20, 22–5, 25–6, 72–7, 90–1, 168
  see also challenge
choice, transformation as 77–8, 81, 159–60

Christians, 'ordinary' 1, 168, see also theology, ordinary
church, as context for sanctification 92
clergy:
  and authority 55, 112–13, 138–9
  in small groups 96–101, 105–7, 113–14
Collicutt, Joanna 15, 83, 92
Collins, Helen M. 51, 56, 64
comfort, challenge to 117–19
commentaries 99, 102–3, 137, 138–49
communities:
  Base Ecclesial 32
  and change 27
  interpretive 4, 9, 19
  transformation 13, 17–18, 31, 42, 46
conflict-in-context 30, 31, 32, 33, 123, 134, 135
conformation to Christ 18, 21, 37, 168
congregation, and interpretation 22
context, and reader 2, 8, 45–6, 90
Contextual Bible Study 5, 8, 45–6, 92, 112–13, 115, 141–2, 150, 165, 168
conversion 14, 18, 21, 75
Craigie, P. C. 155
Cranton, P. 42
crisis:
  as catalyst 27, 30, 33–4, 78–9, 89, 134
  and transformation 3–43
critical realism 10, 52–4, 57
Croft, Stephen 2
Crossan, John Dominic 13
culture, and challenge 129–30

INDEX OF NAMES AND SUBJECTS

Dakin, T. J. 162
de Wit, Hans 1, 2, 4, 5, 11 n.1, 35, 45, 63, 168
  and transformation as process 73, 91
dilemma, disorientating 12, 24, 27–8, 31, 32, 33, 41, 78–9, 84, 134
discipleship 2, 26, 160
disorientation 12, 24, 27, 28–9, 31, 32, 33, 41, 78–9, 84, 134
Donahue, B. 46, 47
Douglas, T. 35–6, 38, 58
Dugud, Iain 13
Dulles, Avery 20

Eagleton, Terry 3
Eddo-Lodge, R. 56
Egelke, M. 25
engagement with the Bible:
  and choice of materials 137–58
  contextual 5, 8, 44–6, 90, 92, 150
  creative approaches 157
  deep 44–5
  in evangelical churches 66–7, 70, 114, 139, 167
  and experts 112–15, 148, 171
  group-based 44–5
  and theology 1, 18–19
  transformative 1–2, 9, 19–25, 35, 43–8, 54–5, 62, 88–90, 134–6
espoused theology 7, 53, 91, 135–6, 157–8, 168
evangelical churches, and Bible study groups 66–7, 70, 114, 139, 167
evolution, and transformation 74–5, 118
Exile, as transformative 12–13
Exodus, as transformative 12

expert:
  challenge to 99–100, 106–7
  and I Corinthians 3 110–11, 113
  deferring to 96–101, 113–14, 148
  internal/external 95–6, 99, 101, 102–110
  as key theme 65, 95–115, 171
  and transformative biblical engagement 112–15, 168–9
  and use of materials 137–8

faith, and biblical interpretation 20–1
Fee, G. D. 133
fellowship see relationships
feminist theology 22–3
Fiorenza, Elizabeth Schüssler 22–3
Fish, Stanley 4, 9
Fleischer, B. J. 156, 158
focus groups 36, 57, 61–2, 72–4, 169, 177
Ford, David G. 21, 23, 25, 65, 84
formation, and transformation 18, 46–7, 92
Fowler, James W. 30, 99
Freire, Paulo 27, 114
French Jr., J. R. P. and Raven, B. 112, 113

Gadamer, Hans-Georg 21, 45
gatekeepers 57, 170
Geertz, Clifford 53
gender, effects in small groups 128–9, 135, 170–1
Getu, Makonen 25–6, 77, 167
Gorringe, Timothy 86, 89, 131, 158, 161
Graham, Elaine 1
Green, Laurie 32–4, 51, 164–6, 167

Grenz, Stanley and Olson, Roger 6–7, 96, 106, 109, 112, 127
Grey, M. 22
Grimell, Jan 65
group norms, in small groups 38–9
groups, created/natural 35–9, 58; see also small groups

Hansen, G. W. 133
Hardy, Daniel 19, 146
Hare, A. P. 37
Harris, T. A. 41
Haughton, Rosemary 18
hermeneutics:
  collaborative 125, 135
  congregational 6, 137
  of place 46
  of suspicion 23
  turn to the reader 2, 3–4, 5, 9
Heron, A. I. C. 19, 85
Heron, John 41, 42, 43, 120, 127
Holladay, Tom 109, 114, 151
Holy Spirit:
  and engagement with the Bible 19, 85, 103
  and transformation 16–18, 42, 79–80, 92, 168
Hopewell, J. F. 2
house groups 36–7
Hull, John 78, 117

individuality 24, 48
information, and transformation 24, 32, 86
interpretation:
  and meaning 3–4, 9, 21
  multiple 124–7, 148
  and ordinary readers 112–13, 165
  see also small groups
interviews 56–7, 61, 169

Iser, Wolfsgang 4

Jarvis, Peter 121
Jesus:
  and call to transformation 13–15
  as revelation 20
Johnson, David W. and Johnson, Frank P. 37–9, 41, 78
Johnson-Miller, Beverly 18, 26

Kahl, W. 5, 19
Kim, Yung Suk 22, 23–4, 29
Kleisser, T. A. et al. 2, 4
Kolb, D. A. 32

Lanser-van der Velde, A. 130
Latini, Theresa 120, 135
Lawrence, Louise 8, 46, 55, 112, 113–14
Le Grys, Alan 18
leadership of groups 66, 157, 164–6
  and challenge 120–1, 165–6
  and expertise 111, 165–6
  and People's Theologian 164–6
  and preparation 156–8
  responsibility 41, 169–71
  shared 67, 101
learning:
  and challenge 119–21, 135
  transformative 26, 41–2, 120
Lees, Janet 46
Let's Do Theology Spiral 32, 34, 51, 164, 165
liberation theology 22, 23, 32, 45
literacy, biblical 1
Loder, James E.:
  and community 19
  conflict stage 29–30, 31, 32–3, 123, 134, 135
  and conversion 14, 18, 76

and process of transformation 29–30, 75–6, 167
Lonergan, Bernard 14, 22
Longenecker, R. N. 134
Loughlin, Gerard 4
Luther, Martin 19, 85

McGrath, Alister 50, 53
McLaren, Brian 69, 102, 104–5, 144–9
Maslow, Abraham 39–40, 40
materials:
  Bible study guides 138–44
  choice 138–9, 145–6, 149–50, 154–5, 156–8
  and expert 137–8, 148, 158
  as key theme in research 65–6, 137–58, 171
  and Romans 4 154–6, 157, 166
  and transformative engagement 156–8
  use 140–4, 146–9, 151–4, 166
  see also commentaries
meaning:
  and context 8–9
  and interpretation 3–4, 9, 21
  and interpretive community 4, 9, 19
  perspectives 26–8, 38, 41–2, 120–1
  schemes 26–7
mediators 137–8
Mesters, Carlos 22, 113
methodology, research 10, 49–71, 169
  and accessing small groups 57–8
  audio recording 58, 59, 62, 64
  and critical realism 52–4, 57
  data analysis 63–6
  focus groups 36, 57, 61–2, 72–4, 169, 177
  identification of themes 64–6, 171
  influence of race and ethnicity 56
  mixed-method 56–7
  and observation 57–70, 169
  pilot study 62–3
  questionnaires 55, 56–7, 60–1, 62, 67–70, 87, 131, 169, 172–3, 174–6
  and reflexivity 54–6, 57, 63
Mezirow, Jack 8, 23, 30
  and disorientation 12, 27–8, 31, 32, 33, 84, 134
  and perspective taking 18, 38, 89
  and transformative learning 26, 41–2, 75, 86, 92, 120–1, 135, 167
mission and discipleship groups 36–7
Moo, D. L. 132–3
Morris, Leon 110

normative theology 7, 19, 50–1, 53, 91, 96–8, 135–6, 157
nurture 81

observation, ethnographic 57–60, 62, 169
Ogden, Greg 43
Old Testament:
  and transformation 12–13
  use by St Paul 154–6, 157
operant theology 7–9, 51, 53, 91, 135–6, 158, 169
orientation 12, 24, 27, 28–9
Osmer, Richard 51, 53

Pastor Tom *see* Holladay, Tom
Paul (apostle), and transformation 14, 15
People's Theologian 164–6

Perrin, Ruth 47–8, 62–3, 142, 150
perspectives:
  meaning 26–8, 38, 41–2, 120–1
  multiplicity 53–4, 107
  new 24, 26–8, 31, 33–4, 85, 86–7
Peterson, David 76, 80, 92
Phillips, Peter 1–2
Pike, M. A. 125
power *see* authority
practical theology 7–8, 9–10, 32–3, 49–52, 145
  and critical realism 52–4, 57
  and human agency 79–81, 92
  and mixed-method research 56–7
  as normative 7, 50–1, 53
  and reflexivity 54–6, 63
  and the Trinity 80, 85
prayer, and small groups 55, 59, 62, 67, 69, 70–1, 80, 138–9, 152–3
Prior, John Mansford 53
Purves, Andrew 50, 79, 80, 92

questionnaires 55, 56–7, 60–1, 62, 67–70, 87, 131, 169, 172–3, 174–6

race and ethnicity, influence on research 56
Raths, L. 95, 105, 137
rationality, judgmental 52, 53, 57
reader:
  and context 2, 8, 45–6, 90, 92
  expert 95–115
  ideal 4
  implied 4
  ordinary 3, 4, 5–9, 19, 21, 46, 95, 112–13, 165, 167, 169

reader-response criticism 3–4, 9, 125
reading:
  counter-reading 25
  intercultural 30–1, 45, 78, 130
realism:
  critical 10, 52–4, 57
  ontological 53
reflection:
  and learning 24, 41, 135
  theological 1, 6–7, 12–13, 32, 112
reflexivity 49, 54–6, 57, 63
relationships:
  importance 35, 47, 85–8, 89, 105, 128, 131, 134, 152, 160–3
  and married couples 60, 62, 68, 69, 70, 128, 170
relativism, epistemic 49, 52, 53–4
reorientation 28–9, 30, 31–2, 33
repentance, and transformation 81
research:
  contribution 167–9
  further 170–1
  implications 169–70
  limitations 170
  qualitative 59, 65, 170
  see also methodology, research
resistance, to transformation 77–8
resurrection, as transformation 14–15
revelation, divine, and the Bible 20, 89
Riches, John 13–14, 46, 113, 150, 165
Ricoeur, Paul 3
Rigney, D. 103
Robertson, E. H. 44–5, 115
Rogers, Andrew 6, 22, 63, 125, 137
Root, Andrew 53, 79, 92
Ryle, Gilbert 53

INDEX OF NAMES AND SUBJECTS

sanctification 75–6, 92, 117–18
Schipani, Daniel 30–2, 33, 75, 78, 121, 161, 167
Schneiders, Sandra 18, 20–1
See-Judge-Act model 32
self-examination 27, 42
Shapiro, Tim 119
small groups 35–48
  age range 55–6, 65, 67–71, 114–15, 170
  and church traditions 57, 68–71, 102, 146
  church-related 36
  development 35–7
  educational settings 41–2
  and formation 46–7
  gaining access to 57–8
  group norms 38–9
  and individual needs 39–40, 47–8, 88
  and mutual support 47, 160
  outcomes 30, 35, 43, 47, 61, 93, 167–8, 172–3
  and participant expectations 31, 78, 88, 150, 161
  participants 66–71
  and prayer 55, 59, 62, 67, 69, 70–1, 80, 138–9, 152–3
  purpose 36, 39, 43–4, 47, 61, 159–63, 166
  size 37, 43
  and transformation 1–2, 9, 12–13, 37–42, 62, 72–93, 135, 167–8
  as transformative 85–8, 89
  use of set texts 61–4
  values 69, 161, 162–3
  see also challenge; engagement with the Bible; leadership; materials
social constructivism 52, 107
spirituality, and theology 19

Stackhouse, John 19
stages in transformation *see* transformation, as process
Steiner, G. 3
Stevens, R. P. 8, 139
Swinton, John and Mowat, Harriet 49–51, 53–4, 159, 168, 169

Tanner, B. L. 155
Taylor, J. B. 13
teachers, as facilitators 114–15
text:
  and meaning 3–4
  and reader 3, 8, 21
  and social location 22–3
  text-generated challenge 122–5, 135–6
Theological Action Research 7, 135–6
theology:
  academic 6–8, 19, 95, 169
  contextual 22–3
  and engagement with the Bible 1, 18–19
  espoused 7, 53, 91, 135–6, 157–8, 168
  feminist 22–3
  folk 6–7, 127
  formal 7, 53, 91, 106, 114, 135–6, 158, 169
  lay 6
  liberation 22, 23, 32, 45
  ministerial 6, 8, 106, 109, 112–14
  normative 7, 19, 50–1, 53, 91, 96–8, 135–6, 157
  operant 7–9, 51, 53, 91, 135–6, 158, 169
  ordinary 2–3, 5–8, 95, 164–6
  professional 6, 96–7, 106, 109, 112

and spirituality 19
voices of 7–9, 53, 104, 135, 157–8, 168, 169
see also practical theology
Thielman, F. 16
Thiselton, Anthony 2, 19, 21, 23, 25, 125
Tindale, R. S. and Anderson, E. M. 36
Todd, Andrew 4, 8, 47–8, 125
Tompkins, J. P. 3
transformation:
 in the Bible 12–18
 of communities 13, 17–18, 31, 42, 46, 164
 of creation 14, 17–18, 93, 168
 definitions 25–6, 34, 37, 90, 93, 167–8
 eschatological 14–15
 factors in promoting/hindering 77–81, 156–66, 167–8, 169–71
 and formation 18, 46–7
 identification 76–7, 91
 as mystery 44, 87, 168
 and new perspectives 24, 26–8, 31, 33–4, 85, 86–7
 as ongoing 12, 17, 19, 22
 and participant expectation 31, 78, 88, 150, 161
 as process 24–5, 25–34, 72–7, 90–1, 167
 and small groups 1–2, 9, 12–13, 37–42, 62, 72–93, 135, 159–66
 transformative learning 26, 41–2, 75, 85
 types 24
 see also change
transition, and transformation 73
trigger events 30, 134
trust, in small groups 31, 33, 43, 121, 161

Tuckman, Bruce 43

Van Maanen, J. 58–9
Vanhoozer, Kevin 3–4, 85
Vanier, Jean 42
Veling, Terry 33
Village, Andrew 5–6, 8, 21, 56, 127
voices of theology 7–9, 53, 104, 135, 157–8, 168, 169

Walton, Roger 36, 46, 47, 56–7, 169
Ward, Pete 7, 49–50
Ward, Pete and Dunlop, Sarah 6
West, Gerald 5–7, 45–6, 112
Whitaker, D. S. 37, 39, 162
Williams, Rowan 149
Wink, Walter 43–4, 157, 162, 163
 and transformation as mystery 44, 87, 168
 and transformation as process 26, 73, 91
women
 and challenging others 128–9, 135
 and transformative learning 27, 41–2, 92
Woolf, M. A. 73
Wright, Tom (N.T.) 67, 88, 122, 126, 130, 132, 133, 138–9, 140–4, 148
Wuthnow, R. 43, 47–8, 60, 172–3

Yong, Amos 19

Index created by Meg Davies